CONTENTS

Contents

SOCRATES

BY

W. K. C. GUTHRIE

F.B.A.

Master of Downing College and
Laurence Professor of Ancient Philosophy in the
University of Cambridge

CAMBRIDGE UNIVERSITY PRESS

CAMBRIDGE

LONDON · NEW YORK · MELBOURNE

Published by the Syndics of the Cambridge University Press
The Pitt Building, Trumpington Street, Cambridge CB2 1RP
Bentley House, 200 Euston Road, London NW1 2DB
32 East 57th Street, New York, NY 10022, USA
296 Beaconsfield Parade, Middle Park, Melbourne 3206, Australia

ISBN 0 521 09667 7

First published as Part 2 of
A History of Greek Philosophy, Volume III
(Cambridge University Press, 1969)
Reprinted separately as a paperback, 1971, 1977

Printed in Great Britain
at the University Press, Cambridge

SOCRATES

LIST OF ABBREVIATIONS

Most works cited in abbreviated form in the text will be easily recognizable under the author's or editor's name in the bibliography. It may however be helpful to list the following:

PERIODICALS

AJP	*American Journal of Philology.*
BICS	*Bulletin of the Institute of Classical Studies* (London).
CP	*Classical Philology.*
CQ	*Classical Quarterly.*
CR	*Classical Review.*
GGA	*Göttingische Gelehrte Anzeigen.*
HSCP	*Harvard Studies in Classical Philology.*
JHI	*Journal of the History of Ideas.*
JHS	*Journal of Hellenic Studies.*
PCPS	*Proceedings of the Cambridge Philological Society.*
REG	*Revue des Études Grecques.*
TAPA	*Transactions of the American Philological Association.*

OTHER WORKS

CGF	*Comicorum Graecorum Fragmenta*, ed. Meineke.
DK	Diels–Kranz, *Die Fragmente der Vorsokratiker.*
KR	G. S. Kirk and J. E. Raven, *The Presocratic Philosophers.*
LSJ	Liddell–Scott–Jones, *A Greek–English Lexicon*, 9th ed.
OCD	*Oxford Classical Dictionary.*
OP	*Oxyrhynchus Papyri.*
RE	*Realencyclopädie der classischen Altertumswissenschaft*, ed. Wissowa, Kroll *et al.*
TGF	*Tragicorum Graecorum Fragmenta*, ed. Nauck.
ZN	Zeller–Nestle (see bibliography).

PREFACE

The third volume of my *History of Greek Philosophy* (Cambridge University Press, 1969) was divided into two parts, entitled respectively 'The World of the Sophists' and 'Socrates'. By issuing the two parts separately in paperback form, the Press hopes to make them more easily and cheaply available to students. This book reproduces the second part, with the minimum of alterations necessary to allow it to appear as a separate publication. Mentions of 'vol. I' or 'vol. II' in the text refer to the earlier volumes of this work.

Books have most frequently been referred to in the text and notes by short titles, and articles by periodical and date only. Full particulars of books, and titles and page-references for articles, will be found in the bibliography. The fragments of the Sophists, and other texts relating to them, are included in the *Fragmente der Vorsokratiker* of Diels and Kranz (abbreviated DK). The texts in an 'A' section of DK (*Testimonia*) have their number preceded by this letter, and those in a 'B' section, purporting to be actual quotations from the philosopher in question, are designated 'fr.' (fragment).

Translations, from both ancient and modern authors, are my own unless otherwise stated.

W.K.C.G.

DOWNING COLLEGE CAMBRIDGE
MARCH 1971

I

In 1894 Edmund Pfleiderer observed that, since innumerable writers, many of them men of the highest reputation, had written about Socrates and Plato, anyone undertaking the task once more must surely, *in tanta scriptorum turba*, ask himself like Livy: *Facturusne operae pretium sim?* I should not like to have to count the number of books and articles about Socrates that have appeared in the seventy-odd years since Pfleiderer wrote, but I must hope that yet another presentation of him, in the context of the history of Greek philosophy and especially of the philosophic preoccupations of his own century, will prove worth while. The enormous bulk of the scholarly literature means that my own reading in it has been even more—much more—selective than for earlier periods of Greek thought.[1] I have tried to make the selection representative of at least the more recent work, but it is probably inevitable that some of my readers will look in vain for their favourite items. I hope however that I have made myself sufficiently familiar with the ancient evidence to be entitled to views of my own, and it would not be safe to assume that the omission of a writer or a theory is necessarily due to ignorance. In putting Socrates into his setting in the history of Greek thought, it is impracticable to take note of every theory about him, including those which seem to me (though others may differ) to be highly improbable. I shall not, for instance, say much about what may be called the pan-Antisthenean school, who see Antisthenes lurking anonymously in many of Plato's dialogues and disguised as Socrates in Xenophon's *Memorabilia*.[2]

In a review in *Gnomon* for 1955 (259 ff.) Dr Olof Gigon, considering that in spite of over 2,000 years of inquiry the problem of Socrates had not yet been tackled in a properly methodical way, outlined what he saw as a programme of the required research. It is perhaps the best that could be devised, and I have tried to keep its principles in mind in my own work, even if not proceeding in the same order. Yet the final effect of it was a feeling

[1] The bibliographies of V. de Magalhães-Vilhena's two books on Socrates, published in 1952, cover about 96 pages of titles, and the literature of the last sixteen years could add considerably to their number. He also provides a survey of all previous opinion from the eighteenth century. C. J. de Vogel's article on *The Present State of the Socratic Problem* (*Phron.* 1955) deals mainly but not entirely with Vilhena and is a useful starting-point for an exploration of recent views. Useful bibliography will also be found in Coleman Phillipson's *Trial of Socrates* and Gigon's commentaries on Xen. *Mem.* 1 and 2.

[2] For Joël's theory see *The Sophists*, p. 310, n. 4. Perhaps the climax of pan-Antistheneanism is the description of the simple word φρόνησις in Chroust's *S. M. & M.* (128) as 'a typical Antisthenean–Cynic term'. On p. 204 the equation of σωφροσύνη with τὰ ἑαυτοῦ πράττειν at *Charm.* 161b is said to be 'an Antisthenean definition'. The cult frequently causes its devotees to overlook completely parallels between Xenophon and Plato. For more about it see p. 27 below.

that, in spite of the application of the most scientific methods, in the end we must all have to some extent our own Socrates, who will not be precisely like anyone else's. The first step in Gigon's programme is to set apart all texts whose character makes them necessarily consider the historic Socrates alone. The remainder will be those whose aim is other than a historical report: his personal friends, comedy, the attack of Polycrates (which incidentally no longer exists) and certain later material. As to these we are to consider several questions, of which the first is how big a part is played by apologetic or polemic. It sounds perfect, until one finds that the first to be mentioned in the list of purely historical texts is the indictment of Socrates in 399. If this gives us 'the historic Socrates alone' we must accept without question that he was a corrupter of youth and a disbeliever in the city's gods. Did polemic play no part in the statement of those who wished him brought to trial and demanded the death penalty? Another is Xenophon's story of how Socrates rebuked him for asking the Delphic oracle a leading question (p. 28 below); but some scholars have seen a strong apologetic purpose behind this story. The fact is that no one was left indifferent by this altogether unusual character: everyone who has written about him was also reacting to him in one way or another. If then every man must have his own personal Socrates, I can do no more than present mine. It will be based on the fairest assessment of the evidence of which I am capable.

4

I

PROBLEM AND SOURCES

(1) GENERAL

It is a bold—some will say over-bold—procedure to try to separate Socrates from Plato. In the dialogues of Plato it would seem that he has so blended his own spirit with that of Socrates that they can never again be separated. I thought so myself until I came to write an account of the Sophistic movement; but the study which this necessitated has made me see Socrates as squarely set in his contemporary world of the Sophists, Thucydides and Euripides and an eager participant in their arguments. Certainly it has been impossible to leave him out of the previous sections describing fifth-century controversies. Plato, for all his reverence for Socrates as the inspiration and starting-point of his own reflections, is a more sophisticated philosopher and marks a new and fateful development in the history of thought. I would even claim that in reading Plato himself, without any checking or supplementation from other sources, one gets a strong impression that he was an essentially different philosophical character from the master through whose mouth he so often expresses the results of his own maturer and more widely ranging mind. He was still passionately concerned with the questions which excited the previous two genera-tions—whether law and morals were natural or conventional in origin, whether 'virtue' could be taught, whether intelligence or inanimate nature was prior, whether all values were relative, the nature and standing of rhetoric, the relation between being and seeming, know-ledge and opinion, language and its objects—and to him Protagoras and Gorgias, Prodicus and Hippias were still opponents whose challenge had not been adequately met; but to meet it called for some-thing far more radical and comprehensive than the simple ethical intellectualism of Socrates. It called for nothing less than a new vision of the whole of reality, involving metaphysics, human psychology and not least cosmology, for the physicists' conception of a world

5

arisen from soulless matter had proved a powerful support for the sophistic denial of a scientific ethic based on anything but the exigencies of a particular immediate situation. To provide this total solution Plato, a genius of a far more universal stamp than Socrates, was supremely fitted. Since he claimed to have found what Socrates all his life was seeking, and since the personal impact of Socrates had been for him an unforgettable experience of his most impressionable years, he could see nothing improper in putting into Socrates's mouth some (not all) of the discoveries which in his eyes provided the final justification of Socrates's life and death and the answers to the questions that he had asked.

This distinction can only be maintained on the assumption that our sources of information about Socrates are sufficient to give a reliable portrait of him as a man and a philosopher. Any account must begin with the admission that there is, and always will be, a 'Socratic problem'. This is inevitable, since he wrote nothing,[1] and all that we know about him and his thoughts comes from the writings of men of the most varied character, from philosophers to comic poets, some of whom were passionately devoted to him while others thought his influence pernicious. Two things are frequently said of him which, if they both were true, would preclude us from making any significant remarks about him at all. It is claimed on the one hand that his teaching is indissolubly linked with his whole personality, and on the other that we can know nothing about the historical person Socrates because the accounts of him which we have not only are somewhat distorted, as might be thought inevitable, by being filtered through the minds of his pupils or opponents, but were actually never intended by their authors to be anything but fiction.[2] It will be the purpose of the

---

[1] That is, nothing philosophical. If the *Phaedo* is to be believed (60 c–d), he wrote a hymn to Apollo and versified the fables of Aesop in his last days in prison. For references to spurious Socratic works see Chroust, *Socr. M. & M.* 279, n. 791.

[2] Examples: for the first statement (*a*) Jaeger, *Paideia*, II, 36 f.: 'The whole of Socratic literature, with one voice, denies that Socrates's doctrine can be detached from his individual self'; (*b*) Zeller (*Ph. d. Gr.* II. i, 44): 'There is no thinker whose philosophical importance is more closely attached to his personality than is the case with Socrates.' For the second statement: (*a*) Chroust, *S. M. & M.* xiii: 'From its very inception this [*sc.* the Socratic] tradition was intended to be fiction and nothing else'; (*b*) 'L'œuvre, la vie et la mort de Socrate sont une fiction littéraire' (quoted by Ritter, *Sokr.* 61 f., from the summary of Dupréel's *La légende socr.* on its dust-cover). Ritter comments that in this way scholarly critics have happily consigned the person of Socrates, as they did that of Jesus, to the realm of myth ('mit nicht geringerem Scharfsinn—und eben so dumm').

following pages to show that the first statement is true and the second false.

The existence of the Socratic problem makes it necessary to start with an examination of our sources of information. These are for practical purposes four: Aristophanes, Xenophon, Plato and Aristotle. Of the rest of the Socratic literature which grew up in the period immediately following his death, virtually nothing has survived except a few fragments of his follower Aeschines, and the later sources say little of interest which is not taken from Plato or Aristotle. Of our four surviving writers two were philosophers of very different philosophical temperaments, one a retired general who, though endowed with a strong literary and historical bent, had been for most of his life a man of action and always remained so by temperament, and the fourth was a writer of comedies with a strong admixture of satire and farce. With these diverse characters and gifts they naturally saw different things in Socrates and have left us different impressions of him. Albert Schweitzer wrote that in the matter of historical information we are much better off with Jesus than with Socrates, because Jesus was portrayed by simple uneducated people, but Socrates 'by literary men, who exercised their creative ability upon his portrait'.[1] The idea of the 'Socratic legend' as a serious theory seems to have owed its inception to the book of E. Dupréel,[2] and by some scholars it has been taken for granted as needing no further proof. Yet the assumption that all the writers I have mentioned *intended* their accounts to be no more than fiction is so extraordinary as to require indisputable evidence before it is believed. The nearest to such evidence that can be produced is probably the *a priori* argument in the preface to A. H. Chroust's book that

Whenever we possess an ample literary tradition about a certain historical personality, but are yet unable successfully to reconstruct the historicity of that person, we are compelled to assume that the whole literary tradition was never really intended to concern itself with the historical reporting of fact.

---

[1] *The Quest of the Historical Jesus*, Eng. tr., 1954, p. 6.
[2] *La légende socratique et les sources de Platon* (1922). A similar thesis, reducing the Socratic literature to the status of romantic fiction, is put forward by Gigon in his *Sokrates* (1947), on which the comments by C. J. de Vogel in *Mnemos.* 1951 are pertinent.

We must *surmise*, therefore, that this tradition was aimed primarily at creating a legend or fiction.

On the next page this becomes '*As has been pointed out*, from its very inception this tradition *was* intended to be fiction and nothing else'.[1] Evidently therefore the theory of a deliberate fiction stands or falls by our ability or otherwise to elicit from the sources a credible historical figure. If the reader when he reaches the end of this book thinks that we have done so, he need not trouble himself with the theory, but, until the attempt has been made, judgment must be suspended.

Should it be considered to have failed, it need not on that account have been waste of time. We shall at least have learned what Socrates meant to many people, and there remains the possibility of regarding him not as a historical but as a symbolic or eternal figure, in which guise he has been proved an incalculable influence on the history of thought. Thus A. W. Levy has written:

The problem of the historic Socrates is, I believe, insoluble, but the quest to find the meaning of Socrates for ourselves is perennial . . . One can as legitimately ask a philosopher what stand he takes on the meaning of Socrates's life as one can ask what is his theory of the nature of sense-data or his belief about the objectivity of moral values.[2]

For myself however I do not think that our position concerning knowledge of the historical Socrates is as hopeless as is sometimes alleged. The 'question' is at least in part the creation of scholars themselves, who for some reason when they hear the name of Socrates abandon the ordinary canons of comparative evaluation of evidence in favour of one-sided reliance on a single source. Disparity between the authorities is not a thing to cause despair. If they agreed exactly, then indeed we might suspect either that we were getting a very one-sided view of him, because they were all similar people looking for

[1] Chroust, *S. M. & M.* xii and xiii. The italics are mine. M. Treu also argues that it is *a priori* (von vorne herein) mistaken to look for the historical Socrates in the *Memorabilia* (*RE*, 2. Reihe, xviii. Halbb. 1772 f.).

[2] *JHI*, 1956, 94 and 95. As an instance, Professor Ayer's claim about the controversy over the objectivity of values (quoted in *Sophists*, p. 165) could certainly be described as taking a stand on the meaning of Socrates's life, for Socrates as we know him both lived and went to his death in the conviction that the moral problem: 'What am I to do?' cannot be adequately answered without an antecedent knowledge of objective standards of value. In this he has not only his contemporaries the Sophists but the whole tradition of British empiricism against him.

and admiring the same sort of thing, or that he was himself a rather simple and uninteresting figure, which he clearly was not. He was a complex character, who did not and could not reveal every side of himself equally to all his acquaintances, since by reason of their own intellectual powers and inclinations they were not all equally capable of observing and appreciating them. If then the accounts of, say, Plato and Xenophon seem to present a different type of man, the chances are that each by itself is not so much wrong as incomplete, that it tends to exaggerate certain genuine traits and minimize others equally genuine, and that to get an idea of the whole man we must regard them as complementary.[1] The important thing is that of all four main authorities we have writings sufficiently voluminous and self-revealing to leave us in no doubt about *their own* character, mentality and tastes; and this knowledge of the writers themselves is a most valuable aid in comparing and evaluating their impressions of Socrates.

To make this comparison, and neglect no one who had access to Socrates himself or to those who knew him, is absolutely essential. The earlier tendency to pick out one source as authentic, and belittle the rest, became somewhat discredited when every one of the four had found his chosen champion and been held up in turn as the only true mirror. A. Diès speaks entertainingly of how few scholars have, as he puts it, had the courage to mount the quadriga and drive all four horses. Most have preferred to disqualify all but one whom, rather than guide, they allow to run as he pleases. Plato was the first to enjoy this privilege, then Xenophon, then Aristotle; one or two backed Aristophanes, then round came the wheel to Plato again in this century with the British scholars Burnet and Taylor.[2]

[1] It is scarcely any longer possible to say anything new about Socrates. After making the above point repeatedly in lectures, I saw the following by W. W. Baker in *CJ*, 1916–17, 308f.: 'This great figure of Socrates was not one-sided but many-sided ... If Socrates was many-sided, it is natural that men who themselves had different tastes and interests should have *seen* different sides. Therefore the pictures they draw, though different, may be entirely true.' It is astonishing how few scholars have taken this elementary point. (Kierkegaard argued somewhat similarly in a puckish way when he said that although we have no completely dependable conception of Socrates, 'still, we have in exchange all the various nuances of misunderstanding, and with such a personality as Socrates I believe this serves us best'. See his *Concept of Irony*, 158f. His American translator thinks he may have had his tongue in his cheek and Hegel in mind.)

[2] Diès, *Autour de P.* 157–9. See also Stenzel in *RE*, 2. Reihe, v. Halbb. 888: 'He who thinks it permissible to orientate himself from a single source must inevitably, from the standpoint of his own modern thought, intensify still further the exaggeration of his source' (and much more

One very curious argument is quite commonly found, that if something appears to have been widely asserted in the Socratic literature (the writings about Socrates of those in his immediate circle or their associates), that is evidence that it is not genuinely Socratic. This is clearly implied for instance in Chroust's reference to the refusal of Socrates to be perturbed at being condemned to death (*S. M. & M.* 23), which is found in both Xenophon and Plato:

Both Xenophon and Plato may have borrowed 'the philosopher's willingness to die' from Antisthenes; or Xenophon (*Memor.* 4.8.1) may have derived it from Plato who, in turn, is probably dependent on some Antisthenian dictum [when he was a close disciple of Socrates and present at his trial!]. The Stoics, who in this are admittedly under Cynic influence, made much of this 'readiness to die'.[1]

Again, though there are differences between Plato's and Xenophon's accounts of Socrates and his teaching, at many points they coincide. Some critics, however, will not allow us to regard this as any confirmation of the truth of what they say about him: their conclusion is simply that Xenophon has copied Plato. This is not critical method but uncritical theorizing. No doubt Xenophon read Plato's dialogues and the other Socratic writings,[2] but similarity between them is not necessarily evidence that Xenophon was a mere borrower, and it is still less justifiable to extend the argument to the rest of his Socratic writings on the ground that if he sometimes borrowed he did so always. Is it not more likely that, as Diès put it, 'Xenophon et Platon exploitent un fonds commun de Socratisme'?[3]

Before going on to consider the main authors one by one, a word is in place about the so-called 'Socratic *logoi*' or discourses featuring

that is to the point). Vilhena's massive work is once again directed to establishing Plato's dialogues, rightly understood in the context of their time, as the sole historical source. His examination of Xenophon and Aristotle leads him to an entirely negative conclusion, and a full consideration of Aristophanes is deferred.

[1] We cannot doubt that the attribution of such readiness to Socrates is historical. As De Strycker justly points out (*Mél. Grég.* 208), his attitude is confirmed not only by the manner of his death but also by his solitary championship of the law against an infuriated *demos* in the case of the generals after Arginusae (pp. 59 f. below).

[2] Chroust has collected references to a number of 'suggestive similarities' between passages in Xenophon and the Platonic dialogues on p. 230, n. 39, of his *S. M. & M.*

[3] A. Diès, *Autour de P.* 228. See also Field, *P. and Contemps.* 140 f., Stenzel in *RE*, 837 f.

Socrates. In the *Apology* (39 d) Plato makes Socrates utter a prophecy: if the Athenians think that by silencing him they will escape future censure, they are wrong. Others will speak, of whom as yet they know nothing because his authority has restrained them, and being young they will speak all the more harshly. This was true, as Plato knew. He himself (still in his twenties when Socrates died), Aeschines, Antisthenes, Xenophon and others, poured out so many writings to his memory, mostly in the form of conversations in which he played the leading role, that these 'Socratic conversations' (Σωκρατικοὶ λόγοι) achieved the status of a literary genre. The flow was stimulated by opposition, such as that of Polycrates who, probably in the late 390s, composed an *Accusation of Socrates* which is now lost but is mentioned and criticized by Isocrates (*Bus.* 4) as well as later writers.[1] Xenophon, in writing his own version of Socrates's defence and attitude to death, speaks of 'others' who have described them before him and says that he owes his own information to Hermogenes. (Hermogenes, Aeschines and Antisthenes were all of the intimate circle who were with Socrates in his last hours. See *Phaedo*, 59 b.) We know of seven Socratic dialogues by Aeschines (*Alcibiades*, *Axiochus*, *Aspasia*, *Callias*, *Miltiades*, *Rhinon*, and *Telauges*) from which a number of quotations survive, the fullest remains being those of the *Alcibiades*.[2]

For the supposition that 'Socratic *logoi*' had the status of a literary genre of their own our main authority is Aristotle. At the beginning of his *Poetics* he introduces the subject by classifying different kinds of 'imitation' (*mimesis*), of which poetry is one, according to their media. Painters imitate through the medium of colours and shapes, others through the voice,[3] poetry through rhythm, language and harmony, dancing through rhythm alone. There is also an art which

[1] For information on Polycrates see Chroust, *S. M. & M.* chapter 4, and Dodds, *Gorgias*, pp. 28 f. Many scholars believe that, when Xenophon speaks of what 'the accuser' said of Socrates, his reference is to Polycrates rather than to the actual accusers at the trial, and that the *Gorgias* and possibly other dialogues of Plato were written in reply to his attack.

[2] For Aeschines see Field, *P. & Contemps.* 146–52, who gives a complete translation of the *Alcibiades* fragments. He seems to have looked somewhat sourly on his fellow-companions of Socrates, determined to show the worst sides of Callias (in his *Callias*, Dittmar, 193 ff.), Hermogenes and Critobulus, calling Hermogenes a slave to money and Critobulus stupid and dirty (in the *Telauges*, see frr. 40 and 44, Dittmar 290 f.). Plato and Xenophon give a different impression.

[3] Cf. Plato *Soph.* 267 a.

imitates by language (*logos*) alone, either in prose or verse. It has no name, for (1447b9) 'we have no common name for a mime of Sophron or Xenarchus[1] and a Socratic *logos*', and should still lack one if their imitation were in verse. I have quoted this sentence in its context because it is sometimes said that Aristotle is here putting the Socratic conversations 'into the same class with' the mimes of Sophron (the Syracusan contemporary of Plato whose *mimoi* depicted realistic *genre* scenes of everyday life) in such a way as to justify the conclusion that in substance the former could claim no more historical veracity than the latter. In fact he is citing them only as random samples of the whole genus of 'imitation through language alone'. All that they are said to have in common is the medium of *logos*, as painters effect their imitation through colour,[2] and *mimesis* could cover the whole range of verisimilitude from Homer or tragedy ('the imitation of a serious action') to Zeuxis's painting of grapes, so realistic that the birds pecked at it. It is true (and this may well be what made Sophron and the Socratic *logoi* occur to Aristotle's mind together) that Plato was said to have been a great admirer of Sophron and to have introduced his work to Athens.[3] Probably he saw in the form and presentation of its material a useful precedent for the realistic setting and conversational style which he adopted as the best medium for interpreting to the world the character and philosophy of his master, and developing its implications. This is especially likely as the mime had up to then been a very humble and popular form of entertainment, and its elevation to the plane of literature seems to have been due to Sophron himself. It

[1] Xenarchus was Sophron's son, but little else is known of him. See Ziegler in *RE*, 2. Reihe, XVIII. Halbb. 1422.

[2] The much-discussed fragment of Aristotle's dialogue *On Poets* (72 Rose, from Ath. 505 c), with its doubtful points of reading, adds nothing. In Ross's translation (p. 73) it runs: 'Are we then to deny that the so-called mimes of Sophron, which are not even in metre, are *logoi* [to accept Ross's 'stories' here would be misleading] or imitations, or the dialogues of Alexamenos of Teos, which were written before the Socratic dialogues?' (If the MS πρώτους, emended by Kaibel to πρότερον, is correct, the only difference is that the otherwise unknown Alexamenos is himself being called the first writer of Socratic dialogues. See on the text Natorp in *RE*, I, 1375.) Aristotle was evidently making the same point in his lost as in his surviving work on poetry. His only other reference to the Σ. λ. is at *Rhet.* 1417 a 18, where he says that mathematical λόγοι are not concerned with character or moral purpose as Socratic are.

[3] The earliest reference to Plato's interest in Sophron is a quotation from the historian Duris (fourth–third century B.C.) in Athenaeus (504 b). See also D.L. 3.18. In later times the story was frequently told that after his death a copy of the mimes was found under his pillow. (References in *RE*, 2. Reihe, v. Halbb. 1100. It was said that the plays of Aristophanes were found with them.)

remains in the highest degree improbable that from the point of view of historical fidelity there was anything in common between the dialogues of Plato, in which Socrates is shown conversing with other well-known historical figures like Protagoras, Gorgias or Theaetetus, and a series of mimes with titles like *The Sempstresses*, *The Mother-in-law*, *The Fisherman and the Farmer*, *The Tunny-fisher* or *The Sorceresses*. They are 'true to life' in a different sense, and their heirs are Theocritus and Herondas, not Plato.[1] The practice among Socrates's friends of making notes of his conversations at the time, then writing them up and referring back to Socrates himself to check any doubtful points, is attested on pp. 23 f. below.

The historical value of the Socratic literature is to be judged from its own purpose and character; that is, mainly from the internal evidence of the writers—Plato and Xenophon—whose works have survived. And, as Field wisely reminded us, 'we must not fall into the error of ascribing a precisely similar purpose to all of it'.

(2) XENOPHON

Xenophon was an almost exact contemporary of Plato. Probably born within five years of him (430–425), he is known from the internal evidence of his works to have lived until after 355.[2] He was an Athenian citizen, son of Gryllus of the deme Erchia.[3] In 401, in spite of a warning from Socrates (*Anab.* 3.1.5), he joined the ill-fated expedition of Cyrus in Asia, with which his name is primarily linked in most people's minds as the author of the immortal *Anabasis*. Just how long his acquaintance with Socrates lasted we cannot say, but, since Socrates was executed in 399, it could have been almost as long as Plato's. He missed the

---

[1] Detailed comparison between the Platonic dialogues and the mime will be found in Reich, *Der Mimus*, vol. i, chapter 5. If I have not used him as an authority, it is because I find in this chapter some misunderstandings and a truly astonishing exaggeration. One example, in the face of which I find comment impossible, should suffice. Of Plato's portrait of Protagoras he writes (p. 390): 'He has become a type, matched by few in world literature, such as are—besides Hamlet, Falstaff, Don Juan and Don Quixote—above all the figures of mime, Samio and Ardalio, the stupidus, the μωρὸς φαλακρός, Maccus and Pulcinello, Hans Wurst and Kasperle and Karagöz.'

[2] See the discussion in M. Treu, *RE*, 2. Reihe, XVIII. Halbb. 1571 ff. The precise date of his birth is not now ascertainable. Gigon (*Comm. on Mem.* 1, 106; but cf. *OCD*, 962) has revived an early theory that it was a few years earlier (441/o), whereas others have made him a little younger than Plato. (See Phillipson, *T. of S.* 27 with n. (q).)

[3] Authorities in *RE*, VII, 1899.

poignant last scenes of Socrates's life, the trial, the conversations in prison, and the drinking of the hemlock in the presence of his intimates, which so heightened and intensified the feelings of Plato and others about him; but his own attachment was so strong and lasting that in later years he made a point of inquiring about these events from another friend of Socrates, and wrote his own version to counteract the misleading impressions which, as it seemed to him, were being created by others already current. 'When I think', he said at the end of this little work (*Apol.* 34), 'of both the wisdom and the nobility of this man, I cannot refrain from writing of him nor, in writing of him, from praising him.' Set beside this the closing words of the *Phaedo*—'our friend, the best, as we should claim, of any of his generation known to us, and the wisest and most just'—and they afford together a moving testimony to the effect of this remarkable man on others of the most diverse character.

Xenophon might be described as a gentleman in the old-fashioned sense of the term, implying as well as a certain not ignoble type of character a high level of education and general culture. It is a plant that thrives best in an environment of wealth, especially inherited wealth, and there is a certain resemblance between Xenophon and the best among the aristocracy which occupied the great country houses of England in the eighteenth and nineteenth centuries—men whose hearts were not only in the management of their estates and the service of their country but also in the great libraries which some of them amassed with considerable discrimination and also used. He was soldier, sportsman, and lover of country life, methodical in his work, temperate in his habits, and religious with the religion of the plain and honest man. As a writer he employed a clear, easy, straightforward Attic prose on subjects which at least have the charm of variety, and as treated by him seem to put us in astonishingly close touch with the life of his period and class. In these qualities it would be difficult for anyone to surpass the man whose works include the first-hand story of the retreat of Cyrus's Greek force across the Anatolian plateau, a history of Greece from the time when Thucydides left off, a treatise on housekeeping and husbandry, a manual of horsemanship (and one on hunting if the *Cynegeticus* is a genuine work of Xenophon), another on 'ways and means' with suggestions for improving the finances of Athens, and, of course, a series of works designed to display the character of Socrates and preserve his memory from detractors.

On the debit side we must put a certain literal-mindedness and tendency to prosiness, a pedestrian outlook which is sometimes frankly dull, and little sign of any capacity for profound philosophical thought. Here we are concerned with his portrayal of Socrates, as to which it is fair to say that if Plato had been as capable as Xenophon of coping with the retreat across Anatolia or discoursing on the finer points of horsemanship or the virtues of different kinds of soil, he would have been unlikely to display at the same time the philosophic genius and the deep insight into character and motives which so obviously mark his own interpretation of Socrates's life and make one feel that it is penetrating much further than Xenophon's. Xenophon honoured and respected intellectual ability, but all the more, we may suspect, when he saw it combined, as it was in Socrates, with high physical courage, a good war record and general contempt of danger. So much of Socrates he appreciated and loved, and he felt a generous indignation at the harsh treatment that Athens had meted out to him. Much that he saw in Socrates was, I am convinced, characteristic of the real man. When however we find in the Socrates of Plato something far less common-place, far more paradox, humour and irony and above all a greater profundity of thought, it would be wrong to suppose that these were foreign to Socrates simply because they do not appear in Xenophon's portrait. The impression of uniqueness, and the powerful impact, favourable or unfavourable, which he made on everyone who met him (and of these the most hardened sceptic can scarcely feel a doubt), are more comprehensible if we suppose that he had in him much of what Plato discovered as well as what appealed to the prosaic commonsense of Xenophon.

The works in which Xenophon introduces Socrates (apart from the story in *Anab.* 3.1) are four: *Oeconomicus*, *Apologia*, *Symposium* and *Memorabilia*. A reading of them at once makes plain that they differ considerably in character and purpose. The *Oeconomicus* is a highly practical treatise on estate management and farming, in which out of compliment to his dead teacher and friend Xenophon writes of a favourite pursuit of his own in the form of a dialogue between Socrates and a young man seeking his advice. Verisimilitude is assisted by making the last two-thirds of the work a report by Socrates of a conversation which he himself had had with a gentleman farmer, in which he questioned him about his pursuits, although even in this part we find that Socrates has something of his own to contribute. Readers of Plato, knowing their Socrates, may be amused to find this devotee of the city, who never left it of his own free will because 'trees and the open country have nothing to teach me' (*Phaedr.* 230d), singing the praises of agriculture not only as the healthiest of occupations but because it gives the mind leisure to attend to the interests of one's friends and city and is a training in the leadership of men, and solemnly declaring that 'the earth teaches justice too to those capable of learning' (*Oec.* chapters 5 and 6.9). Nevertheless Socrates knew himself to be a peculiar character marked out for a unique mission. He never claimed that his life of self-chosen poverty in the city, with no regular occupation, was the right life for others; and there are several touches in the dialogue sufficiently individualistic to show that the choice of Socrates as chief speaker is something more than an empty compliment. In making Socrates the exponent of one of his own favourite subjects, Xenophon was not neglecting what he remembered of his character or had learned from the talk and writing of others. So for instance Socrates claims to be richer than his wealthy young friend Critobulus because he has sufficient for his needs whereas Critobulus's commitments exceed his income (2.4). At 6.13 we read of his consuming interest in visiting the workshops of all sorts of craftsmen—builders, smiths, painters and sculptors.[1] At 11.3 he makes a joking reference to the comic poets' picture of him as a chatterer, a measurer of the air and a penniless beggar. At 17.15 he digresses briefly from the subject of weeds to remark on the value of an apt simile. Finally, his conversation

---

[1] In *Mem.* 3.10 Xenophon shows him conversing about their craft with a painter, a sculptor and an armourer. The precepts on management and farming, and certain other details, are obviously Xenophon's own, but it was a brilliant touch to remind a reader at this point of Socrates's insatiable eagerness to acquire information about every sort of craft and profession from the men who practised it. (Cf. also *Mem.* 2.7.6 and Plato, *Apol.* 21b–22d.) With questions about the secrets of their art he bombarded manual workers of every sort, poets and politicians: why not also farmers and estate owners?

with Ischomachus is not only a lesson in agriculture but an illustration in that particular field of the truth that one can be unaware of one's own knowledge, and that the best form of teaching is to elicit by questions this knowledge which the pupil already possesses but has been unable to formulate or use. 'Can it be, Ischomachus, that asking questions is teaching? I am just beginning to see what was behind all your questions. You lead me on by means of things I know, point to things that resemble them, and persuade me that I know things that I thought I had no knowledge of.'

Here is the Socratic method in a nutshell, question and answer, 'mental midwifery' and all. It is a clever (and again a truly Socratic) touch, that this time Socrates casts himself in the role of pupil but in reality, through narrating the conversation to one of his own young men, is acting as his guide to the method. Xenophon is not usually credited with an appreciation of the Socratic irony, the affectation that everyone else was wiser than he, but surely it is present here in double measure: in his pretence to Critobulus that he had to put himself under the instruction of Ischomachus not only in the technicalities of farming but even in the method which was peculiarly his own; and in the delighted surprise with which, in the dialogue-within-a-dialogue, he hails his discovery of what Ischomachus had been after with his questions. There is even an open acknowledgment of the Socratic theory, which Plato seized upon with such avidity, that learning is recollection, the bringing into full consciousness of knowledge that was latent in the mind already.[1] For instance, Socrates is quite sure that he does not know how big a hole should be dug when planting a fruit tree, but he has used his eyes as he walked about the fields, and in answer to Ischomachus's questions has to admit that he has never seen one more than $2\frac{1}{2}$ or less than $1\frac{1}{2}$ feet deep, nor more than 2 feet broad, and can even suggest a reason for the appropriate depth. We may well doubt whether the real Socrates was as observant of these things as he was of the characters of his fellow men, but Xenophon has simply used an example from his own sphere of interest to illustrate a pedagogic principle that he had learned from Socrates. The recollection in this

---

[1] ἐλελήθη ἐμαυτὸν ἐπιστάμενος, 18.10. Cf. Plato, *Meno* 85 d οὐκοῦν οὐδενὸς διδάξαντος ἀλλ' ἐρωτήσαντος ἐπιστήσεται, ἀναλαβὼν αὐτὸς ἐξ αὑτοῦ τὴν ἐπιστήμην.

instance is of observations of practical, workaday life, and the author of the *Memorabilia* would be the first to admit that Socrates applied his method to more philosophical, and particularly ethical, teaching. Yet Socrates was not averse to taking his analogies from 'shoemakers, carpenters and smiths' or even, in all probability, from farmers as the Sophists did.[1] Whether he raised the theory of recollected knowledge from an educational aid to a metaphysical doctrine of an immortal soul recalling in this life eternal truths that it has learned in the Beyond, as Plato makes him do, is another question, and must be left till later. The object of the present section is simply to suggest, from an independent reading, that E. C. Marchant goes very wrong when he says (Loeb ed. xxiv): 'The thoughts and reflections... are so entirely Xenophon's own that we may wonder why he did not frankly produce a treatise on the management of an estate instead of a Socratic dialogue.'

The *Apologia*, a brief pamphlet of some eight pages, does not, like its Platonic counterpart, consist simply of the speeches supposedly made by Socrates at his trial. It begins with a statement of purpose. To describe once again the bearing of Socrates at the time of his condemnation and death will not be otiose. Previous writers have put beyond doubt the lofty tone of what he said, but, since they omitted to give the reason for it, it has appeared to spring from a lack of understanding of his predicament. Xenophon therefore applied to Hermogenes, one of the philosopher's closest friends who was with him at the end, and Hermogenes explained the reason, that in Socrates's opinion it was better for him to die than live because he had reached an age when he could only look forward to a gradual failing of his powers, and this would be particularly intolerable to one who had lived such a perfect life hitherto. What follows is partly in Xenophon's own words and, as he tells us himself, 'I have not tried to relate all that was said at the trial, but have contented myself with demonstrating, first, that Socrates's whole concern was to act with reverence towards the gods

---

[1] *Mem.* 1.2.37, and of course analogies from everyday crafts and their tools are frequently employed by the Socrates of both Xenophon and Plato, e.g. the shuttle and the awl at Pl. *Crat.* 388a–b, the pruning-knife at *Rep.* 353a. The common fifth-century analogy between education and farming is used by Socrates at *Phaedr.* 276b and e and (*ex parte Protagorae*) at *Theaet.* 167c. (See *The Sophists*, pp. 168 f.)

and justice in his dealings with men; and secondly, that he did not think it proper to beg and pray for his life, but rather considered it time for him to die.' His method of doing this, as is obvious to anyone who takes the trouble to read this rather pathetic little work, is to put all his reverence for Socrates into the philosopher's own mouth, thus producing an impression of intolerable smugness and complacency. If Socrates had really said such things about himself,[1] far from exciting the love and admiration of men as wise as Plato and as talented and high-spirited as Alcibiades, he would have repelled them more speedily and surely than the ostracizer was repelled by Aristides the Just, who, after all, was only given that standing epithet by other people.

There are a few features in common between Plato's and Xenophon's versions of what happened at the trial, though they have been blunted and coarsened by Xenophon's less sensitive mind and by the fact that his information was at second or third hand and probably put together from various sources besides Hermogenes. In so far as they agree, however, they provide evidence that such points were in some form or another really made, or such incidents really occurred. Both agree that Socrates thought it at least possible that death was better for him than life, and there is a reference in Plato to his advanced age (38c), though this is by no means given as his reason for thinking so. Xenophon's Socrates has not prepared a speech in his own defence, Plato's says that he will speak 'at random, using whatever words come into my head' (17c). Both introduce the 'divine sign' (pp. 82 ff. below), Xenophon as forbidding him to prepare a defence in advance, Plato as having uttered no warning against his coming to trial, thereby indicating that, whatever the outcome, it must be good. In both cases the effect is an indication that death will mean no harm for Socrates. Both agree on the substance of the charges brought against him, which are confirmed as

---

[1] E.g. §5: 'Do you not know that up to now I would not allow that any man has had a better life than I have, for I have had the supreme pleasure of knowing that I have lived my whole life piously and righteously'; and §18: 'If no one can disprove what I have said about myself, do I not justly deserve the praise of both gods and men?' Plato's Socrates says (*Apol.* 21 a–b) that Chaerephon asked the Delphic oracle whether anyone was wiser than he, and the oracle replied 'no one'; whereat he was astonished and incredulous, because he knew he was not wise in the least. Xenophon's, reporting (§14) only that Chaerephon 'asked the oracle about me', says Apollo told him that no man was either more liberal or more just or possessed of greater prudence and self-control (σωφροσύνη); and he accepts the reply without comment, except to say that Apollo at any rate did not call him a god, as it did Lycurgus, but only the wisest of men.

historical from an independent source (p. 62 below). Both agree that Chaerephon consulted the Delphic oracle about Socrates and received a favourable reply, though Xenophon tells the story more clumsily and makes Socrates speak about it in a different and more laboured way. Both report that an exchange of remarks took place between Socrates and Meletus, and that Socrates was unwilling to offer an alternative penalty in the ordinary sense, though only Plato refers to the suggestion of free meals in the Prytaneum and the offer of a sum of money put up by his friends. Finally, both mention his refusal of the offer of his friends to arrange his escape after condemnation, the subject of Plato's *Crito*. There is some slight internal evidence that the *Apology* of Plato was among Xenophon's sources, but the differences are too great to allow of the supposition that he simply took over these facts from Plato. Even if he had done so, we should still have been faced with the question whether Plato, who claimed to have been present at the trial, had himself invented them.

To conclude, Xenophon's *Apology* is of little or no independent value, and may be set aside in favour of a serious consideration of Plato's writings on the same subjects. It teaches us something about Xenophon, that, when he was trying to live up to the demands of a serious and solemn subject like the justification of Socrates's conduct through his trial and approaching death, he was by no means at his best.[1]

The *Symposium* is a longer and a more elaborately composed work, which naturally invites comparison with Plato's of the same name. Apart from Socrates, none of the participants are the same, but some are

---

[1] Every kind of opinion has been put forward about the *Apology*. Its authenticity has been denied (by Schenkl, Wilamowitz and others) and reasserted. The reliance on Hermogenes has been called fictitious (e.g. by Gigon and Treu; and the fact that in *Mem.* bk. 4 Xenophon repeats some of the same matter on the same authority is, oddly enough, said to confirm this), and again both genuine and Xenophon's only source (von Arnim). The *Apol.* has been said to have borrowed from Plato's as well as other Socratic 'apologies' (Treu) and again to have been written before Plato's (von Arnim, whose imagination soared to recounting how Plato's when it appeared made Xenophon ashamed of his own so that he wrote *Mem.* 1.1.4 and bk. 4 to replace it, as well as to answer the attack of Polycrates; Maier on the other hand, *Sokr.* p. 15, thought his *Apol.* itself showed knowledge of this attack). Alternatively, it was written after Plato's not in imitation but to oppose the sober truth to Plato's 'magnificent fiction', and is a highly trustworthy source (W. Schmid, *Gesch.* 224 f.). See in general Diès, *Autour de P.* 220–2, Hackforth, *CPA*, 11–21, Edelstein, *X. u. P. Bild*, 138–50, and Treu in *RE*, 2. Reihe, XVIII. Halbb. 1888–94. If it is true that Anytus lived until after 386 (Wilam. *Ar. u. Athen*, II, 374f.) then the *Apol.*, which mentions his death, cannot have been written before that date.

known from the pages of Plato nevertheless. We meet Hermogenes the brother of Callias (known to us from the *Phaedo* and *Cratylus*), Critobulus the son of Crito (mentioned in the *Apology* and *Phaedo*), and Plato's uncle Charmides, after whom he named a dialogue. The host is Callias son of Hipponicus, whom Plato portrayed as the richest man of Athens with an extravagant passion for Sophists[1] and cast as host to the gathering of Sophists so vividly described in the *Protagoras*. Of special interest is the presence of Antisthenes, of whom we know all too little. He was undoubtedly a figure of considerable importance in the context of Sophistic and Socratic thought, yet Plato ignores him completely except for the bare mention of his name among those present at Socrates's death. In Xenophon he appears as a somewhat ill-mannered, disputatious and tactless person, and at the same time quick to take offence at any suspected aspersions on himself. It is easy to believe that this was the man who quarrelled with Plato and gave an insulting title to the dialogue that he wrote against him (see *The Sophists*, p. 310 with n. 2).

Whatever else may be said about the work, it presents a most vivid and realistic picture of that curious institution of the time, the *symposion* or 'drinking-together', a mixture of after-dinner conversation over the nuts and wine with cabaret entertainment hired by the host. Plato with his more purely philosophical interests does not give us such a typical example. At his *symposion*, as soon as dinner is over, the proposal is made and accepted that the drinking should be moderate and the entertainer dismissed, so that the company can embark immediately on a discussion of a set subject, each stating his views in turn. Xenophon's aim is to portray the whole man Socrates, not simply the philosopher, and for this, as he tells us, he decided it was important to show him in his lighter and more unbuttoned as well as his serious moods.[2] It is therefore only in the middle of a varied programme of

[1] The joke about the huge sums that he has spent on them (Plato, *Apol.* 20a, *Crat.* 391c) is repeated by Xenophon (*Symp.* 1.5). On Xenophon's characterization of him see Dittmar, *Aesch.* 207–10. Aeschines wrote a dialogue named after him.

[2] *Symp.* 1.1. Cf. *Mem.* 4.1.1. Dittmar noted (*Aesch.* 211) that in Plato's *Prot.* (347c ff.) Socrates appears to condemn outright the hiring of entertainers at symposia as unworthy of educated men. But he misses the irony of the passage. The point of it is that Socrates chooses to put the understanding of poetry, which Protagoras has just advocated as 'the most important part of education' (338e), on a level with such cabaret turns. (In Plato's *Symp.* the suggestion that the flute-girl be dismissed comes not from Socrates but from Eryximachus.)

entertainment that Socrates suggests turning to *logoi*.[1] Admittedly the dancing-girl's achievements inspire him to make a few observations on the comparative powers of men and women (rudely interrupted by Antisthenes with a personal remark about Xanthippe), but he breaks into the start of a discussion on whether virtue is teachable with a suggestion that they attend instead to the business in hand: the dancer is ready to begin. The humour in the dialogue, of which there is plenty, consists of personal banter, never subtle and often crude. The main subjects of more serious talk are, first, a series of speeches and discussions in which each symposiast is asked to say what is the accomplishment or possession on which he most prides himself and why; and secondly a speech by Socrates on Eros which is brought in rather suddenly and awkwardly without natural connexion with what has gone before. The Syracusan master of the boy and girl entertainers has gone out to prepare with them for a little mythological scene of Dionysus and Ariadne, and Socrates suddenly 'raised a new topic' while they were waiting, namely the praise of Love. A eulogy on Love by each of the diners in turn is of course the sole theme at Plato's symposium, which may be the reason for its sudden appearance here (there are one or two pretty clear signs that Xenophon knew Plato's),[2] but it is likely also that Love was a fairly constant theme at such gatherings in real life. The erotic element runs like a thread throughout Xenophon's conversations, much more crudely and outspokenly expressed than in Plato, and no secret is made of the intentionally aphrodisiac effect of some of the performances. As for Socrates, though as ready to join in the jokes as anyone, his theme, as one would expect, is that 'love of the soul is greatly superior to love of the body'.

Structurally the composition creaks at every joint. Rather than lead naturally from one subject to another, Xenophon will say, 'So that subject dropped. Then X said...' or 'that was the end of that conversation'. Unable to trust his readers to catch the tone of his writing, he will tell us laboriously, 'Thus they mingled jest and earnest in their

[1] They had already enjoyed instrumental solos by a flute-girl and boy-citharist, acrobatic dancing by a girl with hoops and among knife-blades, a dance by the boy, a comic parody of it by the professional buffoon, and an accompanied song by the boy.

[2] On the complex relation between the two see Maier, *Sokr.* 17–19, and other authorities referred to by Treu, *RE*, 1872. Perhaps predictably, an assumed but unknown dialogue of the ubiquitous Antisthenes figures prominently as a conjectural common source.

talk', or 'So then this *logos* was conducted seriously'. Nevertheless the scenes have an authentic stamp, all the more perhaps for his naivety, and few would want to miss such things as the 'beauty competition' between young Critobulus and the Silenus-like Socrates or the latter's complaint that Antisthenes loves him not for himself but only for his looks. That the *Symposium* is an imaginative work can hardly be denied, and Xenophon's claim to have been present must be taken as a transparent dramatic device. He begins: 'In my opinion, it is worth recording the behaviour of good men not only when they are serious but also when they are amusing themselves, and I wish to relate things which I know because I was present when they took place.'[1] There is no other reference to his presence, he takes no part in the conversations, and indeed, from the time in this first chapter when he describes the meeting of the friends and their adjournment to the house of Callias, it is impossible to suppose that he was among them. In any case he was probably, as Athenaeus already objected, only a child at the time.[2] What we may without undue credulity allow him is that his playlet was at least to some extent based on conversations which he had heard at different times and on his personal recollections of the characters and idiosyncrasies of its real-life actors, supplemented no doubt after his return from Asia by talk with surviving friends of Socrates and perusal of their reminiscences. Phillipson very reasonably says[3] that, if his Socratic writings were not composed until, perhaps, between 387 and 371, this is no objection to such a supposition. Memoirs and autobiographies are often written many years after the events and people to which they refer. In an age when books were less amenable to quick and easy reference, memories were better, and Xenophon, as a devoted Boswell, would no doubt have made notes at the time of conversations of Socrates to which he had listened. This practice among Socrates's pupils is mentioned by Plato. In the *Theaetetus* Euclides of Megara speaks of having been told by Socrates of a discussion he had had with Theaetetus and, when asked whether he can repeat it, replies (142d): 'Certainly not from memory, but I made some notes at the time, as

[1] οἷς δὲ παραγενόμενος ταῦτα γιγνώσκω δηλῶσαι βούλομαι.
[2] Ath. 216d. The dramatic date of the *Symp.* is fixed at 422 by the victory of Autolycus in the Panathenaic pancration (*Symp.* 1.2, cf. Ath. *loc. cit.*).
[3] *Trial*, 29, and cf. Schmid, *Gesch.* 231.

soon as I got home, and later on wrote out what I could recall at my leisure. Then, every time I went to Athens, I questioned Socrates upon any point where my memory had faded and made corrections on my return. In this way I have pretty well the whole conversation written down.' The narrator of Plato's *Symposium*, Apollodorus, who has been an associate of Socrates for three years, says that during that time he has 'made it his care to know what Socrates says and does every day' (172c). He learned the conversation at Agathon's house from another admirer of Socrates, obtained confirmation of some points from Socrates himself (173b), and is now ready to pass it on like a precious inheritance to others. Plato's half-brother Antiphon 'worked hard at getting by heart' the discussion between Socrates, Zeno and Parmenides (*Parm.* 126c). One may admit the dramatic value of such passages, but they would be impossible without a foundation in a known practice of the disciples. To record or commit to memory Socrates's conversations, and repeat them to one another, was obviously a labour of love among them.[1] If Xenophon included among things that he had 'heard Socrates say' conversations which in fact had been related to him in this way, or written down, by those who *had* heard them, the conventions of the time would allow it to be an innocent enough procedure.

Whatever Xenophon's sources of information and method of composition may be, we recognize in the Socrates of his *Symposium* a number of traits which can be justifiably regarded as genuinely Socratic. Such are his mock modesty (1.5); his cultivation of bodily health by exercise and avoidance of excess (2.17 and 24f.); his addiction to the method of question and answer (4.56ff.); his equation of beauty (καλόν) with practical utility or fitness for function (5.4ff.; Treu compares *Mem.* 3.8.4ff., 10.9ff., 4.6.9, to which one could add many passages from Plato); and his praise of a love which, though spiritual rather than physical, does not thereby become pallid and lacking in passion (ἀνεπαφρόδιτον, 8.15 and 18.)[2]

---

[1] Cf. also D.L.'s report of Simon the cobbler (2.122), who used to make notes of all he could remember of what Socrates said on visits to his shop. (For details on Simon, Zeller, *Ph. d. Gr.* 241f. with notes.)

[2] I have said nothing about the so-called 'sympotic literature', a shadowy phenomenon which some have assumed to have been already in existence in the fifth century, so that the *Symposia* of

I have left to the last the main Socratic work of Xenophon, the four books of *Memorabilia*.[1] What has just been said about the credibility of the *Symposium* applies in even stronger measure to them. Their character is governed by his motive, which he states thus (1.3.1): 'To support my opinion that Socrates benefited those who consorted with him, both by actions revealing his own character and by his conversation, I will set down what I can remember of them.' This then is the work in which he has collected all possible material bearing on his chosen subject, and it is not surprising to find occasional repetitions of what he has said elsewhere, e.g. in the *Apology* (cf. *Mem.* 4.8), and even internal repetitions and sometimes inconsistencies. The occasional claim of the author to have been present at the actual conversations he records is perhaps not to be taken more seriously than when it occurs in *Symposium* or *Oeconomicus*,[2] but his earnest desire to reproduce accurately the substance of what he has learned is, in accordance with his purpose, beyond doubt.[3] This purpose is not to write a life of Socrates, nor even to give a complete portrait of his character, but by

Plato and Xenophon represent only links in a chain ('ein Glied innerhalb der sympotischen Literatur', Treu, *RE*, 1872), or alternatively the tip of an iceberg of which the rest lies submerged beneath the waves of time. Treu refers to the article on this subject by Hug (*RE*, 2. Reihe, VIII. Halbb. 1273 ff.), but what Hug says is quite different. As a form of prose literature, the symposium is a post-classical phenomenon owing its inspiration entirely to the work of Plato and Xenophon who were not intermediaries but the originators of the whole genre. 'Aber erst durch den sokratisch-platonischen Dialog wurde die naturgemässe und bequeme Form für eine Literaturgattung gegossen, die Symposion-Literatur, welche... eine ununterbrochene Reihe von Plato bis Macrobius bildet.' 'Durch ihre [*sc.* Plato's and Xenophon's] häufige Nachahmung wurden die literarischen Symposien eine eigene Literaturgattung.' (See Hug, 1273 and 1274.)

[1] In Greek ἀπομνημονεύματα. Schmid (*Gesch.* 225, n. 5), distinguishes this word as 'personal recollections' from ὑπομνήματα, written notes or memoranda. The Latin title dates only from the sixteenth century, and *Commentarii*, which occurs in Gellius (14.3), has been suggested as a better translation. See Marchant, Loeb ed. vii.

[2] Schmid's attempt at a distinction, on the ground that the *Mem.* belong to a different 'Literaturgattung', has not been generally supported. The claim is however, as Treu remarked (*RE*, 1771), genuinely intended 'to legitimize the author's right to speak about Socrates'. It is in fact rarely made, unambiguously in only four places (1.3.8, 1.4.2, 2.4.1 and 4.3.2). To these are usually added 1.6.14 and 2.5.1, but I do not think that ἐμοὶ ταῦτα ἀκούοντι and ἤκουσα ἄλλον αὐτοῦ λόγον necessarily imply the presence of Xenophon at the conversation in question. Contrast ἤκουσα αὐτοῦ διαλεγομένου at 2.4.1 and the emphatic language of 4.3.2, ἐγὼ δέ, ὅτε πρὸς Εὐθύδημον τοιάδε διελέγετο, παρεγενόμην. 1.3.8 is the only occasion on which he himself takes part in the talk.

[3] For a reasoned defence of the *Mem.* as historical in intention, and an estimate of their historicity in effect, see Simeterre, *Théorie socratique*, 7–19. For the date or dates of its composition see his summary of the evidence on p. 13. On pp. 19–21 he gives a bibliography to date of works on the historical value of Xenophon.

illustrating in speech and action his inherent goodness and the beneficial effect of his companionship, example and advice, to refute his detractors and in particular those who, at his trial or afterwards, brought specific charges against him. He is not concerned to fill in the historical, biographical or local background, and however much we should now treasure such information it is pointless to blame Xenophon, as he is sometimes blamed, for not doing what he did not set out to do.

He starts by repeating the legal indictment against Socrates and refuting its two charges in turn, namely offences against the state religion and corruption of the young. Under the latter head he introduces a series of points which are not known to have been made by the prosecution and are known from Libanius to have occurred in the later 'Accusation' of Socrates by Polycrates (written some time after 393), and in dealing with these he speaks no longer of 'the prosecution' (οἱ γράψαντες) but of 'the accuser' (ὁ κατήγορος). This apologia, it appears, is a combined reply to both.[1] It occupies only the first two chapters of Book I, after which Xenophon turns from the negative task of rebuttal to the positive benefits which resulted from Socrates's teaching and example, and it has all the appearance of a self-contained pamphlet. The structure of the *Memorabilia* has given rise to wildly different opinions. To some they are a consciously and carefully constructed whole, to others a confused and clumsy collection of material for whose arrangement Xenophon is not to be blamed, since he obviously never intended it to be published and it was thrown together by a careless editor after his death.[2] Such judgments are inevitably in large measure subjective, and need not detain us here.

Enough has probably been said in estimation of the historical value of the work, which is made more probable by the feebleness of some

---

[1] The allusions to Polycrates were first detected by Cobet. The charges are partly political in character (Socrates was said to have fostered oligarchy and to have attacked the Athenian method of election by lot), and it is suggested that such matters could not be brought up at the trial owing to the amnesty of 403 (Chroust, 73). See also pp. 61–3 below.

[2] Gigon in his Commentary argued against Maier and Wilamowitz for conscious composition by Xenophon himself, and he is supported by Treu (*RE*, 1779). By way of contrast Chroust (*op. cit.* 5) speaks of 'the obvious lack of an orderly and articulate arrangement', and concludes that 'the whole *Mem.* could neither have been the result of one single uniform draft, nor have been edited by Xenophon himself'. Similar opinions are expressed by von Fritz in *Rh. Mus.* 1935, p. 20, and Schmid, *Gesch.* 229.

of the arguments used against it. If many of the ideas must be 'Xenophon's own' because they reappear elsewhere in his writings, is it not possible that he owed them to Socrates whom he so much admired? Those who like to detect 'Antisthenean elements' everywhere say for instance that, since Antisthenes's ideal was to teach by example rather than theoretical discussion, it is 'Antisthenean' when Xenophon tells us of the moral influence of Socrates's own conduct. Apart from the fact that Antisthenes claimed to be in all things following Socrates, the information is most useful as illustrating how different disciples' accounts of Socrates supplement each other to give between them a picture of the whole man: we know enough of Plato and Xenophon to be sure that it is his ideas that would especially appeal to the former, his conduct and practical advice to the latter. Again, the Antisthenes-cult can lead its devotees to ignore completely any parallels between Xenophon and Plato. At *Mem.* 1.2.53 Socrates says that once the soul has left a body, even of a near relation, it may be disposed of quickly and unceremoniously. Chroust compares this to 'Cynic lack of piety towards the dead'. No thought of the *Phaedo* enters his head, where in answer to Crito's question how they are to bury him Socrates smilingly replies (115c) 'Anyhow you like, provided you can catch me', and explains that, since the corpse will no longer be Socrates, its disposal is of no importance. Nor does he think of Aristotle, who says (*EE* 1235a39) that in Socrates's opinion corpses were useless, and could be disposed of as such.[1] Finally, when Diogenes Laertius five or six centuries later tells an anecdote in which a saying is attributed to Antisthenes, and Xenophon gives the same saying to Socrates, the same critics expect us to believe Diogenes rather than the man who was personally acquainted with Socrates and with a number of his friends.[2] There is indeed something in the claim that, in accordance with his avowed purpose of winning over the ordinary Athenian, we must be prepared to find him putting a somewhat one-sided emphasis on the conventionally virtuous side of Socrates rather than on his uniqueness

[1] Gigon (*Mus. Helv.* 1959, 177) assumes that Xenophon and Aristotle are both drawing on a 'Grundtext' now lost.

[2] For a treasury of such examples of the Antisthenes-cult, which was inaugurated by Joël's *Echte u. xenoph. Sokr.*, see Chroust, *S. M. & M.* chapter 5. It is to be noted that, in Chroust's own words (p. 102), 'with the exception of a few meagre fragments, all the writings of Antisthenes have been lost'.

and eccentricity.[1] Yet even this did not prevent him from letting Socrates argue for his disturbing paradox (known also from Plato) that the sinner who knows what he is doing is more righteous than the involuntary one (*Mem.* 4.2.19f.).

Before leaving Xenophon it is worth recalling a story of which the truth can hardly be doubted, and which gives a valuable insight into his personal relations with Socrates. In the *Anabasis* (3.1.4) he tells how, when he received a letter from his friend Proxenus inviting him to join the expedition of Cyrus, his first reaction was to show it to Socrates and ask his advice. Socrates was doubtful of the effect on Athenian opinion of Xenophon's linking himself with the pro-Spartan Persian prince, and advised him to consult the oracle at Delphi. Being keen to accept, Xenophon somewhat disingenuously put his question in the form 'to what god should he sacrifice and pray in order to ensure a successful outcome of the enterprise he had in mind?', and the oracle obligingly supplied the names of gods. Socrates told him frankly that he had done wrong in not asking first whether he should go at all, but added that, as he had put the question in this way, he must carry out the god's orders. The Athenians did in fact pass sentence of banishment on Xenophon, and there is something rather touching in the pains he takes to make it clear that Socrates was not in any way responsible for his unpatriotic conduct. One of the complaints against Socrates was that his young associates, of whom Alcibiades was the most notorious, had had discreditable political careers, and Xenophon elsewhere shows himself particularly anxious to exonerate him from the charge.[2] Here he does so even when the story must be against himself. It also shows that the occasions in the *Memorabilia* on which Socrates's younger friends turn to him for immediate practical advice are based on a genuine aspect of their relationship, though Plato preferred to concentrate on their more general and philosophical difficulties like the nature of names or (half-way between the two) the way in which *areté* is acquired.

---

[1] So Zeller, *Ph. d. Gr.* 2.1, 95, and Taylor, *VS*, 31: 'He carefully suppresses, as far as he can, all mention of the personal peculiarities which distinguish Socrates from the average decent Athenian.' Since Xenophon was something of an 'average decent Athenian' himself, perhaps 'was less aware of' would be truer than 'carefully suppresses'.

[2] See especially *Mem.* 1.2.12ff. Plato in the *Symp.* shows the same desire to dissociate Socrates from Alcibiades's unprincipled conduct

(3) PLATO

Mann kann einem Lehrer einen schöneren Dank nich abstatten, als es Platon gerade damit tat, dass er so über ihn hinausging.

The finest possible expression of gratitude to a teacher is to go beyond him in just the way that Plato did.

Julius Stenzel

When in my book on the Sophists I tried to describe the whole intellectual ferment of the fifth century B.C., I naturally could not omit Socrates, perhaps its most important, and certainly its most controversial, figure. In referring there to his opinions, I depended mainly on Plato, as I did also, to a considerable extent, for the views of the Sophists Protagoras, Prodicus and Hippias. It may fairly be said, therefore, that in that book I prejudged, or begged, the question of Plato's trustworthiness as a source for Socrates. On their relationship as I see it I have said a little already (pp. 5 f. above). It is here that one feels most acutely the inevitable subjective element in anyone's treatment of Socrates. Perhaps this is in itself some evidence for the kind of man he was. 'This', said L. Versényi, 'was what the maieutic method aimed at: that each should come to know himself rather than Socrates.'[1] At any rate it is best to state one's position frankly at the outset. For the personal appearance, character and habits of Socrates[2] we may go with confidence to both Plato and Xenophon, and we find indeed a general agreement in their accounts of these matters. But for our chief concern, the contribution of Socrates to philosophical, and in particular ethical, inquiry, I believe it is best to rely primarily on those who were themselves philosophers and so best capable of understanding him. That means in the first place Plato, but also Aristotle in so far as he was a student and associate of Plato and had learned from him the relation of his own thought to the unwritten teaching of his master.

[1] *Socr. Hum.* 159. Did the author realize that even in that sentence he was accepting Plato as a reliable source? It is from Plato that we learn of the 'maieutic method' as characteristic of Socrates (pp. 58 n. 3, 124 f. below). Or take the boldly sceptical remark of Schmid about the one work in which, if anywhere, most people would claim that there was a large amount of historical truth (*Gesch.* 243): 'Although Plato was present at the trial (Plato, *Ap.* 34a, 38b), to regard the *Apology* as historical is out of the question.' If it is out of the question to regard the *Apol.* as historical, why believe its statement that Plato was at the trial?

[2] Those who are wondering what place these have anyway in an account of his philosophical views may be referred back to the quotations from Jaeger and Zeller on p. 6, n. 2 above.

Plato, then, it is here claimed, is the chief, and Xenophon only an auxiliary, source of our knowledge of Socrates as a philosopher. But this brings us immediately to the crux of the whole Socratic question, namely the relation between the teachings of Socrates and Plato. The very fact that Plato was himself a philosopher means not only that he was better placed than others to understand the full import of Socrates's teaching, but also that in his own hands philosophy was bound to progress. His lifetime was prolonged for over fifty years after Socrates's execution, and his love and admiration for his master did not lead him to suppose that he could best honour his memory by merely writing down, as nearly as possible verbatim, what he recollected of his conversations, with no attempt to develop their implications. Piety itself demanded that he should defend the outlook of Socrates against criticisms inherent in the development of philosophy after his death, and how could this be done without adding fresh arguments to what the living Socrates actually said? This is of course the normal relationship between the work of master and follower in the philosophical world. Here however we have not only the complication that the master himself left nothing in writing by which the innovations of his successor could be checked: we have the altogether unusual situation that the successor wrote no impersonal treatises but a series of dialogues, sometimes highly dramatic in form, in many of which his predecessor is the chief speaker; and a limitless field for controversy is provided by the question how far what is ascribed to Socrates in a Platonic dialogue represents the views of the historic Socrates.

Our own answer to this question will only be completed with the completion of the whole account of Socrates, for it is bound to crop up at various points in the exposition itself. But a few principles may be briefly laid down first. I have said already that it is difficult not to think of Socrates as a man of (to use a crude distinction) the fifth century and Plato of the fourth, one who had had time and talent to think out a fuller reply to the Sophists than Socrates had done in the heat of personal contact and argument with them. Reading our authorities on Socrates gives a vivid impression of a highly individual character whom one feels one knows not only as a thinker but as a whole person. In this of course the dramatic form of Plato's writings, far from being a hindrance, is a tremendous help.[1] This feeling of personal acquaintance gives a certain encouragement (may I even say a certain right?), when a particular philosophical point is in question, to say: 'No, I can't imagine that Socrates himself would have put it like that', or 'Yes, that is just what I should have expected Socrates to say'. If this sounds an impossibly subjective criterion, I can only say that, provided it is based on a reading of all the sources, I do not believe that any better one presents itself. Indeed on this basis a large measure of agreement was being reached, at least in England, when in the first quarter of this century the subject was once more thrown into the melting-pot by the contentions of two Oxford scholars, both occupying chairs in Scotland, whose knowledge of their subject and general powers of judgment inevitably commanded respect: A. E. Taylor and John Burnet. Their thesis obtains little if any support today,[2] but reference to it may be a useful way of leading up to what I regard as a more historical approach.

The Burnet–Taylor thesis was that whatever in a Platonic dialogue is put into the mouth of Socrates must be assumed to be substantially what Socrates said in his lifetime. If this were true, much of what has through the centuries been thought of as Plato's most characteristic contribution to philosophy would not be his at all, but only a reproduction of his master's voice. This applies in particular to the famous 'Theory of Ideas', which is expounded through the mouth of Socrates in some of Plato's greatest dialogues like the *Phaedo* and *Republic*. On it Taylor wrote (*Socrates*, 162):

For my own part, I feel with Burnet that it is inconceivable that any thinker should introduce an eminently original doctrine of his own to the world by representing it as something which had long been familiar to a number of living contemporaries who were certain to read his work and detect any misrepresentation.

The main argument for this point of view might be described as 'the argument from outraged propriety',[3] and it receives its greatest support from the *Phaedo*, which purports to relate the conversation on the last

---

[1] Ritter on p. 31 of his *Sokrates* gives an admirable summing-up of the way in which Plato presents a consistent and rounded picture of a real, living and exceptional individual and makes credible both the devotion of his followers and the opposition and hatred of his enemies.

[2] For an effective reply to it see A. M. Adam's article in *CQ*, 1918.

[3] 'An offence against good taste and an outrage on all natural piety', Burnet (*Phaedo*, p. xii).

day of Socrates's life up to the last moving moment when, surrounded
by his most intimate friends, he drank the hemlock. How improper it
would have been for Plato at any time, but above all in describing this
last solemn scene, to misrepresent Socrates as putting forward a doctrine
which was in fact his own invention and not something taught by
Socrates at all!

This argument errs because it looks back from the present day on
all the consequences of Plato's theory, which have admittedly been tremendous. But it is no unique event in the history of philosophy and
science that something which proves afterwards to have been a turning-
point should have been first introduced naturally, almost unconsciously,
by its author, to whom it seems no more than an inevitable consequence
of things that have been said before. A parallel will be helpful. The
'Copernican revolution' is certainly such a turning-point, yet of the
De revolutionibus of Copernicus, in which the epoch-making hypothesis
was announced, T. S. Kuhn has written:[1]

It is a *revolution-making rather than a revolutionary* text . . . A revolution-
making work is *at once the culmination of a past tradition and the source of a
novel future tradition.* As a whole the *De revolutionibus* stands almost entirely
within an ancient astronomical and cosmological tradition; yet within its
generally classical framework are to be found a few novelties which shifted
the direction of scientific thought *in ways unforeseen by its author.*

Briefly the matter stands thus. Socrates said that you cannot discuss
moral questions like how to act justly, or aesthetic questions like
whether a thing is beautiful, unless you have previously decided what
you mean by the concepts 'justice' and 'beauty'. (This we know from
Xenophon and Aristotle no less than Plato.) Until these are fixed, so
that we have a standard in our minds to which the individual actions
or objects may be referred, we shall not know what we are talking
about, and discussion may be frustrated because the parties are attaching
different meanings to the same words. If this is right, said Plato, then
we must believe that such a thing as justice or beauty really exists, for
otherwise what is the use of trying to define it? It is no good looking

[1] *The Copernican Revolution*, 134. I have italicized words which seem to me particularly
significant for our present purpose. Cf. also what is said about the relation of Platonic to Socratic
forms on p. 121 below.

32

for a universal standard if it is only imaginary. He taught therefore the existence of a Form or 'Idea' (in Greek *eidos* or *idea*) of these and other concepts, which was not a *mere* concept existing in our minds but had an eternal and unchanging nature independent of what human beings might think it was. This is the famous *chorismos*, or affirmation of the *separate* existence of the Ideas—separate, that is, both from the particular instances of them in the world and from our thought of them; and belief in such independently existing Forms constitutes what is known as 'Plato's Theory of Ideas'. That it arose out of the Socratic demand for definitions, and went beyond it in this way, is confirmed by Aristotle.

This was seen by later philosophers, from his immediate pupil Aristotle onwards, to constitute a new conception of reality, and further reflection, and discussion with his colleagues in the Academy, revealed serious difficulties in it to Plato himself. Yet in his own mind, I am sure, it would seem to constitute no more than the obvious and only possible defence of Socrates's teaching, and to do no more than bring its implications into the open. 'Before you can know that a thing is beautiful you must be able to say what beauty is.' It could not have been long before someone raised the pertinent question: 'Yes, Socrates, but are you asking us to define what is real or not? For, if beauty, justice and such are only creations of our imagination, surely you are wasting our time.' By trying to answer this question in a sense favourable to Socrates rather than to Gorgias, how could Plato have thought that he was acting otherwise than from motives of piety, and why should he have hesitated to put the necessary defence of Socratic doctrine into Socrates's own mouth?

The justification, then, in Plato's mind for putting a doctrine into Socrates's mouth was not that the doctrine *tel quel*, in its complete form, had been taught by Socrates, but that it could appear to Plato to be based on one of Socrates's fundamental convictions, and constitute a legitimate projection, explication and defence of it. This criterion may help us to put our fingers on some of Socrates's other beliefs. Did he, for instance, believe in the immortality of the soul? Many scholars have thought that in the *Apology* Plato makes him speak as an agnostic on this point, but in the *Phaedo* he asserts it unequivocally and offers a series of elaborate and highly metaphysical proofs involving the doctrines of transcendent forms, of reincarnation, and of knowledge as recollection of truths learned in the other world. It is neither improper nor unlikely that Plato should have added these proofs on his own account, drawing them from his other great source of inspiration, the Pythagorean philosophy, *provided that Socrates was convinced of immortality in the first place.* If he was not, we must agree with Burnet and Taylor that it would have been unthinkable for Plato to have foisted the conviction on him in narrating the last hours of his life. But if Plato knew that Socrates died in the faith that his soul—his true self—would survive the death of his body, it was both natural and proper that he should make him defend that faith in what seemed to him, Plato, the most convincing manner. Again, the idea of the philosopher-kings in the *Republic*, with all the substructure of psychology, epistemology and ontology that supports it, undoubtedly goes beyond anything that Socrates ever said and develops his teaching in ways peculiarly Platonic; but it has its base in the firm conviction of Socrates, which he preached in season and out of season, that politics was no place for the amateur, because government was a *techné* and depended on expert knowledge as much as architecture, shipbuilding, shoemaking, or any other craft.

The general point is well made by Stenzel in his article on Socrates in the *RE*. He writes for instance (867): 'In my opinion the decisive question here is not "what new thing has Plato introduced?" but "what trait, what view, what tendency in Socrates gave him the objective (or at least subjective) right to strengthen a trait in this or that direction, to produce a line already drawn?"' Stenzel's own example (872) of a case where the borderline between Socrates and Plato can be detected is the nature and influence of goodness, a constant theme of Socrates's talk, which Plato took over and sought to raise to a theoretical plane as the highest object of knowledge. By comparing *Meno* 87 e and 88 a–b (where goodness, practical benefit and right usage are equated) with the introduction of the form of goodness in the *Phaedo* (76 d) and goodness as the 'greatest object of learning' at *Rep.* 504 d ff., he shows how the Platonic doctrine developed out of Socrates's insistence on the identity of good with useful or profitable (ὠφέλιμον) and of virtue with knowledge. These, one may add again, are known to be Socratic from Xenophon and Aristotle as well as Plato.[1]

I will only add here the chronological fact that Plato was born in 427. We do not know when he first met Socrates,[2] but if he were eighteen he could have known him for about ten years, and only when Socrates was already in his sixties. It must be admitted, then, with Diès (*Autour de P.* 170), that 'Platon a donc, en somme, peu vu de la vie de Socrate'. But, as Diès goes on, Socrates would have talked of his earlier years to his young friends, and there were plenty of others to satisfy Plato's unquestionable curiosity about them, notably his older relatives Charmides and Critias.

(4) ARISTOTLE[3]

Unlike Plato, Xenophon and Aristophanes, Aristotle, who was not born until 384, did not have the benefit of personal acquaintance with Socrates. He had however the inestimable advantage of having worked for twenty years in the Academy under Plato's headship, which must have given him an unrivalled opportunity for knowing just what we want most of all to know: the relation between the philosophies of Socrates and Plato. Xenophon has painstakingly amassed, from his own memory and other sources, recollections of Socrates and his conversations, and used them, to the best of his ability and in his own, sometimes rather heavy-footed and platitudinous way, to construct a defence of his life and example. Plato offers a series of philosophical and literary masterpieces, the dramatic dialogues in which it is not easy to distinguish what goes back to Socrates himself, what has been transformed by the sheer artistry of the writer, and what is the result of Plato's own reflections on the consequences of his master's thought and his attempt to buttress it against criticism. Aristotle, whose interest is purely

[1] Of the hundreds of books and articles on the subject, I would suggest, to supplement this brief essay, Diès, *Autour de P.* book II, chapter 2 (*Le Socrate de Platon*); Ritter's *Sokrates* (especially pp. 48 ff.); Stenzel in *RE*, 2. Reihe, v. Halbb. 865 ff.; and De Strycker in *Mél. Grégoire*, II, 199–230. Note especially in De Strycker's excellent article his four criteria for deciding whether a particular passage in Plato is historically Socratic or not.

[2] According to Diog. Laert. (3.6) he became his 'hearer' when he was twenty.

[3] The texts of Aristotle relating to Socrates are conveniently collected in Th. Deman, *Le témoignage d'A. sur Socrate*.

philosophical, tells us in a few crisp sentences where in his opinion the thought of Socrates ends and that of Plato begins. He if anyone ought to know, and his contribution to the problem is invaluable. I have no intention of trying to guide the reader through the extraordinary maze of conflicting views which have been put forward on this point, but it may save discussion if I allow myself to quote from one or two of those with whom I should wish to ally myself as having said the most obvious and sensible things.[1]

Sir David Ross has expressed his views in the introduction to his edition of Aristotle's *Metaphysics*, pp. xxxiii–xlv, and his presidential address to the Classical Association in 1933 (*The Problem of Socrates*). Both should be read in full, but here is a quotation from the latter:

Can we seriously suppose that in twenty years' membership of the school [*sc.* Plato's] he did not, just as he learned a great deal about Plato's later views which we find nowhere in the dialogues,[2] learn much from Plato or from older members of the school about the origin of the ideal theory? It is in the last degree improbable. And we have direct evidence that it is not true. For one thing, he could not have learned from the dialogues that Cratylus was Plato's first master; nothing in the *Cratylus* or elsewhere in Plato suggests it.[3] And, what is more important, the statement that it was Plato and not Socrates that 'separated' the universals and called them Ideas shows that he did not take at their face value the many passages in the dialogues in which Socrates does both these things; are we not bound to infer that there was a well-understood tradition in the school on the subject; that it was known that the dialogues were Plato's chosen method of expounding his own views, and not studies in biography? . . . That Aristotle credited Plato and not Socrates with the introduction of the ideal theory is con-

---

[1] With Aristotle as with every other source learned opinion has swung from one extreme to the other. He is independent of Plato and Xenophon and the only source for the real Socrates (Joël); he is dependent on Plato, whose dialogues have no historical value, so that the only historical source is Xenophon (Döring); or he is dependent on both Plato and Xenophon and may therefore be omitted (Taylor and Maier). Deman (*Témoignage d'Ar.* 11–21) gives a summary of earlier scholarship which may save a reader from wading through a morass of tedious and frequently perverse argument. I am surprised that so sympathetic a critic as Ritter (*Sokr.* 46f.) should have been seduced by Taylor and Maier into leaving Aristotle out of his assessment of sources.

[2] He also learned something about the difference between Plato's and Socrates's manner and style of speaking. It was not from Plato or Xenophon, but from some other Socratic *logos* if not even more directly, that he learned of the retort of Aristippus when Plato had expressed himself somewhat too didactically: 'Our friend Socrates never spoke like that' (*Rhet.* 1398 b 31).

[3] Gigon in *Mus. Helv.* 1959, 187, suggests that Aristotle's source here was Aeschines.

firmed—though confirmation is unnecessary—by the familiar passage in the *Ethics* in which he confesses his hesitation to attack the theory because it had been introduced by his friends. Would he have spoken thus of Socrates, who died fifteen years before he was born?[1]

G. C. Field writes, referring to the influence of Socrates on Plato (*CQ*, 1923, 113f.):

In his twenty years' association with Plato, Aristotle must have had constant personal intercourse with him and with others who knew him. It is really impossible to suppose that Aristotle would be reduced to mere conjecture or to a reading of Plato's works when he wanted to know anything about him. At least for twenty years of his life he had far more direct and certain sources of information than that.

In his compilation of Aristotle's evidence, Th. Deman writes (*Témoignage*, 106): 'There is no reason to charge Aristotle with inaccuracy. It is up to us to discover his methods and use his witness in a way which consorts with our own historical demands.'

The significance of the last sentence is this. One can usually trust Aristotle to distil the essence of one of his predecessors in philosophy, as it appeared to him, in the tersest and driest terms. This is most valuable for comparison with the wordy and scarcely philosophical expositions of Xenophon or the easy conversational flow of Platonic dialogue, flitting naturally from subject to subject 'wherever the wind of the argument blows' (*Rep.* 394d). But the terms in which he sums it up are his own: he explains earlier ideas in his more advanced and analytic vocabulary. This may not be in our eyes a sound historical procedure (though common enough among philosophers today), but guided by our knowledge of his own philosophy and terminology we can without too much difficulty make allowances for it (it is not for nothing that we have enough Aristotelian material to fill twelve volumes in translation), and his purely philosophical judgments will then form an invaluable supplement to the more personal records of Xenophon and Plato. He says for instance that Socrates, when Plato

---

[1] *Class. Ass. Proc.* 1933, 18f., supported by Diès, *Autour de P.* 210–18, Robin in *REG*, 1916. As Ross says, his case is strong enough without the final reference to *EN* 1096 a 11ff., as to which a captious critic could object that Aristotle might have said the same thing (διὰ τὸ φίλους ἄνδρας εἰσαγαγεῖν τὰ εἴδη) even if Plato had taken over the theory from Socrates and given it circulation in his writings.

came in contact with him, was not concerning himself at all with natural philosophy but solely with ethics, and that he had great influence in turning the whole current of philosophy in that direction; that his method was to look for the universal and ask for definitions, but that he did not 'separate' the universals: it was Plato who assumed that the object of a definition must exist apart from its instantiations in sensible form. In the Socratic search for the universal Aristotle saw the germ of a logical method, and being himself, unlike Socrates, keenly interested in logic for its own sake, he gave Socrates credit for this in his own language by saying that we may fairly ascribe two things to Socrates: inductive argument and general definition. Socrates, who had other aims in mind, would no doubt have been surprised to hear it put in those terms, but in grasping the historical significance of the Socratic method Aristotle has shown considerable insight.[1]

Aristotle had no personal interest in Socrates. He weighed his thought as dispassionately as he could, his purpose being, as with all his predecessors, to study their ideas and test them by the touchstone of his own philosophical assumptions, in order to discover how far they might be said to have contributed to the advancement of philosophy and still be useful for incorporation in a modern system, and how far they must be discarded as mistaken. There is no emotional involvement, as there was for Plato and Xenophon, who were frankly concerned to defend the memory of their friend, 'the most righteous man of his time', and as there was for Aristotle himself in his relations with Plato. (The emotional tension crystallized in the later paraphrase of *EN* 1096a16, *amicus Plato sed magis amica veritas*, was genuine enough.) With Socrates he could always be cool and critical, as in his brief and crushing comment on the doctrine that no one does wrong except through ignorance: it is 'in plain contradiction to experience'.

For his knowledge of Socrates he had of course the writings of Plato, Xenophon,[2] Antisthenes, Aeschines and other Socratics, and the

---

[1] See the further quotations from Ross on p. 108 below.

[2] *Eud. Ethics* 1235 a 35–b 2 reproduces fairly closely *Mem.* 1.2.54. When however Taylor claims that *Rhet.* 1393 b 4 ff., because it refers to Socrates's disapproval of election by lot as giving power to the ignorant, shows clear dependence on *Mem.* 1.2.9, he is talking nonsense. See Deman, 58 f. Joël (*E. u. X. S.* 206–10), though a little apt to see contrasts too starkly in black and white, has proved pretty conclusively that in general the Socrates of Aristotle owes nothing to Xenophon's.

'so-called unwritten opinions' of Plato to which in one place he refers.[1] Above all he had the earlier Platonic dialogues and the personal instruction of Plato himself. He came to Athens at the early age of seventeen because the fame of Plato's school had reached his northern home. As it happened Plato was away in Sicily at the time, but the dialogues were written, and nothing could be more natural than that the enthusiastic youngster should prepare for the great man's return by reading them. That he did so is confirmed by the fact that he could think of no better inspiration for his own early efforts at writing. The death of his friend Eudemus prompted him to compose a dialogue on immortality on the lines of the *Phaedo*, and the central figure of his *Nerinthos* was a farmer who had been so impressed by reading the *Gorgias* that he abandoned his field and his vines to submit his soul to Plato. In this Aristotle was probably lagging behind the rest of the Academy, who by 367 under Plato's guidance were deep in the onto-logical and epistemological difficulties raised by the theory of trans-cendent forms, and tending more and more towards mathematical solutions of philosophical problems. One may feel some sympathy for the young boy, who in his maturity was to express his regret that 'for the moderns, philosophy has become mathematics' (*Metaph.* 992a32), if at this stage he found their discussions a little difficult to follow and turned with relief to the more Socratic topics of ethics and immortality as treated in these dialogues. But if as a philosopher Plato had left Socrates behind, one may be sure that he had not forgotten him as the greatest single influence on his life, nor would he be reluctant to answer the eager questions of his latest recruit.

(5) COMEDY

Surely the oddest place in which serious information about a philo-sopher has ever been sought is the Athenian comedy of the fifth

[1] At *Phys.* 209 b 13 he says that Plato's description of the 'receptacle of being' in the *Timaeus* differs from that ἐν τοῖς λεγομένοις ἀγράφοις δόγμασιν. Ross (*Metaph.* 1, xxxv) speaks of him as drawing on these for his knowledge of Socrates as well as Plato, but it is more probable that they contained Plato's later doctrines, formed at a time when his interests had diverged greatly from those of Socrates, and would not have much to say about Socrates himself. From Aristotle's description it does not sound as if they were actually never committed to writing, but rather that they were unpublished notes for use within the school.

century, with its farcical knockabout business, broad sexual humour, and grotesque phallic costumes. But though the object was certainly to raise a laugh, many features of the plays were there because they stemmed from the ritual origin of comedy and represented a tradition which the poet was not free to abolish.[1] Within its framework he aimed his criticism at the manners and customs of the time and at specific individuals of whom he disapproved. The phenomenon has no modern parallel, though serious criticism by comic means is familiar enough in satire and the political cartoon.

Aristophanes is the only contemporary comedian of whom we still possess complete plays, but he was not the only one to make fun of Socrates, who was evidently thought of as a peculiarly good subject. He was mentioned to our knowledge by four other writers of the Old Comedy, Callias, Ameipsias, Eupolis and Telecleides, of whom Ameipsias at least brought him on to the stage in person. Aristophanes too makes passing reference to him in other plays besides the *Clouds*. Not all the remarks are uncomplimentary. Ameipsias in the *Connus* says that along with being foolish, going hungry, having no decent coat and being 'born to spite the cobblers' (since he never wore shoes), he had great powers of endurance[2] and never stooped to flattery. Eupolis spoke of him as not knowing or caring where his next meal was coming from. Apart from this he is represented as squalid (literally 'unwashed'), thievish, and as an endless talker indulging in time-wasting dialectical subtleties. His name was linked, naturally enough, with that of Euripides, in the insinuation that Socrates wrote his plays for him. Callias spoke of one who had come under his influence as acquiring a 'solemn and lofty mien'.[3] The *Connus* of Ameipsias called Sophists *phrontistai*

[1] Chapter 4 of Murray's *Aristophanes* gives a good account of the part played by traditional elements.

[2] καρτερικός; Xenophon uses the same word, *Mem.* 1.2.1. Socrates's one old coat (τρίβων, not χλαῖνα) was a byword. Cf. Plato, *Prot.* 335 d, *Symp.* 219 b. It became a sort of uniform for ascetic philosophers, especially the Cynics, who claimed to model themselves on Socrates. (D.L. 2.28 in quoting these lines does not say which play of Ameipsias they come from, but I agree with all scholars since Meineke (*CGF*, 1, 203) that the *Connus* is by far the most likely.)

[3] Callias *ap.* D.L. 2.18. The line τί δὴ σὺ σεμνὴ καὶ φρονεῖς οὕτω μέγα; is surely lifted from a tragedy. Cf. Eur. *Alc.* 773 οὗτος, τί σεμνὸν καὶ πεφροντικὸς βλέπεις; other references are to Ameipsias in D.L. 2.28 (poverty and endurance), Eupolis, Kock, 1, p. 251 (poverty and loquacity), Aristophanes, *Birds* 1282 (associated with long hair, hunger and dirt), 1553 (unwashed, cf. *Clouds* 837), *Frogs* 1491 (time-wasting logic-chopping; the words Σωκράτει παρακαθήμενον λαλεῖν remind one of Callicles's criticism in Plato, *Gorg.* 485 d).

(thinkers), and Socrates was nicknamed *phrontistes* and in Aristophanes presides over a private *phrontisterion* or thinking-shop.[1]

However, the main source for the Socrates of comedy is the *Clouds* of Aristophanes, in which he is the chief figure.[2] Like all other sources of information on Socrates, it has aroused the most diverse opinions. In the eyes of some it exhibits a 'passionate hatred' (Ritter); Aristophanes has heaped on Socrates's head 'everything he knew about the Sophists that was hateful and unreasonable' (Zeller). Alternatively it carefully exonerates Socrates from the immoral teaching of the Sophists: his would-be pupil comes to him *expecting* to learn how to cheat, and is encouraged in this by the chorus, but in fact Socrates only teaches him all sorts of unpractical and unworldly things. Socrates is not responsible for what the Unjust Argument says, and is accused of nothing worse than wasting time in talk and finicky argument (Gelzer). Taking a different approach we are told on the one hand that Aristophanes aimed his shafts at a general tendency of the time: warmongering (*Acharnians*), modern poetry (*Frogs*), or subversive educational ideas (*Clouds*). For dramatic purposes these must be embodied in a single individual, but the element of personal attack is subordinated to the general aim, and no one would expect to see anything but the most general resemblance to the chosen victim. Socrates in the *Clouds* is 'in effect the abstract principle of evil'. So Cornford, who argued that the characters, though bearing historical names, were made to wear one or other of a

[1] Athenaeus (218c), discussing the dates of Protagoras's sojourn in Athens, says that Ameipsias in the *Connus* οὐ καταριθμεῖ αὐτὸν ἐν τῷ τῶν σοφιστῶν χορῷ. This was for long taken (and still is by many) as evidence that the chorus of the *Connus* consisted of φροντισταί, but Rogers (*Clouds*, xxxvf.) long ago pointed out the utter impossibility of a comic chorus being composed of twenty-four named individuals or of a man like Protagoras being represented not by an actor but by a member of the chorus. (Dover, *Clouds*, l–li, does not seem to think these are impossibilities.) The word obviously has its general, semi-humorous meaning of a troop or company, as at Plato, *Prot.* 315b, *Theaet.* 173b, and elsewhere, and the explanation of the phrase is that at some point or points in the play the Sophists then resident at Athens are named, and Protagoras was omitted from the list. The *Connus* won second place in 423 when the *Clouds* (first version) came third, and as I have just said it presented Socrates in person. Connus, according to Plato (*Euthyd.* 272c and 275d, *Menex.* 235e), taught Socrates music.

Socrates is ὁ φροντιστής at *Clouds* 266 and Xen. *Symp.* 6.6 (ἆρα σύ, ὦ Σ., ὁ φροντιστής ἐπικαλούμενος;). The use at *Mem.* 4.7.6 has an obvious apologetic purpose. Cf. Plato, *Apol.* 18b.

[2] K. J. Dover's recently published (1968) edition of this play did not become available to me until I was about to deliver my completed typescript to the press. Consequently I have only been able to add a note here and there in reference to it.

set of stock masks and were 'to the almost complete sacrifice of realistic portraiture, conformed to the traditional traits of those masks'. The masks represented a few set types—the Boastful Soldier, the Learned Doctor (these have had a long history), the Cook, the Parasite—which in a particular play were attached to the name of a well-known contemporary, Lamachus or Socrates, Euripides or Cleon. In the case of Socrates, 'almost everything he had to say and do was notoriously foreign to the real philosopher's nature and pursuits'. The proper comparison is Shakespeare's Falstaff, and his relation to the real Sir John Falstaff, the 'magnificent knight' of whom Fuller wrote that 'to avouch him by many arguments valiant is to maintain that the sun is bright'.[1] In a lecture Cornford once drew a more amusing parallel.

In one of Mr Shaw's plays there is a professor of Greek who, in moments of enthusiasm, quotes his own translation of Euripides. He can be identified with a personal friend of the author, well known for his pacific and rationalist opinions, who after the war became a member of the League of Nations Assembly. Some centuries hence critics may argue, on the strength of *Major Barbara*, that this gentleman had a past lamentably inconsistent with his ostensible character. Before the war he had been the director of an armament firm and, earlier still, the adherent of an unconventional religious organization, frequenting the lower quarters of the town for the purpose of indulging in corybantic rites.[2]

On the other side we have Taylor, for whom the old comedy 'dealt throughout in personal burlesque, not in satire on generalized social "types"... A successful burlesque must be founded on notorious fact, or what is believed to be such.' It is caricature, admittedly, but we should be 'foolish not to ask ourselves what are the real facts which explain the caricature, and whether we cannot discern them reappearing from a different angle of vision in what we are told by Plato or Xenophon' (*Socrates*, 18f.).

[1] See Cornford's *Origin of Attic Comedy*, ch. 8. That the masks in the old comedy represented types rather than actual portraits is by no means certain. Cornford argued strongly that they did (*op. cit.* 169 n. 1, 170), but the case for portraiture is probably stronger. See Schmid in *Philol.* 1948, 211, and the evidence in M. Bieber's *RE* article *Maske* (xxviii. Halbb. 2087). Add now Dover, *Clouds*, xxxiii with notes.

[2] Unpublished. The name of the professor in question will be found on the flyleaf of *The Origin of Attic Comedy*, which is dedicated to him. It is a curious coincidence that A. Diès (*Autour de P.* 160) speaks of A. E. Taylor presenting Socrates as 'le général d'une antique Armée du Salut'.

Taylor's last piece of advice is surely sound. If we can recognize, even through the veils of caricature and burlesque, some of the traits which we find in the more serious accounts of Socrates given by others of his personal acquaintance, we may regard this as confirmation of their historical verisimilitude, and perhaps even feel encouraged, with due caution, to use Aristophanes in amplification of knowledge already gained. If on the other hand there seems to be nothing in common between them, it will be the comic poet rather than the others who feels entitled by his medium to lead us into a world of fantasy.

First, then, a summary of the play. Strepsiades, a blunt, uneducated farmer, has married an aristocratic wife with expensive tastes, who abets their son Pheidippides in his extravagances. This elegant youth cherishes a passion for horses which has got his father deeply into debt. Unable to sleep for the thought of his creditors, he bethinks himself of a set of people who, if their palm is crossed with silver, will teach one how to outwit an adversary, be one's cause right or wrong. They keep on the premises both *logoi*, the stronger and the weaker, the latter of which can win an unjust cause (112 ff.). Anyone who is acquainted with the Greek Sophists as portrayed especially by Plato will recognize the type at once—the professors of rhetoric, Protagoras let us say (though a little unfairly), or Gorgias or Polus. But no: the people he has in mind are Socrates and his school, who combine such instruction with strange theories about the heavens. If his son will agree to go to school with them, he can soon learn the way to bilk a creditor. Pheidippides is appalled. What? Join that set of pale-faced, bare-footed impostors? He could never look his fellow-sportsmen in the eye. He refuses point-blank, so there is nothing else for it: the old man must go himself, slow-witted and forgetful as he is, and try to learn the new hairsplitting logic.

He knocks at the door, and a comic scene ensues in which the disciples of Socrates are revealed in various indecorous poses as they pursue their researches into geophysics, astronomy, geometry and geography,[1] and one of them explains (with a warning that these things

---

[1] Instruction in the special sciences like mathematics and astronomy was offered by some Sophists. Cf. Plato, *Prot.* 318e, 315c, and *The Sophists*, p. 45.

are religious mysteries, only to be revealed if Strepsiades is determined to join the disciples) how the Master applies his brilliant intellect to such questions as the length of a flea's jump, which end of a mosquito produces the buzz and, more practically, how to filch a supper for the school (143–79). Socrates himself is discovered suspended above the stage in a basket. He is contemplating the sun and other astronomical phenomena, and gives a scientific explanation of the necessity for the mind to be raised up from the earth's damp vapours and mingled with its kin, the air, if it is to think clearly about such matters.[1] Strepsiades explains his wishes and promises payment on oath, whereat Socrates chides him for invoking non-existent gods, and asks him if he wants to know the truth about religion and consort with 'our own deities', the Clouds. He agrees, and is put through a mock initiation ceremony, which Socrates promises will make him 'a rattling talker, a wide boy, a slippery customer' (260). Socrates then prays to Air, Aither and the Clouds, and the Clouds appear in the form of goddesses. They are genuine clouds, as they themselves make plain in one of those odes of pure poetry which so surprisingly irradiate the buffoonery of an Aristophanic comedy, and Socrates expounds their role as weather-controllers, the supplanters of Zeus, in the current scientific jargon of vortices, compression, and natural necessity. But they are also, he says, the patron deities of Sophists, and can bestow wit and cleverness, skill in debate, verbal juggling and the like (317f.). For Aristophanes atheistic natural science and dishonest debating tricks are evidently but two sides of the same thing, sophistry.

The Clouds address Socrates with respect as 'high priest of the finest nonsense', a 'meteorosophist' in his own way the equal of Prodicus,[2] and promise their favours to Strepsiades on conditions: he will need a good memory, intelligence and powers of endurance, and to achieve his aim of victory, in action, counsel and speech, must be prepared to bear cold and subdue his taste for food, wine and physical

---

[1] Kinship of the *psyche* with the air went back to Anaximenes, but the theory was being developed and popularized at the time of the *Clouds* by Diogenes of Apollonia, with particular emphasis on the connexion between pure, dry air and the power of thought. See vol. II, 374.

[2] Even if we accept Dover's interpretation of the joke here (Clouds, lv f.), which does not seem to me to be certain, there remains the fact that Socrates is addressed as a μετεωροσοφιστής.

exercise.[1] When he has promised to put up with all this and more, and to renounce all gods except Chaos, the Clouds and the Tongue, they promise to make him the best speaker in all Greece, whose words will carry the day in the Assembly more often than any other's (432).[2] But his aims are much more modest: let them only teach him how to pervert justice and give his creditors the slip. Praising his spirit, they promise him this and more. Through their teaching he will become famous and rich, for men will flock to his doors to learn the secrets of his success. They then hand him over to Socrates, whom they describe as their minister (πρόσπολος, 436), to put him through his paces, and the two retire together to the inner sanctum of the *phrontisterion*.

After the parabasis, out they come again with Socrates swearing by all the gods in the scientific pantheon that he has never met a more hopelessly stupid and forgetful pupil. But he will give him another chance. In the following scene he tries to instruct him in the more theoretical branches of the learning in which the Sophists specialized— poetry, metre, rhythm, and the rules of grammatical gender.[3] When Strepsiades objects that not these, but the 'unjust argument', is what he came to learn, he is told that these are a necessary propaedeutic (658). Socrates relents so far as to set him to think out by himself something relevant to his own affairs (695), and present it for criticism, adding a little advice on method: 'Let your subtle thought go free, think out the subject bit by bit, dividing it aright and examining it, and if one of your thoughts defeats you, let go and leave it, and then again set it in motion and weight it up' (740 ff.). The old man's first idea (involving getting a witch to draw down the moon so that the end of

---

[1] 412 ff. The last was certainly not a genuine Socratic trait, but the poor physical condition of his disciples seems to have been thought suitable material for a joke. They are pale creatures who cannot stand the open air (103, 198 f.). The origin of it may have been his fanatical follower Chaerephon, noted for his emaciated appearance. He is mentioned at *v.* 104, called 'half-dead' at 504, and was nicknamed 'the Bat' (*Birds* 1296, 1564). The παρὰ προσδοκίαν is effective, and (*pace* Merry *ad loc.*) spoiled by the κάδηφαγίας of D.L. 2.27, a feeble repetition of ἀριστᾶν. According to Xenophon (*Mem.* 1.2.4) Socrates disapproved of *over*-exertion; one should take as much exercise as is agreeable to the soul. Rogers suggested that the γυμνάσια may be mentioned as places resorted to for idle or immoral purposes, and passages illustrating the connexion of pederasty with the palaestra have been collected by H. Reynen in *Hermes*, 1967, 314 f.

[2] This echoes the profession of Protagoras to teach a man ὅπως τὰ τῆς πόλεως δυνατώτατος ἂν εἴη καὶ πράττειν καὶ λέγειν (*Prot.* 319a, *The Sophists*, p. 38).

[3] See *The Sophists*, pp. 205, 221 (Protagoras). Hippias taught περὶ ῥυθμῶν (Plato, *Hipp. Maj.* 285d).

the month, when payment is due, would never come) so impresses Socrates that he consents to propose specific financial problems, and adds the lucid advice that the pupil should 'not keep his mind close to himself,[1] but slacken it off into the air like a cockchafer tied by the foot to a thread' (762). However, after one more successful attempt, he produces a solution (suicide) that even Socrates cannot stomach, and after further evidence of his forgetfulness he gives him up for good. On the chorus's advice Strepsiades makes another attempt to enlist Pheidippides by dazzling him with his new learning about the non-existence of the gods and the importance of distinguishing the names for the male and female of animals. In the end he gets him to Socrates, and begs that he be taught the Just and Unjust Arguments—or the latter at least. Socrates replies that Pheidippides will learn 'from the Arguments themselves'; he will not be present.[2]

Enter the Just and Unjust *Logoi* (also known in Protagoras's terms as the Stronger and Weaker). They have a little preliminary sparring. There is no such thing as justice, says the Unjust. Where can it be found? 'With the gods', replies the Just, to be countered with the stock reference to Zeus and his unfilial treatment of his father. The chorus intervene and persuade them to have a set debate (reminiscent of the dialogue between Vice and Virtue before Heracles in Prodicus's fable), with the tutelage of Pheidippides as the winner's reward. The Just speaks first, and commends the 'old education', when boys were taught to be seen and not heard, to walk in well-ordered troops, coatless in any weather, to have good manners, defer to their elders, be modest, chaste and hardy, avoid the baths and brothels, and train hard for athletic success. Such an upbringing produced the heroes of

[1] This cannot possibly mean, as some critics would like it to (e.g. Murray, *Aristoph.* 96), that Socrates is telling Strepsiades to forget his money problems and fix his mind on higher matters. His own instructions were ἐκφρόντισόν τι τῶν σεαυτοῦ πραγμάτων, and he has just set him the specific problem of how to get out of an action for damages of five talents.

[2] The absence of Socrates does not imply, as has been suggested, that he dissociates himself from the ἄδικος λόγος. Given the idea of bringing the personified arguments on to the stage, contemporary theatrical practice made it impossible for him to remain, since the same actor would be needed to play one of the *Logoi* (Dover, lxvii). The theory that the poet wishes to exonerate Socrates from the immorality of the Unjust *Logos* is far-fetched. It is Socrates who 'keeps the *Logoi* on the premises', and Socrates who personally hands back Pheidippides to his father with the assurance that he has learned his lesson well and can secure an acquittal however plain the guilt. Strepsiades is under no illusions. When his son's new morality recoils on his own head, he curses him 'along with Socrates and the worse *Logos*'.

Marathon. This, of course, is both the 'just' and the 'stronger' case, but the Unjust Argument retorts that, though he is called the weaker (simply because he taught how to confute the old rules, which has been worth a fortune to him), he will easily beat it. For warm baths he can invoke Heracles, strongest and best of all the heroes.[1] Unchastity is not only enjoyable but is indulged in by Zeus himself.[2] What matters is to follow 'the necessities of nature'.[3] So it goes on till the Just *Logos* admits defeat. The two depart, Socrates and Strepsiades enter again, and Socrates asks the old man whether he is satisfied with what his son has heard already, or wants him to have personal instruction from himself. Strepsiades begs him to take the boy in hand and sharpen his wits both for petty lawsuits and other purposes, and Socrates promises to turn him out 'an accomplished sophist' (1111).[4] A choral interlude represents the teaching period. Socrates comes out again and assures Strepsiades that the lesson is well and truly learned. Strepsiades need never henceforth be convicted in any court, though there be ten thousand witnesses of his default. He receives Pheidippides with joy and triumph, and sure enough Pheidippides can tell him a trick to avoid the day of reckoning. They go into the house to celebrate with a dinner, but Strepsiades is brought out again by the arrival of the creditors, whom he tries to worst by a marvellous mixture of the 'unjust argument' that Pheidippides has taught him with the rest of the new cleverness that he has learned from Socrates, which in his eyes is obviously all alike and ought to be equally effective. 'How can you expect to be paid when you make mistakes in your genders?' 'What right have you to your money when you are ignorant of the natural laws governing the rainfall?'[5] That natural philosophy and practical astuteness are not in fact unconnected he shows by an argument from analogy, applied by the Socratic method of question and answer (1286 ff.): What is interest? The growth of a sum of money month by month.

---

[1] Warm springs were regularly called baths of Heracles because of the story that the first one sprang out at Thermopylae to refresh him after one of his labours.

[2] For the unprincipled use of mythology at this time as an excuse for human failings see *The Sophists*, pp. 228 f.

[3] Cf. Antiphon, *The Sophists*, p. 108.

[4] Dover argues *ad loc.* that this conversation is between Strepsiades and the Unjust *Logos*, since there would be no time for the actor to change his clothes and reappear as Socrates.

[5] This has been quoted in the general context of fifth-century thought in *The Sophists*, p. 114.

Is the sea larger now than last year? No. If then the sea, with all the rivers that run into it, grows no larger, what reason can there be for money to grow?[1]

Having rid himself of the creditors by blows rather than the persuasiveness of his arguments, Strepsiades returns within, but the chorus have just time to prophesy an unhappy ending to his affair when out he comes again, crying and lamenting as Pheidippides rains blows on his head. They have quarrelled at table over the moral tone of the old and modern poets, and armed with the New Logic Pheidippides has no difficulty in proving that it is right for sons to beat their fathers. That it is not *nomos* is no objection: he has learned the worthlessness of established *nomoi* (1400), which have no other sanction than human persuasion, and can be altered at will (1421 ff.). We should take example from the animal world.[2] The poor old man is almost convinced that his treatment is just, when Pheidippides tries to comfort him by adding that he can as easily prove the rightness of beating his mother too. Not all his marital trials can make Strepsiades swallow this culminating evidence of depravity, which finally convinces him that his whole recourse to the New Thought has been wrong. Overcome by repentance, he curses his son, Socrates and the Weaker Argument together and turns reproachfully on the Clouds who have encouraged him in his wickedness. They blandly reply that it was his own idea, and if they seem to have egged on a 'poor foolish old man', it was with the highest moral intentions: when they see someone planning evil, they let him carry on to the inevitable downfall, thus teaching repentance and a proper respect for the gods. Strepsiades (with astonishing magnanimity, one might say, but Aristophanes's old men, even if rogues, are always

[1] In thus associating, through caricature, natural philosophy with sophistic argument, Aristophanes was hardly being unfair (cf. *Sophists*, pp. 114, 116), and argument by analogy in ethical contexts was in itself characteristic of the Platonic Socrates. It was common in earlier and contemporary natural philosophy (e.g. Empedocles's famous comparison of respiration to the action of the clepsydra, or the 'like-to-like' analogies for the behaviour of atoms in Democritus; see vol. II, 220 ff., 409) and in the Hippocratic Corpus. See in general Lloyd, *P. & A.* part 2. These scientific analogies have already been caricatured in the *Clouds* (234), when Socrates compared the absorption of moisture by cress and by the human mind. Among the Sophists we saw analogy used in the comparison of education to husbandry (*Sophists*, pp. 168 f., 256), and it was probably much more common than the scanty remains of their teaching allow us to see.

[2] The dethronement of οἱ καθεοτῶτες νόμοι (v. 1400) at this period was a major theme in Sophistic teaching. Socrates of course was firmly opposed to it. That the human race could learn from the animals is reminiscent of Democritus fr. 154. See *The Sophists*, p. 104 with n. 4.

rather endearing characters) admits that this is hard but just. The real villains are Socrates and his crew, and they must be punished. The play ends with Strepsiades setting fire to the *phrontisterion* and smoking out Socrates and his disciples, 'above all for their crimes against the gods'.

I have summarized the play at some length in the hope that it will carry its own answer to the question how far it is likely to give a true portrait of the historic Socrates, or at least to the question how far Aristophanes intended to implicate Socrates in the immoral side of sophistry. There has been a tendency of recent years to argue that Socrates is discharged without a stain on his character, that Aristophanes in fact is at pains to distinguish his teaching from immoral sophistry, and that much of the comic effect lies in the contrast between what the rascally old man hopes and expects to be taught and what he actually finds when he joins the *phrontisterion*: a band of unworldly, pale-faced students living in poverty with their heads in the clouds, studying mathematics and the secrets of nature. Instead of ways to cheat his creditors, Socrates teaches him the true explanation of meteorological phenomena and the niceties of metre and grammar. There is no attack on his honour, says Murray, and Wolfgang Schmid repeats it: Aristophanes never impugns his honour, and he never tells Strepsiades how to cheat his creditors. The worst that he is accused of, adds Gelzer, is garrulity and waste of time in finicky argument.[1] According to Erbse, the Unjust Argument does indeed use a 'Sophistic-Socratic method', but in a context in which Socrates would have allowed it. Socrates, he thinks, is doing his best to cure Strepsiades of the immoral hopes that he entertains of philosophy, and the play demonstrates the irreconcilability of Socratic teaching with the moral dangers of Sophistic. The themes are sophistic, for instance language

[1] Murray, p. 94, Schmid, 224, Gelzer, 92. The chief upholders of this view are Murray in his *Aristophanes* (who had been much impressed by Taylor's *Varia Socratica*), Wolfgang Schmid in *Philol.* 1948 (not to be confused with Wilhelm Schmid of Christ–Schmid's *Gr. Literaturgesch.*, whom he criticizes on p. 213, n. 2 for overestimation of Xenophon as a source), and H. Erbse in *Hermes*, 1954. Much of Schmid's article seems to be taken from Murray, and Erbse's special pleading goes too far. Socrates, he contends, is not shown as an atheist (as that was understood at Athens), nor as pursuing natural science further than Xenophon said he did. (For this purpose we are asked to assume that not only stupid old Strepsiades, but Socrates's own pupils in the first scene, have 'misunderstood' him.)

and grammar, but Socrates's aim in his questions about 'the correctness of names' is to *attack* the theory that words were symbols of realities, a theory which must have been held 'in gewissem Umfange' by all the Sophists who taught the subject. (This is a considerable oversimplification of a complicated situation. Cf. *The Sophists*, pp. 209 ff.)

Erbse makes much of the words of the Clouds at the end (1454 ff.). 'Why didn't you warn a poor ignorant old man?' asks Strepsiades. 'This is our way with wicked people, to lead them into trouble so that they may learn to fear the gods.' The old man has misunderstood them from the beginning. They warned him (412–19) of the necessity for perseverance, concentration, hard work, abstinence and so forth. (But they did promise him that the reward for all this would be 'victory in battles of the tongue'!) Erbse does mention that Socrates introduces the Clouds as purveyors of quick wit, verbal juggling, circumlocution and chicanery, argument and counter-argument (320f.), and boasts of the way they support crowds of sophists and undesirables in idleness (331 ff.), but he seems oblivious to the damage this inflicts on his case. However, even if we agreed with the repentant Strepsiades that their cruel deceit was 'hard but just', that would not exonerate Socrates and his crew, whom he still regards as scurrilous deceivers to be smoked out of their nest. This in Erbse's view was no outburst of hate against philosophy on the poet's part but the trifling (*sic: unbedeutender*) price paid by Socrates for a clear indication of the uprightness of his teaching!

This is a highly distorted and over-subtle view which disregards much that is in the play. The Clouds are the queens of sophistry (317f.), the patrons of oracle-mongers, quack doctors, beringed dandies, dithyrambic poets and hordes of Sophists (331 ff.), and Socrates is their minister (436). They promise Strepsiades 'You shall have your wish; it is a modest one' (435), and their astonishing *volte-face* at the end of the play can only be taken as another example of their sophistry. Likewise Socrates, who holds that all other gods are false, promises a training in dishonesty (260), regrets that Pheidippides does not yet seem capable of mastering all the weapons of litigation (874f.), but later guarantees that he has learned the Unjust Argument and can now get his father acquitted of all his peccadilloes (1148ff.). He is the master of 'contrary arguments',[1] for he keeps both the stronger and the weaker, the just and the unjust, on the premises (112 ff.). This is not misunderstanding on Strepsiades's part, for Socrates, when asked to teach them to Pheidippides, can produce them in person and let them speak for themselves. He is in fact a replica of Protagoras, if one assumes (as Aristophanes and other conservatives did) that the rhetorical methods taught by Protagoras were bound to be employed for improper purposes. His atheism too would link him with Protagoras as well as the natural philosophers, and he has certainly turned Pheidippides into a Sophist when the latter declares that the 'established *nomoi*' were made by a man like himself and he has every right to make new ones.[2]

Amid the stresses and anxieties of the Peloponnesian War, which had already continued for eight years when he produced the *Clouds* in 423, Aristophanes was deeply concerned at the decay of the old ideals of conduct, the lowering of moral standards which was corrupting the youth of Athens. This he attributed to a variety of influences in their education and environment which all alike tended to undermine the sense of loyalty to the old-fashioned values and virtues formerly accepted without question. To attack these tendencies through the medium of comedy, they must all be embodied in a single individual, and the obvious person was Socrates. He had lived in Athens all his life[3] and would be known to everyone in the theatre since, as Xenophon said, he always lived in the public eye and was an unmistakable figure with his snub nose, bulging eyes, rolling gait and continuous, insatiable questioning. Whenever distinguished Sophists visited Athens— Protagoras, Gorgias, Hippias, Prodicus—he joined eagerly (if the evidence of Plato and Xenophon means anything at all) in their discussions and took up with enthusiasm their favourite subjects: the relation between *physis* and *nomos* and of language to its objects, the nature of virtue and whether it was teachable, or the meaning of

---

[1] ἀντιλογίαι. Cf. ἀντιλογικός in *v*. 1173, and *The Sophists*, pp. 177 and 264.

[2] Cf. *The Sophists*, p. 114.

[3] On p. xxi of his *Clouds*, Rogers suggests that it would not have accorded with Athenian courtesy and hospitality to make a distinguished visiting Sophist the butt of an entire comedy. But, as he notes on p. xxxv, Protagoras was at least brought on to the stage, not simply referred to, by Eupolis, and the supposition is not necessary. Socrates would be chosen for the advantage, for comedy, of having a man really well known to everyone, whose personal characteristics lent themselves readily to caricature. (James Adam in the introduction to his edition of the *Apology*, pp. xxi–xxiii, is excellent on this.)

justice. Moreover he was well known to gather the young men of Athens around him and set them arguing on any and every subject. If a single Athenian had to be chosen to embody all the influences that Aristophanes disliked, he was the obvious victim. Consequently there is something in a claim once made by Cornford,[1] that we can recognize in the Socrates of the *Clouds* at least three different types which were never united to perfection in any single person: first the Sophist, who teaches the art of making a good case out of a bad one; secondly the atheistic natural philosopher like Anaxagoras; and thirdly the ascetic moral teacher, ragged and starving through his own indifference to worldly interests. With the worship of his new deities and the initiation ceremony in mind, we may add the begging priest or seller of purificatory rites, a type castigated by Plato in the *Republic*, or the diviners and devisers of private mysteries whom he hits at in the *Laws*.[2] How much of each there was in Socrates we shall hope to see as we proceed. Both Plato and Xenophon agree that he was attracted to natural philosophy in his younger days (Plato was a child of four when the *Clouds* was first produced, perhaps seven or eight at the date of the second version); he consorted with Sophists and advocated a freedom of thought and lack of respect for conventional views which might be held to be characteristic of them; and in the ardour of his intellectual and moral mission he certainly neglected his own advancement. But (to anticipate) he turned from natural science when he found that it could teach him nothing about what he had come to see as the most important topic of all, namely the conduct of human life. He disagreed with the Sophists on fundamentals, as well as repudiating their practice of education as a paid profession, whether with private pupils or in public lectures and declamations at festivals. To the third type, the ascetic living in voluntary poverty, he probably bore a stronger resemblance, with his indifference to money, clothes and luxurious feeding, although there is evidence that he was no lover of abstinence for its own sake: it was simply that his mission must come first.

There is (*pace* Taylor) little evidence to connect him with Pythagorean or Orphic sectaries who practised private rites, though he had friends among them like the Thebans Simmias and Cebes of the *Phaedo*,

---

[1] *Camb. Anc. Hist.* VI, 302 f.   [2] *Rep.* 364b, *Laws* 908 d. See *The Sophists*, p. 246.

and this together with occasional fits of rapt withdrawal (pp. 84 f. below) might lend some plausibility to the charge. Having decided that Socrates was to be the *persona* for all this, Aristophanes was not likely to leave out every trait by which he could be recognized. There is little about his personal appearance (probably because the mask was a portrait or caricature, see p. 42, n. 1, above), but lines 362 f. 'You swagger along the streets and roll your eyes from side to side and go barefoot' must have called up a familiar picture to the audience. Other features also tally with the Socrates of Plato and Xenophon. He is poor and of Spartan habits. We see him teaching by asking questions on analogous examples and explaining by means of homely similes,[1] bringing people to 'know themselves' by convincing them of their ignorance (842), and acquiring both an inner circle of genuine disciples and a fringe of 'young gentlemen' who sought him out for the wrong reasons. Pheidippides's treatment of his father after instruction by Socrates can be compared with the later accusation that he undermined the respect of children for their parents.[2] Even the *phrontisterion*, or college, could be a comic version (wildly distorted, but what in Aristophanes was not?) of known features in Socrates's life. In Plato's *Apology* (33 a–b) he claims, no doubt justly, that he never taught anyone privately or grudged that anyone who wished should hear him. Nevertheless he certainly had a small band of young followers linked to him by strong emotional ties. Though a familiar figure in the *agora* and other public places, he did not *always* talk there. In the *Gorgias* Callicles's criticism of a philosopher like Socrates is that he shuns the city centre and the *agora* and retires to whisper with a few young boys in a corner. Xenophon speaks of the common meal which he and his friends enjoyed, and of their habit of reading together 'the treasuries of ancient wisdom in books', and making extracts from them.[3] It has to be remembered that a meal in Greece was a ritual, probably preceded by sacrifice and certainly followed by libation to the gods. The line

---

[1] See 345 f., 234 (cress and the human mind), 385 ff. (thunder explained by analogy with abdominal disturbances). At 1286 ff. Strepsiades has learned to use the method of question and analogy.

[2] Xen. *Mem.* 1.2.49, *Apol.* 20. The comparison was made by Kierkegaard (*Irony*, 209 n.).

[3] *Gorg.* 485 d–e, Xen. *Mem.* 3.14.1, 1.6.14. Xenophon's reference to οἱ συνιόντες ἐπὶ δεῖπνον, who each brought a contribution, suggests a regular practice. The δεῖπνον of the members of the φροντιστήριον comes in at *v.* 175. See also Joël, *E. u. X. S.* 254, n. 3.

between a band of friends joining regularly in a common meal, a religious guild or *thiasos*, and a philosophical school was a thin one, and disappeared altogether in the next generation. Both Plato's Academy and Aristotle's Lyceum were legally registered as *thiasoi* and held organized monthly dinners.[1] Although no formal foundation of this sort can be fairly assigned to Socrates, there may have been enough in the habits of him and his companions to justify turning them into a *thiasos* for comic effect and adding such picturesque details as the ban on revealing its 'mysteries' to any but the initiated disciples (140–3, 258).

Xenophon and Plato make several references to the treatment of Socrates by the comic poets, though not all are certainly to Aristophanes. In the *Oeconomicus* (11.3) he says he is 'supposed to be a chatterer and a measurer of the air and—the silliest kind of accusation— a poor man' and in the *Symposium* (6.6) Xenophon makes a direct reference to the *Clouds* when the impresario rudely asks Socrates not only whether he is 'the one they call *phrontistes*' but also whether he can tell him how many feet away a flea is, 'for this is the sort of geometry they say you do' (cf. *Clouds* 145 f.). At *Phaedo* 70b–c Socrates says drily that if, as a man condemned to death, he discusses the possibility of immortality, 'not even a comic poet could say that I am a chatterer about things that don't concern me', and the remark in the *Republic* (488e) that in the 'democratic' ship the skilled steersman will be called a 'sky-gazer, a chatterer,[2] and useless' is a fairly obvious reference to the Socrates of comedy. In Plato's *Symposium* (221b) Alcibiades quotes the actual words from the *Clouds* about his 'swaggering and rolling his eyes'. But the most striking allusion is in Plato's *Apology* (18b, 19b–c). What he has to fear, says Socrates, on trial for his life, is not the present legal accusation so much as the slander with which for many years the minds of his fellow-citizens have been misled about him. He will treat these slanderers as his real accusers and as it were read their indictment. It runs thus: 'Socrates is guilty of mischievous meddling in that he searches into the things under the earth

---

[1] See on this Festugière, *Epicurus and his Gods*, p. 25, and Jaeger, *Aristotle*, 325 f.

[2] ἀδολέσχης is the word in all three passages, and seems to have been a stock label for Socrates. It occurs in the *Clouds* (1485; the φροντιστήριον is the οἰκία τῶν ἀδολεσχῶν) and in Eupolis, Kock, 1, p. 251 (Σωκράτην τὸν πτωχὸν ἀδολέσχην). Probably it was applied also to Sophists in general. Cf. Plutarch and Plato quoted in *The Sophists*, of p. 228 with n. 1.

and the things in the sky, makes the weaker argument the stronger, and teaches the same to others.' 'That is the gist of it', he continues. 'You have seen it for yourselves in Aristophanes's play, someone called Socrates swinging around there, saying he is treading the air and a lot of other nonsense that I don't know the first thing about.' Many people have expressed astonishment that, if Socrates thought of the *Clouds* as a major cause of his ultimate condemnation, Plato, who tells us this, could also in his *Symposium* depict him with Aristophanes and the tragic poet Agathon, amicably discussing the art of drama around Agathon's hospitable board. Making all allowance for the *Symposium* as an imaginative work, we cannot doubt that the two were still on friendly terms after the writing of the *Clouds*. What the real situation was, one can only conjecture, but two things may be said. The *Clouds* was produced in 423, when no one had any thought of prosecuting Socrates,[1] and twenty-four of the most unhappy years in Athenian history had to pass before such a catastrophe could occur. Many a politician has enjoyed the cartoons about himself, and the play is extremely funny. One can well imagine Socrates taking up at the time the attitude attributed to him in an anecdote of Plutarch's. Asked if he was not angry at the way Aristophanes had abused him in the *Clouds*, he replied,' Good heavens no. He has his joke against me in the theatre as if it were a big party of friends.'[2] Secondly, the *Clouds* is certainly not introduced in the *Apology* as an originating cause of the slander. Socrates says that he has been falsely accused by many people over many years, and that his hearers, the jury, have had it dinned into them since they were children or adolescents. He does not even know the names of the slanderers, 'unless one of them happens to be a comic poet'. As Burnet pointed out (*Euthyphro* etc., pp. 74 f.), all jurors had to be over thirty, and at the end of a war that had lasted a generation, it was unlikely that many of them were under fifty. The mistaken impression of Socrates went back far beyond the *Clouds*, which is mentioned as an example because all but the comic poets were, as is the way with malicious gossips, unidentifiable.

---

[1] Only the year before, it seems, he had been the hero of the fighting and retreat in Boeotia (p. 59 below). Some have thought this difficult to reconcile with Pheidippides's sneer at 'the pale-faced Socrates and Chaerephon', but Pheidippides is hardly an admirable character, and the laugh would be one in which Socrates himself could join with the rest.

[2] Plut. *De lib. educ.* 10 C, literally 'I am made fun of in the theatre as at a big *symposion*', where all sorts of freedom are allowed because it is all in jest and among friends. See also D.L. 2.36.

NOTE ON THE TWO EDITIONS OF THE 'CLOUDS'

The play as first written was produced in 423, when to Aristophanes's disappointment (cf. *Clouds* 520–6) it obtained third place after the *Wine-bottle* of Cratinus and the *Connus* of Ameipsias, although he himself thought it his best play. He then revised it, and it is the revised version which we possess. It can be dated between 421 and 418 (Merry, *Clouds*, xi; Murray, *Aristoph*. 87), and it was probably never put on the stage or even (to judge from internal evidence) completed. The extent of the revision is stated in one of the Greek 'Arguments' prefixed to the play, which I quote first in Merry's translation:

'This edition is identical with the former one; but it has been to some extent[1] recast, as though the poet had intended to reproduce it on the stage, but for some reason or other had never done so. A general revision too of nearly every part has been effected, some portions having been withdrawn, while others have been woven into the play, and alterations made in arrangement and interchange of characters. The main changes in the play, as recast, are the altered parabasis, the scene between the Just and Unjust Argument, and the burning of the house of Socrates.'

The revision was, it appears, fairly extensive, and the purport of the first clause is somewhat obscure. For our purposes it is important to decide whether the writer of the argument means us to understand that the whole contest between the Just and Unjust *Logos* and the final burning of the *phrontisterion* were additions and did not appear in the acted version at all. This is generally assumed, and some scholars suppose that Aristophanes concluded from his failure that the play had treated Socrates too kindly, and added these two scenes in the revision to make it plain that he really was against him and all the new learning. (So Murray, *Aristoph*. 87 f., 104, and Schmid in *Philol.* 1948, 225. Others, as we have seen, think that in any case Socrates is carefully dissociated from the enormities of the Unjust *Logos*. It is amusing also to note that Kaibel in *RE*, II, 977, thought the failure of the original play due to Aristophanes's error in making Socrates the scapegoat for the sins of sophistry, when the Athenian public well knew that he was neither an atheist nor a 'meteorosophist'.)

But were these two episodes absent from the earlier version? There is much to be said for the arguments of Rogers, which, as they have been generally neglected, I will quote fairly fully (*Clouds*, xv f.):

'Strange to say, some have supposed the writer of the argument to mean

---

[1] ἐπὶ μέρους. Not 'to some extent' but 'in details', Dover, lxxxii.

that the dispute between the two λόγοι had no place in the drama as acted: and some have gone so far as to contend that it contained no reference at all to the λόγοι. This would indeed have been "Hamlet, without the Prince of Denmark". The promise of Protagoras that his disciples should be able τὸν ἥττω λόγον κρείττω ποιεῖν is singled out by Aristophanes as containing the very essence of the Sophistical teaching, and he everywhere makes it the central point of his attack ... The debate of the two λόγοι is the very core of the play. Every preceding scene leads up to it; every subsequent scene looks back to it ... The writer of the Argument pointedly confines his statement to the existing speech of the Just Logic [This is true, and Merry's translation is at this point faulty; literally it should be, not 'the scene between the Just and Unjust Argument' but 'where the Just Argument addresses the Unjust', πρὸς τὸν ἄδικον λαλεῖ], and implies, rather than negatives, the idea of speeches by both λόγοι in the original play.

'*The part of the Play where the Phrontisterion is set on fire*. It is not the conflagration itself that is new, but the part of the written Play which describes it. No doubt the Comedy always ended with the burning of the Phrontisterium, but the present description—the climbing up to the roof, the chopping logic with the rafters, and the actual flames—is a description of proceedings which could hardly have been presented, or described with a view to their presentation, on the Athenian stage. We may therefore readily believe that lines 1482 to 1507, or thereabouts, belong exclusively to the revised version.'

Rogers goes on to conjecture what the original may have been. Whatever may be thought about the practicability of producing the revised finale on the stage, the words of the Argument mean only 'the parabasis of the chorus has been altered, and the part where the Just Argument addresses the Unjust, and lastly the part where the house of Socrates is burned'.

Postscript. The above note was of course written before the appearance of Dover's edition of the play (p. 39, n. 2 above). According to Dover p. lxxxiv, 'the last sentence of the Hypothesis tells us that the parabasis, the contest of Right and Wrong, and the burning of Socrates' school, belong in their entirety to the second version'. This has the support of a scholium which he quotes. Nevertheless the first version did contain a contest at this point (p. xciii, 'I suggest that in the first version the contestants were brought on as fighting-cocks'), and it is not clear to me whom he supposes the contestants to have been. A suggestion that they might have been Chaerephon and Pheidippides is discussed on pp. xcvi f., but not favoured by Dover. Conformably to a principle enunciated in his preface (p. viii), he does not mention Rogers.

II

LIFE AND CHARACTER

(1) LIFE

Socrates was a native Athenian, son of Sophroniscus and Phaenarete, of the deme Alopeke.[1] He was born in 470 or 469 B.C., for the records of his trial and execution put them in the spring of 399, and Plato gives his age as seventy at the time. His father is said to have been a stone-mason or sculptor,[2] and references in Plato to Daedalus as his ancestor (*Euthyphro* 11b, *Alc. I* 121a) do something to confirm this. As doctors traced their descent to Asclepius as eponymous ancestor (so

[1] Apart from a number of mentions in Plato (e.g. *Laches* 180d, *Gorg.* 495d), his father and deme were recorded in the official indictment (D.L. 2.40). That his mother was called Phaenarete and was a midwife is difficult to believe but seems to be true. In Plato's *Theaet.* (149a) Socrates compares his own function in life to the midwife's art. As the midwife helps women in bringing their bodily children to birth, so Socrates practises on men, and the children which he assists into the world are offspring not of the body but of the mind. Like Greek midwives too, he is incapable of childbearing himself. That is, he has no ideas of his own, and can be of service only by assisting others to bring their brain-children to the light. This light-hearted simile he introduces by saying, 'Haven't you heard that I am the son of a fine upstanding midwife (μαίας μάλα γενναίας τε καὶ βλοσυρᾶς) called Phaenarete? Well, I also practise my mother's art.' βλοσυρός in classical usage meant 'shaggy, hairy, bristling' and so 'virile, burly' (LSJ; Lehmann, quoted by Webster, *Myc. to Hom.* 94, supposed the word to be originally connected with vultures, but its etymology is uncertain). It seems a strange word to apply to one's mother. That she was a midwife might be what made Socrates think of the joke in the first place, but that she was a midwife called Phaenarete—'she who brings *virtue* to light'—takes some believing. On the other hand (*a*) Theaetetus's reply to the question 'Haven't you heard . . . ?' is 'Yes, I have heard so'; (*b*) In the *First Alcibiades* (131e) Socrates refers to himself as 'son of Sophroniscus and Phaenarete' where the mention of her name has no special point; (*c*) Phaenarete was at any rate an Attic name, for it occurs in an inscription (Ritter, *Sokr.* 6, n. 11). It was also the name of the mother of Hippocrates of Cos (*RE*, VIII, 1802).

[2] λιθουργός or λιθοξόος (*RE*, 2. Reihe, v. Halbb. 1104), generally translated 'stonemason' but perhaps rather higher in the artistic scale. Aristotle (*EN* 1141a 10) applies λιθουργός to Phidias. λιθοξόος does not occur till later. Lucian (*Somn.* 9) speaks of a boy apprenticed to his uncle in this craft, who is told in a dream that he might become a Phidias but takes instead the advice to follow Socrates and desert it for 'culture' (παιδεία, §12). Run-of-the-mill sculptors would be wanted to turn out the herms and Apollos and such for every house and street, which would no more be original works of art than the monumental sculpture of our cemeteries. Many of these workers lived in Alopeke, which lay on the road from Athens to the marble quarries of Pentelicon (*RE*, I, 1597). There is no express mention of Sophroniscus's profession in Plato, Xenophon, Aristophanes or Aristotle, and the best evidence is probably Aristoxenus fr. 51 Wehrli. (For other late mentions see *RE*, *loc. cit.*) Burnet did not believe in it (*Euthyphro*, etc., p. 50).

Eryximachus in Plato, *Symp.* 186e), sculptors would naturally trace their line back to Daedalus. The justification for the mythical genealogy is that it was regular Greek practice for a craft to be handed on from father to son. Accordingly it was said that Socrates himself was brought up in the sculptor's craft, which he may have practised in his earlier years (Zeller, *Ph. d. Gr.* 52, nn. 1 and 2), before he 'deserted it for *paideia*' as Lucian later put it (*Somn.* 12). Sophroniscus seems to have been a respected citizen who could hold up his head in any company, since Plato makes Lysimachus son of Aristides speak of him as a lifelong friend whom he held in the highest esteem. It is unlikely that he was poor, or that Socrates's later poverty was anything but self-chosen, as Plato in the *Apology* (23b) says it was.

The Peloponnesian War involved him in much active service, and he earned high praise for his courage and coolness, especially in adversity, and his powers of endurance. Plato mentions three campaigns in which he took part, the siege of Potidaea at the beginning of the war, the defeat and subsequent retreat of the Athenians at Delium in Boeotia in 424 ('I was with him in the retreat,' says Laches in the dialogue that bears his name (181a), 'and if everyone were like Socrates, our city would never have come to disaster'), and the battle of Amphipolis in 422. It was during the expedition to Potidaea that he saved Alcibiades's life, and performed feats of endurance which are mentioned by Alcibiades in the *Symposium*.[1]

We next hear of him in the public eye in 406, when he resisted the demand that the generals who failed to rescue the men from ships wrecked in the victorious action of Arginusae should be tried together instead of having their cases considered separately. This was illegal, and it happened to be the turn of his 'tribe' to be *prytaneis*, which meant

[1] Plato mentions all three campaigns at *Apol.* 28e, Delium again at *Laches* 181a and *Symp.* 220e, and Potidaea at *Symp.* 219e and *Charm.* 153a. Whether or not he has embellished Socrates's heroic behaviour, he would hardly have invented the fact that he was present at these engagements. The doubts of Burnet and Gomme are answered by W. M. Calder III in *Phronesis*, 1961. A story known from later writers told how Socrates saved some of those retreating with him at Delium by insisting on taking a different route from the others, warned by his 'divine sign' (Plut. *Gen. Socr.* 581e, Cic. *Div.* 1.54.123). According to Strabo 9.2.7 and D.L. 2.23 he saved Xenophon's life there by carrying him when he had fallen from his horse. Some have inferred from a fragment of Antisthenes (33 Caizzi) that Antisthenes transferred the rescue of Alcibiades (Pl. *Symp.* 220d–e) to Delium, and that Alcibiades was then turned into Xenophon! (*RE*, 2. Reihe, v. Halbb. 812f.) Such stories show at least that the tradition of Socrates's military service does not depend solely on Plato.

that it was for them to decide what business should be brought before the Assembly.[1] The other members were finally intimidated into agreeing to put the illegal motion, and Socrates alone stood out.[2] He mentions this in Plato's *Apology*, where he says that he has never held any political office, though he has served on the Council as any other citizen might be called upon to do. It was well known that he avoided taking an active part in politics, though one purpose of his talks with young men was to prepare them to play their own part honourably and efficiently,[3] and he preferred to go his own way, irrespective of party, following his inner conviction of what was right. If in this instance his conscience and respect for law ran counter to the decision of a democracy, some two years later we find him resisting with equal courage a demand from the newly established oligarchy of the Thirty. These men were responsible for a series of judicial murders, especially of wealthy citizens whose property they coveted. Attempting to implicate Socrates in their violence, they ordered him with four others to arrest a certain man of substance called Leon of Salamis. Leaders of the revolution like Plato's relatives Critias and Charmides might well think that they could count on him, since they had been members of his circle and knew, too, that he was no advocate of the Athenian democratic system, but they underestimated his attachment to legality. The others obeyed and Leon was arrested and killed, but Socrates simply went home.[4]

He was saved from the consequences of his action by the counter-revolution which restored the democracy. But this only brought him into fresh danger. The times were desperate, and the democrats felt it their plain duty to prevent a repetition of the horrors that were so

---

[1] The Council (*Boulē*) of 500 was divided for convenience into panels of 50 *prytaneis*, acting in rotation for one-tenth of the year each. Their duty was to prepare business for the *Ecclesia* (assembly of the whole people), and any proposal had to be considered by them before being brought before the *Ecclesia*.

[2] Xen. *Hell.* 1.7. 12–15, *Mem.* 1.1.18 and 4.4.2, Plato, *Apol.* 32a–c. For problems connected with details of the incident see Burnet *ad loc.*, Treu in *RE*, 2. Reihe, XVIII. Halbb. 1772, De Strycker in *Mél. Grég.* II, 207ff., Dodds, *Gorg.* 247f. G. Giannantoni in *Riv. crit. di stor. della fil.* (1962) tries to reconstruct Socrates's attitude to the trial as an aid to understanding his political thought, based on fidelity to the laws, and De Strycker (*loc. cit.*) points out how it confirms the historical accuracy of Plato's *Apol.* and makes it likely that Socrates's attitude to the laws in the *Crito* is also historical.

[3] Xen. *Mem.* 1.6.15, Plato, *Apol.* 31c and elsewhere.

[4] Plato, *Apol.* 32c and *Ep.* 7. 324d–e, Xen. *Mem.* 4.4.3. The incident is also referred to without mention of Socrates by Xenophon, *Hell.* 2.3.39, Andocides, *De mystt.* 94, and Lysias, 12.52. See Burnet, *Apol. ad loc.*

fresh in everyone's mind, the reign of terror instituted in the short period of their triumph by Critias and his oligarchic associates. Leading figures in that spell of violence, as well as the traitor Alcibiades, had all been intimate with Socrates in earlier days. Moreover he was notorious for having said things which appeared incompatible with the whole democratic form of constitution as then understood. They could not feel safe until he was out of the way. These were not men of violence like the Thirty. Plato himself, who had every reason for disliking them, pays tribute to the moderation with which they conducted themselves after their restoration.

But by some mischance, some of those in power brought my friend Socrates to trial on an infamous charge, the last that should ever have been brought against him. It was impiety that some of them accused him of, and the others condemned him and put him to death—the very man who had refused to have any hand in arresting one of their own friends when they themselves were in exile and misfortune.[1]

Ostensibly, the chief accuser was Meletus, in whose name the indictment stood. In the *Euthyphro* (2b), Socrates describes him to Euthyphro, who has not heard of him, as 'an unknown young man with straight hair and a skimpy beard', and he can only have been a puppet whose strings were pulled by the powerful Anytus, possibly chosen for the enthusiasm with which he would press the religious charge.[2] Anytus was one of the most powerful democratic politicians, a leader in the fight against the Thirty, and Plato represents him in the *Meno* as abusing the Sophists and uttering dark hints of what the city might do to Socrates himself. His objections to Socrates's behaviour will have been largely political, but to bring political charges against him, or mention his earlier associations with Critias or Charmides, would have been contrary to the amnesty declared by the restored

---

[1] Plato, *Ep.* 7.325 b–c. This is not the best place to discuss the authenticity of the Seventh Letter, on which equally good scholars have taken opposite sides. I cannot believe that these sentences contain anything but Plato's own judgment of the tragedy.

[2] Cf. τοὺς ἀμφὶ Ἄνυτον and πειθόμενοι Ἀνύτῳ, *Apol.* 18b and 31a (also 29c, 30b). There is some evidence of Meletus's religious zeal in the *Apol.* itself, and if (as Burnet and Taylor thought) he was the Meletus who prosecuted Andocides in the same year, there is ample proof of it in the speech for the prosecution which has survived among the remains of Lysias and is described by Burnet as 'almost the only monument of religious fanaticism that has come down to us from antiquity'. (See his *Euthyphro*, etc. p. 9.) The name is not common, but Kahrstedt denies the identity in *RE*, XXIX. Halbb. 503.

democracy, to which Anytus was conspicuously loyal.[1] The accusation
therefore confined itself to offences against the state religion and the
vaguely worded 'corruption of youth'. There was a third accuser, an
otherwise unknown Lycon, whom the *Apology* practically ignores to
concentrate on Anytus and Meletus. He is said to be acting on behalf
of the orators, whereas Anytus represents the crafts or trades as well as
the politicians (he owned a tannery), and Meletus the poets (*Apol.* 23e).
Politicians (not really distinct from orators), craftsmen and poets are
the three classes mentioned later in the speech as having been angered
by Socrates's questioning, and the classification was no doubt made by
Plato with that in mind. We possess the text of the indictment from
two sources, Xenophon and Diogenes Laertius. Diogenes took it from
Favorinus the contemporary of Plutarch, who stated that it was preserved in the Metroön in his day. Xenophon confines himself to the
actual charges, in which only one word, not affecting the sense, is
different in the two copies, so we may be confident that we have them
correctly.[2] The full version runs:

This indictment is entered on affidavit by Meletus son of Meletus of the
deme Pitthus against Socrates son of Sophroniscus of Alopeke. Socrates is
guilty of refusing to recognize the gods recognized by the State and introducing other, new divinities. He is also guilty of corrupting the youth. The
penalty demanded is death.

Both Plato and Xenophon lead one to believe that the second charge
was argued in somewhat vague terms. Plato makes Socrates link it with
the first, trapping Meletus into saying that he turns young men into
atheists, and Xenophon (*Mem.* 1.2) defends him against all possible
charges: encouraging them in licentiousness, gluttony, disrespect for
parents, and immoral interpretations of the poets. He does, however,
give prominence, in his account of what 'the accuser' said (i.e. probably
Polycrates in his pamphlet written some years after the event, p. 346
above), to the charge that Socrates had been the educator of Alcibiades
and Critias, and so was responsible for their misdeeds. His relations

[1] For the amnesty see Aristotle, *Ath. Pol.* 39, Xen. *Hell.* 2.4.43, and for Anytus's strict
observance of it, even to his own disadvantage, Isocr. *In Callim.* 23.
[2] Xen. *Mem.* 1.1.1, Favorinus, *ap.* D.L. 2.40. Xenophon has καινὰ δαιμόνια εἰσφέρων for
D.L.'s εἰσηγούμενος, which may have been the correct legal term (Burnet, *Euthyphro*, etc.
p. 102). Paraphrases occur at Plato, *Apol.* 24b, and Xen. *Apol.* 10, and in part at *Euthyphro* 3b.

with these men, especially Alcibiades, seem to have been a focus of controversy between Socrates's attackers and defenders.[1] Anytus would have Critias very much in mind, as a strong reason for wishing Socrates out of the way, but he was prevented by the amnesty from bringing it into the open. Many years later the orator Aeschines (*In Timarch.* 173) told the Athenians bluntly: 'You put Socrates the Sophist to death, because he was shown to have educated Critias.' The motive was in part political, but also wider, as Zeller has well expressed it (*Ph. d. Gr.* 217):

Socrates, it is true, fell as a sacrifice to the democratic reaction which followed the overthrow of the Thirty; but his political views as such were not the primary motive of the attack on him. Rather his guilt was sought first of all in the undermining of the morality and religion of his country, of which the antidemocratic tendency of his teaching was partly no more than an indirect result, partly an isolated offshoot.

One has to remember the licentiousness and suspected sacrilege of Alcibiades, and the atheism of Critias, as well as their politics.[2]

One need not accuse Anytus and his associates of thirsting for Socrates's blood. They would have been content—probably more content—if he had simply removed himself from the Athenian scene, gone into voluntary exile and let the case go by default. In Plato's *Apology*, Socrates quotes Anytus as having said (presumably in his speech as a prosecutor) that *either* he ought never to have come before the court at all *or*, now that he has come, the judges must award the death penalty in order to save their sons from his influence (*Apol.* 29c). Similarly his friend Crito speaks of the bringing of the case to court 'when there was no need for it to be brought' (*Crito* 45e). Even after the verdict of guilty, it was not necessary for the judges to accept the penalty demanded by the prosecution. According to Athenian law, the accused himself could propose a lighter penalty, and the judges voted again on the question which was to be enforced. If at this point Socrates

---

[1] Diès (*Autour de P.* 166f.) calls Alcibiades the pivot on which turned the greater part of the attack and defence; and he instances the *Accusation* of Polycrates, the *Alcibiades* of Aeschines and Antisthenes, Plato's *Symposium*, Xen. *Mem.* 1.2, and the *Alcibiades* ascribed to Plato. *Republic* 494c–495b is also with good reason taken to be a reference to Alcibiades. Dittmar discusses what the various Socratics, including Plato, say about Alcibiades in his *Aeschines*, 65–177.

[2] On Critias and his relations with Socrates see *The Sophists*, pp. 298 ff.

had proposed banishment, there is every likelihood that it would have been accepted, as according to Plato he realized himself. In his reply to Crito's offer to smuggle him out of the country, he imagines the laws of Athens saying to him, 'At the trial itself it was open to you to elect for banishment had you wished, and thus to do with the city's goodwill what you are now trying to do against it' (*ibid.* 52c). However, Socrates believed, for reasons given in the *Apology* and *Crito*, that to leave Athens would be a betrayal of his mission, and that Athens had become in any case so essential a part of his life that he could not imagine himself living anywhere else. Besides, he was convinced that he had done no harm to the city, but on the contrary a great deal of good. His counter-proposal was, therefore, that he should be granted free meals in the Prytaneum, a privilege awarded to Olympic victors and others who had brought honour and benefit to the State. However, he added, he had no objection to paying a fine, since loss of money was no hurt. He could only afford one mina himself, but some of his friends (including Plato) had offered to collect thirty,[1] and in deference to their wishes he would offer that. So at least Plato tells. According to Xenophon he showed his high spirit by refusing to name a counter-penalty at all.[2] In either case his behaviour hardly left the judges any choice, and it is not surprising that this 'miscellaneous assembly of 501 Athenians, including superannuated officials, old and decrepit artisans, little shopkeepers, and others unable to find more remunerative employment' (as Phillipson called them) voted for the death penalty by a somewhat larger majority than had secured the verdict of guilty.[3]

Normally the sentence would have been carried out at once, but a particular circumstance delayed it. Every year the Athenians sent a ship to Delos on a religious mission, in fulfilment of an ancient vow made to Apollo after the success of Theseus in putting an end to the annual

---

[1] Quite a respectable sum. It has been calculated that at the end of the fifth century a mina had about the purchasing power of £75 in the 1950s. See the Jowett translation of Plato's dialogues, 4th ed. vol. I, 335 n.

[2] *Apol.* 23. Xenophon's protestation that Socrates neither proposed an alternative himself nor allowed his friends to do so, on the grounds that it would amount to an admission of guilt, must be a conscious attempt to contradict Plato. Others too have felt the offer of a fine to be an anticlimax (on which see Phillipson, 373 ff.), and its inclusion by Plato encourages the belief that he, who was present at the trial himself, was telling the truth.

[3] Phillipson, *Trial*, 241. For details of the voting, slightly differently expressed by Plato (*Apol.* 36a) and D.L. 2.41, see Phillipson, 367, and S. Erasmus in *Gymnasium* 1964.

tribute of young lives paid to the Minotaur in Crete. The ship had been dedicated on the day before the trial of Socrates, and from then until its return the city was kept in a state of religious purity which did not allow public executions to take place.[1] During this period therefore Socrates was kept in prison, where his friends were allowed to visit him, thus giving opportunity for conversations such as those related by Plato in the *Crito* and, on the last day of his life, the *Phaedo*.

Socrates was married to Xanthippe, and had three sons, of whom the eldest, Lamprocles, was a 'youth' at the time of his execution,[2] and the youngest, to judge from the *Phaedo* (60a), a small child. Xanthippe's name suggests aristocratic connexions, and she has become a byword for shrewishness, by all accounts deservedly. To omit the tales of later scandalmongers, Xenophon (*Mem.* 2.2.7) represents their son as complaining of her intolerable bad temper, and among the badinage of his *Symposium* (2.10) Antisthenes asks Socrates why, if he holds that women are no less capable of education than men, he has not trained Xanthippe, but is content to live with 'the most troublesome woman of all time'. Socrates replies in the same vein that, just as a horse-trainer must practise on the most spirited and awkward, rather than docile animals, so he, whose ambition was to be able to deal with all sorts of men, had chosen her as his wife in the knowledge that, if he could tame her, there would be no one whom he could not handle. Plato's mention of her in the *Phaedo* (60a) is not against this otherwise universal verdict. That she should remark on the day of his execution 'This is the last time that you will speak to your friends' is commonplace enough ('the sort of thing women do say', as the narrator Phaedo remarks), nor is it surprising that she should be led away 'crying and beating her breast'. The thought of being left husbandless with three young sons was not a cheering one, and in any case such conduct was expected of a Greek wife.[3]

---

[1] *Phaedo* 58a–c, Xen. *Mem.* 4.8.2. Xenophon puts the delay at a month.

[2] Plato, *Apol.* 34d. It could mean anything up to twenty.

[3] This not very important question of Xanthippe's character has aroused surprisingly strong feelings, and scholars have rushed gallantly to her defence. Most of them agree that the odious Antisthenes was responsible for blackening the character of a good woman (though there are in fact no witnesses at all on the other side), and Xenophon's second reference to her is silently ignored. Ritter (*Sokr.* 64), following Joël, argues that, although Antisthenes was admittedly one of Socrates's most devoted followers, he was an insensitive sort of fellow, and his only motive

(2) APPEARANCE AND GENERAL CHARACTER

We must remind ourselves at this point of the impossibility, already mentioned, of separating the teaching of Socrates from his whole personality. Otherwise the reader will soon become impatient at the amount of attention given to matters apparently unimportant and remote from philosophy. As it is, however, even to discuss his personal appearance leads directly to the teleological standpoint which led him to judge the ideals of beauty and goodness by the yardstick of utility and fitness for function. By the same token the teaching itself cannot be taken apart, for whether he was demanding definitions, insisting that virtue was knowledge, claiming that no one does wrong willingly or urging men to care for their souls, whether the ostensible subject of the conversation was shoemaking or love, he was always, as he said himself, 'saying the same things about the same things'.[1]

In appearance Socrates was universally admitted to be extraordinarily ugly, but it was the kind of ugliness which fascinates. His chief features

in falsely insulting Socrates's wife to his face was to enhance the glory of Socrates himself! It should be obvious that Xenophon could never have told the story of Antisthenes's joke and Socrates's reply if the bad temper of Xanthippe were not a well-known fact.

It has been argued more than once that, if Xanthippe's shrewish reputation were deserved, Aristophanes could never have resisted such a gift of comic material. It is just possible that Socrates was not yet married when the *Clouds* was produced, but, if not, it must have been very soon after. I wonder if he did resist it. In the *Clouds* Strepsiades has a wife whose social station is above his, and who insists on an aristocratic name for their son. (Lamprocles was an aristocratic name, as Burnet points out on *Apol.* 34d6.) Her particular penchant was for names ending in -ippos, and the first to be mentioned among her favourites is Xanthippos (*Clouds* 64)! Is it not possible that this name brought the house down? One can only guess why Aristophanes did not make her the wife of Socrates himself, but unlike Antisthenes he may have been prevented by a feeling that to make fun of a friend was one thing but to laugh at his wife without disguise another. Also there is a difference between doing it on the public stage and in the easy familiarity of a private party, where a good deal of wine had already been drunk.

Late sources attribute to Socrates a second wife Myrto, daughter or granddaughter of Aristides, some say bigamously married, others as a second wife after Xanthippe, which is manifestly impossible. The truth of the story was already doubted in antiquity by Panaetius (Plut. *Aristid.* 27, Ath. 13.556b) and others, and the reports are indeed riddled with inconsistencies and justify the contempt with which most scholars regard them. Some of the ancient authorities trace them back to a lost work by Aristotle (while at the same time expressing doubts about its authenticity), but it is most likely that it originated with his younger contemporary Aristoxenus in a context of abuse of Socrates. (See Zeller, *Ph. d. Gr.* 55, n. 2, and 63, n. 5.) Some texts are collected in Deman (*Témoignage*, 38), who also cites some representative scholarly opinion, but see also Aristoxenus frr. 54a and b Wehrli. Needless to say, Joël blamed the whole story on Antisthenes.

[1] Xen. *Mem.* 4.4.6, Plato, *Gorg.* 490e. Its recurrence in the two authors (in conversation with Hippias and Callicles respectively) suggests that it was in fact a well-known reply of Socrates to people who taxed him with tedious repetition.

were a broad, flat and turned-up nose, prominent staring eyes, thick fleshy lips and a paunch, or, as he phrases it himself in Xenophon's *Symposium* (2.18), 'a stomach rather too large for convenience'.[1] He had a characteristic way of looking at people which was unforgettable but hard to describe. We hear of him 'staring with wide open eyes, as his custom was', 'glancing up, as his manner was, with lowered head like a bull', and 'casting his eyes sidelong'. He boasts humorously that with eyes so prominent he can see further to the side than most people.[2] His friends compared him to a satyr and a flatfish (the ray).[3] Xenophon in the *Symposium* (ch. v) describes an engaging 'beauty competition'[4] between Socrates and the handsome young Critobulus, who has challenged him to prove by his accustomed method of cross-examination that he is the more handsome. ('Only', he adds, 'let's have the lamp a bit nearer.') So Socrates begins:

S. Do you think beauty exists in man alone, or in anything else?
C. I believe it is found in horse and ox and many inanimate things. For instance I recognize a beautiful shield, sword or spear.
S. And how can all these things be beautiful when they bear no resemblance to each other?
C. Why, if they are well made for the purposes for which we acquire them, or well adapted by nature to our needs, then in each case I call them beautiful.
S. Well then, what do we need eyes for?
C. To see with of course.
S. In that case my eyes are at once proved to be more beautiful than yours, because yours look only straight ahead, whereas mine project so that they can see sideways as well.
C. Are you claiming that a crab has the most beautiful eyes of any animal?

---

[1] References in Xenophon and Plato to Socrates's appearance and personal habits are collected by E. Edelstein in *X. und P. Bild*, 7f. and 22. Some of their points are confirmed by Aristophanes. D.L. 2.43 speaks of a bronze statue of him by Lysippus erected by the repentant Athenians shortly after his death. Extant representations are of two types, of which one is probably based on the lost Lysippean bronze, and the other on a marble original of Hellenistic date. (They are types A and B respectively in Gisela Richter's *Portraits of the Greeks*.) The idea of a pre-Lysippean portrait, executed in the lifetime of Socrates, is conjectural. The design on the cover of the present book is taken from a head of type A in the Vatican (*Richter, op. cit.* figs. 456–7, 459).

[2] Plato, *Phaedo* 86d (for διαβλέπω cf. Arist. *De insomn.* 462a 13), 117b, Xen. *Symp.* 5.5.

[3] Plato, *Symp.* 215b, *Meno* 80a (pp. 78, 82 below).

[4] Such competitions actually formed part of the games (ἀγῶνες) at Athens and elsewhere, under the name of εὐανδρίαι. They were a feature of the Panathenaea (Arist. *Ath. Pol.* 60.5), and the author of the speech against Alcibiades speaks of winning one ([Andoc.] 4.42). Athenaeus (565 f.) says that the aim was to choose the most beautiful, and speaks of a beauty contest (κρίσις κάλλους) at Elis.

S. Certainly, since from the point of view of strength also its eyes are best constructed by nature.

C. All right, but which of our noses is the more beautiful?

S. Mine, I should say, if the gods gave us noses to smell with, for your nostrils point to earth, but mine are spread out widely to receive odours from every quarter.

C. But how can a snub nose be more beautiful than a straight one?

S. Because it does not get in the way but allows the eyes to see what they will, whereas a high bridge walls them off as if to spite them.

C. As for the mouth, I give in, for if mouths are made for biting you could take a much larger bite than I.

S. And with my thick lips don't you think I could give a softer kiss?

C. By your account I seem to have a mouth uglier than an ass's.

S. And isn't this further evidence that I am fairer than you? The Naiads, who are goddesses, are mothers of the Sileni, who resemble me much more than you.

C. I give up. Let's put it to the vote, so that I may know as quickly as possible what forfeit I have to pay.

When the votes were counted, and every one was found to be for Critobulus, Socrates protested in pained surprise that he must have bribed the judges.

True to his aim, Xenophon is letting the mind of Socrates show through even his lighter talk. The principle followed in the beauty competition appears again in Plato's *Hippias Major* (295 c):

Let us postulate that whatever is useful is beautiful. What I have in mind is this: we do not say that eyes are beautiful when they are without the power of sight, but only when they have that power and so are useful for seeing. Similarly we say that the whole body is beautifully made, sometimes for running, sometimes for wrestling, and we speak in the same way of all living things. A beautiful horse, or cock, or quail, and all utensils, and means of transport both on land and sea, merchant vessels and ships of war, and all instruments of music and of the arts generally, and for that matter practices and laws—we apply the word beautiful to pretty well all of these in the same way.

This lesson of Socrates is repeated by Xenophon in other conversations (*Mem.* 3.8.4–6, 4.6.9). For the closest parallel one must go, perhaps, to eighteenth-century England. At the beginning of his *Analysis of Beauty* Hogarth wrote:

Fitness of the parts to the design for which every individual thing is formed, either by art or nature, is first to be considered, as it is of the greatest consequence to the beauty of the whole.

After illustrations from the size and shape of chairs, pillars and arches, he goes on:

In shipbuilding, the dimensions of every part are confined and regulated by fitness for sailing. When the vessel sails well, the sailors ... call her a beauty: the two ideas have such a connexion.[1]

Socrates gave no thought to appearances, but went regularly barefoot, the one ancient coat he possessed was a standing joke, and his critics called him 'unwashed'. Even his friends had to admit that to see Socrates newly bathed and wearing shoes was unusual, and marked a special occasion such as a party to celebrate his friend Agathon's success in carrying off the prize with his first tragedy.[2] Hardiness, temperance and self-control are the features of his character most remarked on, if one understands temperance as meaning not total abstinence or extreme asceticism, but an indifference to the presence or absence of material pleasures. On the Potidaean campaign he walked over the icy ground in the dreaded Thracian winter unshod and otherwise clad as at home; a practice (says Alcibiades in Plato's *Symposium*) which did not endear him to the soldiers, who muffled up well and wrapped their feet in felt and sheepskins, and thought he wanted to humiliate them. As for drink, he was said to be able to outdrink anyone, yet no one had ever seen Socrates drunk, nor did he drink except to comply with social custom and because he valued the conversation which flowed so easily at a *symposion*. All his appetites and passions, for sex as for food, he kept under strict control.[3] Admittedly our information has to be taken mostly from men who not only knew him well but were his devoted admirers, and may therefore be thought suspiciously partial witnesses. Yet, together with what they tell us about his teaching and his intellectual force, it builds up a portrait of an integrated and credible

[1] Ed. Burke, p. 32. See also Burke's article 'A Classical Aspect of Hogarth's Theory of Art' in *Journal of the Warburg (and Courtauld) Institute*, 1943. The utilitarian side of Socrates's teaching will be developed later (ch. III, §8).

[2] No shoes and one poor coat, Xen. *Mem.* 1.6.2; ἀνυπόδητος Aristoph. *Clouds* 103, 363, Plato *Symp.* 220b. His coat was a stock comic joke. Cf. Ameipsias, p. 40 with n. 2, above. For ἄλουτος see *Birds* 1554, and for his unusual party get-up Plato *Symp.* 174a.

[3] His attitude to sex is discussed in the next section.

character, and the little that we have to the contrary is, unfortunately, not impartial but bears the marks of malice and scandal. That curiously sour character Aristoxenus claimed to have heard from his father Spintharus that no one could be more persuasive than Socrates when he was in a good temper, but he was choleric, and when seized with passion was an ugly sight and would give way to the most violent language and actions. He was also passionate sexually, 'but did not add injury to his licentiousness because he only consorted with married women or common harlots'![1] That Socrates had a passionate nature there is no doubt, and those who were smarting under the lash of his anger may well have felt about it as Spintharus did. If it was rarely allowed to erupt, when it did the effect was devastating. Xenophon gives an instance. Critias had been attempting to seduce a youth in Socrates's circle called Euthydemus. When private remonstrance had had no effect, Socrates, seeing him behaving badly at a talk where Euthydemus and several others of his young acquaintance were present, said before them all, 'Critias seems to be overcome by a swinish desire to rub himself against Euthydemus like a pig on a stone'.[2]

(3) ATTITUDE TO SEX AND LOVE

Socrates's attitude to sex must be looked at more closely, in view both of his constant companionship with youth and of the central part played by *eros* in the Platonic philosophy under Socratic inspiration. The attitude to homosexual relationships in the Athens of his day was different from our own. Romance was seen chiefly in male attachments of the Achilles–Patroclus or Orestes–Pylades type, and it was seriously held that such relationships between men, with varying degrees of overtly sexual content, were far more capable of fostering heroism and other virtues, and leading to a lasting and truly spiritual connexion,

[1] Aristoxenus, fr. 54 Wehrli. It is a pity that those who mistrust the favourable accounts of Plato and Xenophon have nothing better than this sort of gossip to put forward on the other side. Aristoxenus was also the man who accused Socrates of bigamy, said that he had been the παιδικά of Archelaus, and claimed that he demanded pay for his teaching (frr. 57f., 52, 59). He also said that the whole of the *Republic* was to be found in Protagoras's *Antilogika* and that Aristotle founded the Lyceum in Plato's lifetime as his rival (frr. 67, 65).

[2] *Mem.* 1.2.29–30. Mary Renault has reconstructed the scene with remarkable imaginative power in her novel *The Last of the Wine* (pp. 120 f. of the *New English Library* paperback ed.).

than was marriage between man and woman. In Plato's *Symposium* it is taken for granted that attraction between the sexes is purely physical and its object the begetting of children. The position is summed up by Demosthenes: 'We have courtesans for our pleasure, concubines for the requirements of the body and wives for the procreation of lawful issue.'[1] Different Greek states, it is true, had different codes of behaviour. Pausanias in Plato's *Symposium* says that in Elis and Boeotia there were no second thoughts about it, and Thebes is known to have been proud of her 'Sacred Band' of lovers, a model for steadfastness and courage. In Ionia and among Greeks under Persian rule it was condemned, a fact which Pausanias connects with a tyrant's natural wish to discourage intellectual and physical achievement, and strongly knit friendships and associations, among his subjects. At Athens itself, he goes on,[2] the position is more complicated and not easy to understand. It is believed that such love can be a noble thing, and much is forgiven to a lover, but at the same time fathers place their sons in the hands of tutors with orders to guard them strictly against any possible communication with suitors. The explanation, he thinks, is that there is a right and a wrong type of love, one man seeking only physical gratification and making off when his favourite's looks begin to fade, and another loving a boy's spirit rather than his body and offering him an ennobling friendship. The obstacles put in the way, taking time and effort to overcome them, serve as a test, and two things are disapproved of by Athenian society: to give in to a lover quickly, or to give in from motives of fear, greed,[3] or hope of advancement. The

[1] Demosth. *In Neaer.* (59) 122, quoted by Levinson, *In Def. of P.* 106, n. 81. Levinson's description of the general state of opinion in Athens is a good antidote to a theory like Kelsen's that Plato suffered from feelings of guilt, rejection and isolation induced by deviation from a socially recognized standard.

[2] And at Sparta if the text at 182b is sound. It has been questioned (see Bury *ad loc.*) on the grounds that Sparta was a completely permissive state and could not have been associated with Athens in this respect. This permissiveness is referred to by Plato (*Laws* 636b, 836b) and from a number of indications is generally accepted as a fact, though Dover has now argued learnedly that the evidence does not justify supposing that homosexual practices were more prevalent at Sparta than elsewhere or were believed to be so by the Athenians (*BICS*, 1964, 36–8). Xenophon certainly claims (*Rep. Lac.* 2.13–14) that the Lycurgan laws, while encouraging a virtuous association between a man and a boy, regarded physical relations between them as on a par with incest.

[3] Prostitution was forbidden to an Athenian citizen by law, and conviction involved loss of civic rights (ἀτιμία). The chief source of our knowledge of Attic law on homosexuality (which also throws considerable light on current νόμος in its wider sense of conventional attitudes) is Aeschines's speech against Timarchus. For a summary see Dover in *BICS*, 1964, 32f.

motive of the younger must be a belief that his association with the older man will strengthen his character and improve his mind, and the other should act in the knowledge that he can do this. Such love is of value both to states and individuals 'because it compels both lover and beloved to submit to self-discipline for the attainment of excellence'.

The speakers in the *Symposium* are in character. Though Pausanias says some things with which Plato would agree, his conception of love is not the same as the Socratic–Platonic one which comes later, and it may be taken as representative of cultivated Athenian opinion. Lagerborg is certainly right to say, in his excellent study of the subject, that 'In the eyes of the Greeks these tender friendships were by no means something to be ashamed of', and 'In his love of beautiful youths Plato is a true child of his time'.[1] The same is true of Socrates, and it disposes of any theory that either was affected by the feeling that he was a deviant from the established mores of his society. Confusion has been caused by failure to make the requisite distinctions between different forms of these attachments, which might range from romantic and high-minded affection, more easily bestowed perhaps on a youth whose good qualities included bodily beauty, to a more or less promiscuous desire for sensual gratification. The latter was certainly condemned by Athenian opinion, and no less by Socrates and Plato.[2] To deny the truth of Vergil's line 'Gratior est pulchro veniens de corpore virtus' would be hypocritical in most of us. As an instance of the accepted moral level, which yet falls far short of the Socratic, one may quote the words of Critobulus, a much sought-after young man now old enough to take an interest in those younger than himself.[3]

We who are handsome infuse something into our admirers which makes them more liberal with money, more ready to work hard and face danger with honour, and even more modest and self-controlled, since what they desire at the same time fills them with shame. Indeed, it is folly not to choose

---

[1] *Plat. Liebe*, 44 f., 31. For the moral and socially valuable aspects of the Greek code of conduct between men, see especially pp. 42 ff.

[2] In the speech of Lysias which Phaedrus reads to Socrates (*Phaedr.* 231 e) it is the non-lover who feels obliged to meet the point that the object of his desire may hesitate 'for fear of the established *nomos*'; but the whole passage shows that in any case the *flaunting* of a physical relationship was deplored.

[3] Xen. *Symp.* 4.15. For Critobulus's stage in life cf. 8.2 ἔτι καὶ νῦν ἐρώμενος ὢν ἤδη ἄλλων ἐπιθυμεῖ.

handsome men as commanders: for my part at any rate I would go through fire if I had Clinias beside me, and I know that you with me would do the same. So don't think it astonishing, Socrates, that my beauty should be a good thing for mankind, and don't despise beauty as something that quickly fades. A youth, a grown man and an old man can have beauty just as a child can. This is proved by the choice of fine-looking old men to carry the olive-shoots at Athena's festival, on the principle that every time of life has its own beauty.

Phaedrus in Plato's *Symposium* (178–9) utters similar sentiments: That which should be the ruling principle of a man's life, without which neither a city nor an individual can do any great or fine deed—namely a feeling of shame at disgraceful acts and ambition to do what is honour-able—is instilled by nothing, whether kindred, honours or wealth, so much as by love. To have his father or his comrades catch him behaving dishonourably, or suffering through his own cowardice, will hurt a man less than if it is seen by his beloved. To put it at the mini-mum, then, no one can read Plato or Xenophon—or for that matter Aristophanes[1]—without accepting as a historical fact that among the leisured classes at Athens love between males was a perfectly natural and unembarrassing topic either for serious conversation or for jesting. G. Devereux, in an interesting article written from the psychoanalytic point of view ('Greek Pseudo-homosexuality and the "Greek Miracle"', *Symb. Osl.* 1967), makes out a good case for seeing Greek homosexual behaviour as not a true perversion but an expression of adolescence prolonged into adult life. It may have been an unfortunate expression but, as the author points out, adolescence is not an opprobrious term. It is, after all, the same as youthfulness, and it is not the detractors of the Greeks who have spoken of their eternal youth. The relation of this youthfulness to the unparalleled flowering of the Greek genius is admirably brought out by the author in his concluding pages.

In all this, what was the position of Socrates? He is depicted as making free use of the language of love, declaring himself an expert

[1] Hans Kelsen, in his argument that Plato felt socially isolated because homosexuality was severely condemned at Athens, says that Aristophanes 'scourged it with the sharpest scorn and irony' (*Int. Journ. Ethics*, 1937–8, 375). It is possible to put a different interpretation on his highly obscene jokes which must have roused the audience to fits of laughter; otherwise they could not have been there. On the difference between the attitudes of Plato and Aristophanes to homosexuality see Dover, *BICS*, 1964, 36 and 38.

in 'erotics' (τὰ ἐρωτικά) and by nature a lover (ἐραστής). In the *Meno* (76c) he says that he can never resist the fair (who are, of course, not of the opposite sex), and in Xenophon's *Symposium* (8.2) that he cannot remember a time when he was not in love. It is by no means unusual, however, to find someone using the language of erotics and yet being entirely continent in his behaviour. The sexual imagery of religious mystics has often attracted attention.[1] Moreover, whereas at the present time we acknowledge (perhaps decreasingly) at least the residue of a social taboo on such language, Socrates was under no such restraint. All the evidence indicates that, on the one hand, he had his passions under complete control, and used the socially approved association of an older man with his juniors as an educational asset; but, on the other hand, he was by nature susceptible to youthful beauty and did not resist it without an effort. When he speaks of it, though it is usually in a humorous way, there is certainly something behind the jest. The most outspoken passage is the description of Socrates's meeting with the boy Charmides after a long absence in the army. All the company have been praising his beauty, and Socrates agrees that he must be quite irresistible, if only he has a soul to match his outward form. They propose to test this by engaging him in talk, and he sits down between Socrates and Critias.

But then I felt embarrassed, and my former confidence that I could make conversation with him was all knocked out of me. And when Critias told him that I knew the cure for his headache, and he turned his eyes on me with an indescribable look and made as if to question me, and everyone in the palaestra gathered round us, I caught a glimpse inside his clothes and was aflame. I was no longer master of myself, and thought how well Cydias had understood love when, speaking of a fair boy, he warned someone to take care 'that the fawn come not in sight of the lion, to be devoured by him'. Indeed I felt just as if I had been seized by a wild beast.[2]

The rest of the dialogue is devoted to the nature of *sophrosyne*, self-control or temperance.

[1] E.g. Taylor, *Socrates*, 46: 'The almost universal adoption of symbolic language borrowed from sexual passion by the mystics of all times and places seems to point to a real connexion between the mystical and the erotic temperament.'

[2] Pl. *Charm.* 155c–e. Cf. Xenophon, *Mem.* 1.3.13, where Socrates describes 'that wild beast called "youth in bloom"' as more dangerous than a scorpion, because it can inject a maddening poison without ever coming into contact with its victim.

Socrates and Love

A particular joke between Socrates and his friends seems to have been his supposed passion for Alcibiades. It is mentioned several times in Plato, and most interestingly in a fragment of the Socratic Aeschines, where it is compared to Bacchic frenzy.[1]

> For my part, the love I bore to Alcibiades brought me an experience just like that of the Bacchae. They, when they are inspired, draw honey and milk in places where others cannot even draw water from wells. Similarly I, though I have learned nothing that I could impart to a man to do him good, nevertheless thought that, because I loved him, my company could make him a better man.

The irony is apparent. The erotic delusion of Socrates, comparable to those of frenzied maenads, is that by his love he might be able to convert the dissolute Alcibiades to a better way of life. With this goes Alcibiades's own description, in Plato's *Symposium*, of Socrates's impregnable chastity and ability to make him feel ashamed of himself. In the *First Alcibiades* Socrates is arguing generally that a man's self is his mind or spirit (*psyche*) and the body only an instrument which it 'governs' and makes use of for living. This gives him the opportunity to point out what he means by true *eros* and to denounce the current version of homosexual love; for he who loves Alcibiades's body does not love Alcibiades but only something belonging to him.[2] In lighter vein, there is a pleasant exchange in Xenophon (*Symp.* 8.4) between Antisthenes and Socrates. Antisthenes says he loves him, and the Silenus-like Socrates replies, 'But the less said about your love the better, since you love me not for myself (literally "my *psyche*") but for my looks'. Later (8.23) he says seriously, 'to consort with someone who loves the body rather than the soul is slavish'.

We may trust Plato's account of Socrates's philosophy and practice in matters of sex not only because there is no reliable evidence to the contrary, nor because, had he been given to pederasty, the conventions of the time imposed no need of concealment. It is more important that the character which Plato presents is absolutely convincing, but the most unchallengeable part of his evidence lies not in his direct praise of

---

[1] Pl. *Prot.* 309a, *Gorg.* 481d, *Alc. I, ad init.*; Aesch. fr. 11c, p. 273 Dittmar. At *Symp.* 217aff. Alcibiades is made to speak of his own mistaken impression that Socrates wished to sleep with him.

[2] 131c. See further pp. 150 ff. below.

Socrates, but in his own philosophy. Holding the views on *eros* which he did, he could not have been such an admiring disciple had Socrates himself fallen short of them. It must indeed have been the influence of Socrates which helped him to transcend so notably the current morality of his time. He condemned pederasty both in the *Republic* and the *Laws*.[1] More important, because more positive, is the central position occupied by *eros* in his whole philosophy. We cannot discuss this fully here, but briefly it means that a complete and satisfying philosophy of life must have regard to the emotions as well as the reason, since both are integral parts of human nature. Philosophy does not consist in cultivating the intellect to the neglect of everything else. It should mean the use of reason to guide the desires towards other forms of satisfaction than physical, in which they will find, not frustration, but their highest fulfilment. In this process the sexual impulses have their place, for it is through them that the *psyche* is first attracted to what is beautiful. They lead first of all, of course, to the admiration of physical beauty, and if they are indulged at this level by physical debauchery, our life is maimed. But in fact this *eros* in us is a spiritual force, and by shunning its lower manifestations and learning its true nature, we may allow it to lead us upwards (as Socrates is made to expound it in the *Symposium*) from passionate desire for a particular body to an aesthetic enjoyment of visible beauty in general, from that to beauty of character,[2] higher still to the intellectual beauty of the sciences, until by persevering to the end we are granted the sudden vision of Beauty itself, the absolute Form which is perceived not with the bodily eye at all, but with the eye of the soul or mind. On this ultimate, indeed divine level, beauty and goodness and truth are one, and the vision of this supreme reality, says Plato through the mouth of Socrates, is only possible to the man who is by nature a lover, for the power which leads to it is the power of *eros*. That, says Socrates, is what is meant by initiation into the final mysteries of *ta erotika*; and

[1] *Rep.* 403 a–c. At *Laws* 838 e, homosexual intercourse is condemned on the grounds of its barrenness as 'deliberate murder of the human race, sowing seed on rocks and stones where it will never take root and bear its natural fruit'. At 636 c it is called 'unnatural and the height of shameless and incontinent indulgence'. That Plato forbade this intercourse is agreed by Aristotle, *Pol.* 1262 a 32 ff.

[2] It has to be remembered that the single word καλόν, which we translate 'beauty', referred as much to moral excellence as to grace of outward form.

that is a fundamental doctrine of Platonism, a philosophy to a large extent inspired by Socrates himself.

In speaking of Plato as a source, I made it clear that I am far from those who claim that everything which he puts into the mouth of Socrates was, or could have been, said by Socrates in real life. In this magnificent central speech of the *Symposium* he certainly transcends the teaching of the historical Socrates.[1] But, just as he could not have made Socrates propound what he himself regarded as the strongest arguments for immortality if Socrates had been convinced that death was the end of everything (p. 34 above), so it is impossible to believe that he could have attributed the *Symposium* speech to Socrates if the ideas and behaviour of the real Socrates in matters of love had been on the same earthy level as those of many of his contemporaries.

All this agrees well with the testimony of Xenophon already noted (pp. 22, 24 above) that Socrates put love of the soul before love of the body, but did not believe that spiritual love need lack a passionate element. Cicero tells a story which probably goes back to a dialogue written by Socrates's young friend Phaedo. A certain Zopyrus, who professed to read character from faces, said that he saw in the features of Socrates many signs of a vicious and lustful nature—not an unnatural verdict when one thinks of those thick sensual lips. The others present laughed at him, out of their knowledge of the continence of Socrates's life, but Socrates himself stood up for him: the lusts were there all right, he said, but he had conquered them by reason.[2] He was

---

[1] At 209 e the Mantinean prophetess Diotima, from whom Socrates professes to have had this lore, says: 'So far, Socrates, I have spoken of those mysteries of love into which even you could be initiated; but the final revelations, to which they lead up if properly pursued, I doubt if you will be able to grasp.' As others have seen (see Stenzel, *PMD*, 4 f.), it is most probable that with this sentence Plato marks the limit reached by the philosophy of his master. It has included the notion of the union of minds, resulting in pregnancy and parturition in the realm of ideas, linking up with the mental labour-pains which the maieutic skill of Socrates relieves by his successful delivery of other people's mind-children, as described in the *Theaetetus*. This involves the characteristically Socratic pose of knowing nothing himself, and justifies a strong presumption that the whole complex belongs to the historical Socrates.

[2] Cic. *Tusc.* 4.37.80, and cf. *De fato* 4.10. Phaedo's dialogue *Zopyrus* is mentioned as genuine by D.L. (2.105). The story has been called 'schwerlich geschichtlich' by Zeller (*Ph. d. Gr.* 64n.) and 'well substantiated' by Friedländer (*Plato*, Eng. tr. 1, 45). Phaedo is the obvious source, and this guarantees that it is historical at least in the sense that it fitted the Socrates he knew. Henry Jackson (quoted by Adam, *Apol.* xxii) remarked that in outward appearance Socrates 'seemed the embodiment of sensuality and even stupidity'. (Cf. 'stupidum et bardum' in *De fato* 4.10.)

a good man in the sense defined by Antiphon (*The Sophists*, p. 259) and had sympathy and understanding for those weaker than himself. As Zeller well expressed it (*Ph. d. Gr.* 68), he was no impersonal ideal of virtue, but an Athenian Greek of flesh and blood.

Handsome young men then, we know, had a powerful attraction for Socrates, and he was never so happy as when in their company. But they knew that the only stimulus they would get from him was the excitement of his friendship and conversation, of experiencing his intellectual midwifery which made their thoughts seem to flow ten times as fast as before.

(4) EFFECT ON OTHERS

If Socrates was fascinated by youthful beauty, it is no less true that the young were fascinated by him. This ugly, flat-nosed, pot-bellied and pop-eyed man exerted an uncanny power of personal magnetism. Such power is difficult to understand without experiencing it, but his young friends have done their best to communicate it, and may be left to speak for themselves. Alcibiades in Plato's *Symposium*, after comparing him to Marsyas the satyr, who contended with Apollo in flute-playing, and commenting on the remarkable resemblance in personal appearance, goes on:[1]

But you don't play the flute, you say? No, indeed; the performance you give is far more remarkable. Marsyas needed an instrument in order to charm men by the power which proceeded out of his mouth ... But you, Socrates, are so far superior to Marsyas that you produce the same effect by mere words without any instrument. At any rate, whereas most of us pay little or no attention to the words of any other speaker, however accomplished, a speech by you, or even a very indifferent report of what you have said, stirs us to the depths and casts a spell over us, women and men and boys alike. I myself, gentlemen, were it not that you would think me absolutely drunk, would have stated on oath the effect which his words have had on me ... Whenever I listen to him, my heart beats faster than if I were in a religious frenzy, and tears run down my face, and I observe that numbers of other people have had the same experience. Nothing of this kind ever used to

[1] 215 b ff., trans. W. Hamilton. Michael Joyce's more racy version of the brilliant young rake's speech (in the Hamilton–Cairns volume of the collected dialogues) is also well worth looking at.

happen to me when I listened to Pericles and other good speakers; I recognized that they spoke well, but my soul was not thrown into confusion and dismay by the thought that my life was no better than a slave's.

Such language is not to be explained away by any reminder of Plato's apologetic purpose of exonerating Socrates from responsibility for Alcibiades's misdeeds. What it describes goes deeper than mere charm of conversation or power of argument, and is less easy to explain. Meno also is made to describe it in the language of spells and magic, and it can only have sprung from Plato's own experience of an effect exerted almost unconsciously by Socrates and in part independently of the words he used. The most remarkable description of it is in the *Theages*, which, if not written by Plato, is generally agreed to be a production of the early fourth century by one of the Socratic circle. If those who deny it to Plato are correct, its witness is the more valuable for its independence, and Plato's own descriptions justify confidence in what it relates. When all allowance is made for Socrates's *eironeia*, there remains something extraordinary which calls for explanation.[1]

A father, worried about his son Theages[2] who is pestering him with his longing to be trained for political life, brings the boy to Socrates. Theages would like Socrates himself to take him on, but Socrates suggests that the proper instructors are the Sophists, men like Prodicus and Gorgias and Polus. They have something definite to teach and know what they are about. He has no skill or knowledge to impart save in the one art of love, and whether or not young men who consort with him make good progress is not in his control; it is a matter of divine providence. Sometimes his heaven-sent premonitory voice forbids him to take a pupil, and even when it does not, success is not guaranteed. Some acquire lasting benefit, but with others the

[1] For the best short account of the *Theages* see Friedländer, *Plato*, Eng. tr. II, 147–54. He sees no good reason against assigning it to Plato, and dates it on grounds of style to c. 400. W. Janell (in *Hermes*, 1901), who thought it spurious, would identify it as the work of a Socratic composed in Plato's lifetime, between 369 and 366. Other references are in *RE*, XL. Halbb. 2366f. Some have doubted Platonic authorship simply on the grounds of what they see as an irrational, superstitious element, in the treatment of the *daimonion* and the reference to physical contact in Aristides's speech. So Dorothy Tarrant in *CQ*, 1958, 95. If this must always remain a matter of opinion, Friedländer has at least given the opposite opinion a good foundation. See especially his p. 152. (J. M. Rist disagrees, *Phoenix*, 1963, p. 17.)

[2] Theages is also mentioned in the *Rep.* (496b) as one who would have deserted philosophy for politics if ill-health had not prevented him.

improvement lapses as soon as they leave his society.[1] He will tell a story to prove it (130a):

It is the story of what happened to Aristides, the son of Lysimachus and grandson of the great Aristides. This boy spent his time in my company and made great progress in a short while. Then he sailed off on some military expedition, and when he returned he found that Thucydides, Melesias's son, had attached himself to me. The day before, Thucydides had taken offence at something in our conversation, so when Aristides caught sight of me, after he had given me his greeting and so forth he said, 'I hear Thucydides is taking a high line with you and complaining to you as if he were somebody.' 'Quite true', I said. 'Why,' said Aristides, 'didn't he know before he took up with you what a slavery it was?' 'Apparently not', said I. 'No, I'll swear he didn't.' 'And what about me, Socrates?' he said. 'My own position is ridiculous.' 'Why so?' 'Because before I sailed I could talk to anybody and show myself their equal in argument. I even sought out the company of the cleverest people. Now it's just the opposite. If I feel that someone is a man of culture, I run away from him, so ashamed am I of my inadequacy.' 'Did this power leave you suddenly or gradually?' I asked. 'Gradually', was his reply. 'And when you had it', I went on, 'did you get it from anything you learned from me, or in some other way?' 'I will tell you something, Socrates', said he, 'something quite incredible but true. *I never learned a single thing from you*, as you know yourself; but whenever I was with you I improved, even if I was only in the same house but not in the same room, though more so when I was in the same room; and it seemed to me that the effect was much greater if, being in the same room, I kept my eyes on you while you were speaking rather than looking in another direction. But the greatest progress of all I made when I actually sat next you and could touch you. But now it has all leaked away.'

One can imagine the solemn youth as he meditates round-eyed on the magical effect of Socrates's presence.[2] What Plato really thought of 'education by contact' (not an impossible belief for a Greek, as

[1] Similar points are made in the *Theaetetus* (150d ff.), where they are expressly related to the midwife metaphor, and Aristides is mentioned in passing. There however it is said only that, if the *daimonion* permits a pupil's return, he again improves. The possibility of a second lapse, in spite of the god's consent, is not mentioned.

[2] The *Theages* is not devoid of character-drawing or humour. Friedländer (*op. cit.* 326) pointed out that the stiff and heavy style of Demodocus's opening speech, which has been stigmatized as un-Platonic (e.g. by Shorey, *WPS*, 429), might be intentional, as appropriate to the worthy farmer. Inevitably he brings out the stock comparison between plant-rearing and education (pp. 168f. above) including the delightful remark that 'planting' children is much easier work for a man than planting trees! It is in the rearing that the hard work begins.

Dorothy Tarrant pointed out in *CQ*, 1958), he shows in the *Symposium* (175 c–d), where Agathon calls to Socrates to sit beside him, so that by contact with him he may have the benefit of his latest inspiration. Socrates replies that it would indeed be a fine thing if by touching each other we could make wisdom flow from the emptier to the fuller by a sort of capillary attraction. There was nothing physical or magical about Socrates's educational powers, as his wide-eyed young admirers might think, but there was nevertheless more than the mere inculcation of facts or ideas. Friedländer (*op. cit.* 152) rightly contrasts Socratic education through love[1] with sophistic education without love, and the sophistic practice of offering intellectual wares to all and sundry with Socrates's *daimonion* which told him whether there was likely to be the requisite mental and moral affinity between himself and a young man to make the teacher–pupil relationship successful. This is also connected with his maieutic art. Since he teaches nothing but only draws out what is there, he can do nothing with one who has not already conceived in his mind. The others he sent to the Sophists (*Theaet.* 151b). The freedom to choose only those whom his instinct (or his *daimonion*) told him would be able to respond to his 'advances' was his main motive for declining to accept payment (*The Sophists*, p. 39). He certainly taught them to be anyone's equal in argument, but only because he was convinced that clear thinking was the necessary prerequisite of right moral action. Dialectical skill was for him only the means to moral reform, which will always fail unless there is an initial current of sympathy between teacher and disciple.

If Socrates had no literal magic in his touch, Plato nevertheless makes it indisputable that the effect of his personality on his hearers was something unique and uncomfortable. Only those of the right temperament could respond to it, and only if they were prepared to persevere. The first contact induced not the self-confidence of which Aristides speaks, but a depressing sense of helplessness. His method was rooted in his belief that before anyone could be helped on the path to wisdom he must first be convinced of his own need, that is, of his present ignorance and foolishness. Some only waited for this first, negative

---

[1] Although Friedländer does not mention it here, the passage of Aeschines quoted on p. 75 is highly relevant to this.

stage, and left him in what a psychoanalyst might call a state of negative transference, angry with Socrates but also with themselves. Many, he says (*Theaet.* 151c), 'are ready to bite me' when they see their brain-children discarded as phantoms. This aspect of him comes out in the *Meno* (80a), joined, as Alcibiades joined it, with an uncomplimentary reference to his face.

It seems to me that you are exercising magic and witchcraft and spells against me till I am a mass of helplessness. To be flippant, I think that in outward appearance and everything else you are exactly like the flat sting-ray in the sea. Whoever goes near and touches it, it numbs, and numbness is just what you inflict on me. My mind and my lips are literally numb, and I have nothing to reply to you ... In my opinion you are well advised not to go abroad. If you behaved like this as a foreigner in another country, the chances are you would be arrested as a wizard.

Together with the *Symposium* and *Theages* this does suggest something that goes further than the force of rational argument. At the same time his method in itself explains much. To be inexorably compelled to recognize one's ignorance is not a pleasant or comfortable process. That some of the young should have enjoyed trying out on their elders and betters what they had been put through themselves is understandable even if not laudable.

(5) THE DIVINE SIGN: SOCRATES AND THE IRRATIONAL

There is other evidence for a less rational side to Socrates. Both Plato and Xenophon refer frequently to what he called his *daimonion*, divine sign or spiritual guide, often simply 'the customary sign'.[1] In Plato's *Apology* (31c–d) he describes it thus:

I experience a certain divine or daemonic something, which in fact Meletus has caricatured in the indictment. It began in childhood and has been with me ever since, a kind of voice, which whenever I hear it always turns me back from something I was going to do, but never urges me to act. This is what has prevented me from taking part in politics.

---

[1] τὸ δαιμόνιον, τὸ δαιμόνιον σημεῖον, τὸ τοῦ θεοῦ σημεῖον, τὸ εἰωθὸς σημεῖον, ἡ εἰωθυῖά μοι μαντική, φωνή. Stress is sometimes laid on the adjectival character of τὸ δαιμόνιον and it is of course different from δαίμων or θεός. This assists the defence in Plato and Xenophon against the accusation that it is a 'new god'.

The Divine Sign

(Two points in this passage are repeated by Plato elsewhere. In the *Euthyphro* (3b) Euthyphro surmises that the *daimonion* is the basis of Meletus's accusation of introducing strange gods, and in the *Republic* (496c) Socrates says it is the *daimonion* that has kept him from a political career.) After his condemnation he tells his friends (40a–c):

In former times my customary prophetic sign has opposed me assiduously even in quite trivial matters, if I was going to do anything amiss. Now there has befallen me, as you see, what would commonly be considered the worst of all evils; yet neither when I left my house nor when I was taking my place in the court nor at any point in my speech has it opposed me.[1] On other occasions it has checked me in the middle of a sentence, but this time and in this affair it has not opposed me in a single word or action.'

From this he concludes that death, which now awaits him, cannot be an evil.

Of the 'more trivial' occasions of its intervention, Plato tells in the *Phaedrus* (242b) how 'the customary sign' occurred, and he 'seemed to hear a voice' which forbade him to leave after his first discourse on love before he had delivered a palinode; and in the *Euthydemus* (272e) how, as he got up to go from the dressing-room in the palaestra, it made him sit down again, and rewarded him with an exhibition by an egregious pair of Sophists. In the *First Alcibiades* he gives its veto as his reason for having shunned Alcibiades's company.[2] Perhaps its most important function was that mentioned in the *Theages* and *Theaetetus* (151a), of dissuading him from accepting or taking back pupils who could not profit from his highly personal teaching methods. In the former it is even said that this daemonic power contributes to, or collaborates in, the success of the pupils whom he takes, and this is distinguished from a merely negative attitude of non-opposition.[3]

Xenophon is more inclined to attribute a positive as well as negative function to the *daimonion*, and some of his references have a more definitely apologetic purpose. He evidently took seriously the suggestion that in accusing Socrates of rejecting the gods of the state and

---

[1] According to Xenophon (*Apol.* 4, *Mem.* 4.8.5), it did intervene *before* the trial, by preventing him from preparing a defence in advance.

[2] 103a. Similarly in Xenophon (*Symp.* 8.5), Antisthenes complains that Socrates makes the *daimonion* an excuse for not speaking to him.

[3] *Theages* 129e. Cf. ἐφῆκεν at *Alc. I* 106a, and Friedländer, *Plato*, I, 34f.

introducing new divinities Meletus and his associates had the *daimonion* in mind, and he is at pains to show that the inner voice was simply the way in which one of the known gods revealed his will to Socrates, as others were shown it through omens, oracles and the other approved channels of prophecy. He is also bothered by the fear that the divine voice might be thought a delusion because Socrates made a point of having received no warning from it about his approaching trial, when in fact he was condemned to death. Xenophon's reply to this is that Socrates was already so old that death was not far off, and that his execution saved him from the diminution of powers which would otherwise have awaited him, and brought him instead the glory due to a noble end.[1]

The exact nature of the 'divine sign' may be left to students of psychology or religious experience.[2] At this distance of time, and on the evidence available, it probably cannot be decided with certainty. We may be content with knowing that it was something that Socrates himself took seriously, and that therefore his educational activities were for him a matter of genuine vocation. More generally, belief in a special, direct relation between himself and divine forces must be accepted in any account of his mentality which lays claim to completeness.

Other evidence adduced in favour of a less rational streak in Socrates's nature is perhaps less certain. In the *Symposium* (220c) Alcibiades, who was with him on the Potidaean campaign, describes how one day he stood still from dawn, apparently fixed in thought. By noon, he began to be noticed. In the evening he was still rooted to the spot, and some of the Ionians, out of curiosity, brought their bedding outside to keep an eye on him and see if he would stand there all night as well. 'And he stood until it was dawn and the sun rose; then after a prayer to the sun he walked away.' It may be said that, being a profound philosopher, he was all this time engaged in following out a normal train of thought; but even the knottiest of philosophical problems could hardly keep him on his feet, oblivious of his surroundings, for twenty-four hours, and the story, if true, is hard to explain without

---

[1] See *Mem.* 1.1.2ff., *Apol.* 12–13, *Mem.* 4.8.1, *Apol.* 5. The *daimonion* is also mentioned as a compliment to Socrates by Euthydemus at *Mem.* 4.3.12.

[2] Good accounts in English are those of Phillipson, *Trial*, 88–98, and Friedländer, *Plato* (Eng. tr.) I, 32–6. See also H. Gundert in *Gymnasium*, 1954 and the references in his notes.

some element of trance. In any case, this power of complete abstraction or withdrawal from his surroundings must partly account for his notorious hardiness and indifference to physical conditions and fatigue.

Less striking perhaps is the incident which caused embarrassment to his friend Aristodemus, whom he met when he was on the way to dine with Agathon (*Symp.* 174a ff.). He suggested that Aristodemus should join him, and he himself would take the responsibility for having invited him. As they neared the house, Socrates stopped and asked Aristodemus to go ahead. He entered the house thinking Socrates was just behind, but he was nowhere to be seen. A servant of Agathon's, sent to fetch him, reported that he was standing in a neighbour's porch and refused to stir when spoken to. Aristodemus, who knew his odd habit of 'going apart and standing still wherever he happens to be', recommended that he be left alone, and he turned up about half-way through dinner.

(6) SOCRATES AND THE DELPHIC RESPONSE

Not unrelated to all this is another event in his life which must be mentioned before we turn to consider more specifically his teaching and its significance. That is, the reply which the Delphic oracle gave concerning him to his ardent and impetuous[1] young follower Chaerephon. We know of it mainly from Plato's *Apology*, though it is also mentioned, in exaggerated form, by Xenophon.[2] We cannot know exactly when it happened, but although Taylor's argument from the *Charmides*, that it must have been before 430, is weak, to suppose it an

---

[1] *Apol.* 21 a καὶ ἴστε δὴ οἷος ἦν Χαιρέφων, ὡς σφοδρὸς ἐφ᾽ ὅτι ὁρμήσειεν.

[2] Plato. *Apol.* 21 a ff., Xen. *Apol.* 14. The two versions are compared on p. 19, n. 1, above. For some opinions on the historicity and significance of the incident see Edelstein, *X. u. P. Bild*, 34, n. 13, Schmid, *Gesch.* 240 with nn., Ritter, *Sokr.* 62 f., Hackforth, *CPA*, 88–104, Deman, *Témoignage*, 45–7. Wilamowitz, *Platon*, II, 52–4, is particularly sensible. It is impossible that Plato (who makes Socrates offer to produce the dead Chaerephon's brother as witness) should have invented it, though opinions may differ about the extent to which it was responsible for Socrates's 'mission'. On the reported statement of Aristotle that it was the Delphic precept 'know thyself' that gave Socrates the impulse to inquire into the nature of man, see Deman, *op. cit.* 44–8. Aristotle also (according to D.L. 2.23) spoke of a personal visit of Socrates to Delphi, and in Gigon's opinion (*Mus. Helv.* 1959, 176) we may 'confidently' put these statements together and assume that Aristotle was telling a story in deliberate rivalry to Plato's.

event of Socrates's early middle age is consistent with what he says in the *Apology*, and some time in his thirties would suit well.[1] His story is that Chaerephon went to Delphi and had the effrontery (ἐτόλμησε) to ask the oracle if anyone was wiser than Socrates, and the Pythia replied that no one was. 'This', wrote J. B. Bury (*Hist. of Greece*, 580), 'showed a strange insight which we should hardly have looked for at the shrine of Delphi.' Taylor was nearer the mark when he said (*Socr.* 77) that the oracle, which liked to please, naturally gave the answer which the eager young man with his very leading question wanted to receive. It was not even necessary (though the necessity is generally assumed) that Socrates should already have achieved a wide reputation as a wise man for the question to have been asked. He need only have had a small but devoted band of disciples, of whom the lean and earnest Chaerephon, 'the Bat', was fanatical enough to take the question to the oracle. Such a following he had even before he abandoned his enthusiasm for natural science: Chaerephon figures prominently in the *Clouds*.[2]

Socrates himself chose to take the oracle very seriously, and regarded it as a turning-point in his life. Some scholars have doubted this, for two reasons, both fallacious. First, they do not believe that Socrates, though a man of undoubted religious feelings, was the sort of orthodox pietist to allow his whole life to be influenced by the Delphic oracle. Secondly, his first reaction was to say that he was sure he was not wise at all, and to set out immediately to find someone who was wiser than he, so that he could point to him and refute the plain meaning of the god.[3] This he describes as acting in obedience to Apollo, but, they say, that is a contradiction: to set out to prove the god a liar would be a strange way of obeying him.

[1] Taylor, *Socrates*, 78. J. Ferguson in *Eranos*, 1964 argues for a date *c.* 421.

[2] Parke (*CP*, 1961) suggests that the oracle may have been given by lot—the drawing of a white or black bean—and the question of motive may not have arisen. (Amandry published an inscription showing that this method was sometimes used. See his *Mantique Apollinienne*, pp. 33, 245.) This however is doubtful. Parke refers to Xenophon's addition that the response was given πολλῶν παρόντων, and says that this detail (not mentioned by Plato) is likely to be historical even though other details in Xenophon's account are not. I cannot see that it has any better claim than the rest. On the contrary, it is just the sort of thing that Xenophon would add to make the story sound better in the telling. In any case, the oracle's reply as Xenophon gives it is inconsistent with the simple 'yes' or 'no' which could be conveyed by the drawing of a white or black bean respectively.   [3] ὡς ἐλέγξων τὸ μαντεῖον, *Apol.* 21 b.

The first point is a matter of opinion,[1] but granted such a view of his general attitude, there could be a good psychological reason for his response to the oracle in this case. There is plenty of evidence that as a young man he was an enthusiast for the natural science of his time, but later condemned it for its irrelevance to human problems and its neglect of final causes. Presumably he was already feeling dissatisfied with this type of inquiry, perhaps already telling his young friends that it was barren and urging them rather to 'care for their souls', but the change would not be made without doubts and mental struggle. In such a state he could well accept the impulsive act of Chaerephon and its consequences as a sign that he was on the right track, and allow it to make up his mind for him. If the mind is already prepared, the actual occasion for such a call to action need only be trivial, just as, if it is not so prepared, the most solemn adjurations in the name of Heaven may fail to take effect.

The second objection rests on a misunderstanding of the way in which Delphic responses were regularly regarded and acted on. Socrates's description of his first reaction to the oracle is this (*Apol.* 21b): 'What can the god mean? What is his riddle? I know very well that I am not the least bit wise. What does he mean by saying that I am the wisest? He can't be lying: that would not be right for him.' What he set out to refute was the obvious meaning of the oracle, its words taken at their face value, in order to discover the answer to its riddle. Everyone knew that it spoke in riddles, and any sensible man or city would look past the obvious meaning for what was hidden underneath. When the Athenians, threatened by Persian invasion, were advised to rely on a wooden wall, they did not set about building one: they held a consultation, and many opinions were expressed as they sought to solve the riddle, until finally the interpretation of Themistocles was accepted that by 'wooden wall' the god meant the navy.[2] In this case Socrates's solution of the riddle was that the god took advantage

---

[1] Dodds (*Gks. & Irrat.* 185 and 198, n. 36) gives chapter and verse for the statement that 'he took both dreams and oracles very seriously'.

[2] Hdt. 7.142, cf. vol. I, 418. Hackforth (*CPA*, 94) argues that Socrates's procedure in testing the oracle was incompatible with a serious acceptance of its authority because he rationalizes it, saving Apollo's face 'by ingeniously imputing to him what he did not say'. But this was a recognized procedure, entirely compatible with acceptance of the oracle's authority. (Hackforth is also criticized by J. A. Coulter in *HSCP*, 1964, p. 303, n. 33.)

of Chaerephon's question to inculcate the lesson that no human wisdom was worth anything. He simply took Socrates as an example and used his name in order to say that the wisest thing a man could do was to be aware of his own unwisdom (23a–b).

(7) HIS SERVICE TO THE GOD

His method of investigating the oracle's meaning was a tireless interrogation of Athenians in different walks of life in order to discover whether any of them were wiser than he. In this practice he continued after as before his discovery of its lesson, because having learned the lesson himself he felt it to be the god's will that he should impart it to others. This took up so much of his time that he had little left for public or private affairs, 'and my service to the god has brought me into great poverty' (23b). It also, not unnaturally, brought him a considerable amount of ill-will. Whether he really believed himself singled out by Heaven for a special mission, or its dependence on the oracle was simply a playful conceit (and it certainly sounds serious enough), may remain, if one likes, a moot point; but at least his cross-questioning and the odium it brought him are facts, and we may continue the story as we have it in the *Apology*. He first sought out a politician with a reputation for wisdom, and talked to him; and as a result of the talk he decided that, whereas the man appeared both to himself and others to be wise, in reality he was not so. He continued the quest, in spite of animosity and abuse, testing the claims of various professions in turn. After the politicians he tried the poets, those traditional repositories of wisdom and knowledge, 'the educators of grown men', only to conclude, regretfully, that they must indeed, as they claimed, have written by divine inspiration rather than their own wisdom, since left to themselves they seemed to have no understanding of what they had done. Yet because of their poems they laid general claim to a knowledge and wisdom denied to other men. Finally he tried the artisans or handworkers. They had not the same reputation for wisdom as politicians or poets, but the wisdom of these had melted away under examination, and at least the craftsmen must be wise in what pertained to their craft, or they could not carry it out. There was no question of divine inspiration here, and, since Socrates, as he says, was convinced that he knew nothing at all, they could not fail to have more *sophia* than he.[1] Nor was he disappointed. 'And in this I was not deceived: they knew things which I did not know, and in this respect were wiser than me' (22d). But they did not know their own limitations. Because of their command of a small field of technical skill, they imagined themselves qualified to give an opinion on greater matters too, and laid claim to a wisdom which they did not possess. This fault, similar to that of the poets, overshadowed what wisdom they had.

(8) POLITICAL VIEWS

Socrates's opinion of the skilled practitioners of any art or craft is as good an introduction as any to the subject of his attitude to democracy. His appreciation of their skills is genuine. One has only to think of the admiration which he expresses in the *Gorgias* (511 cff.) for the pilot who asks a mere two obols to carry a man, his wife, children and goods from Aegina to the Piraeus, and only two drachmas from Egypt or the Black Sea, for which sum he has preserved lives and goods from all the dangers to which the sea exposes them. But his virtue is in his modesty, which realizes that he is in no way capable of improving, in body or soul, those whom he has landed, or even of knowing whether, in their circumstances, a safe landing is better than drowning. He had the same admiration for skill and good workmanship wherever he saw them, in a shoemaker, an armourer, or a farmer.[2] But he objected to the assumption that mastery of a particular skill qualified a man to give a judgment outside his own sphere. The practice of some modern newspapers, which assist their circulation by publishing the opinions of famous footballers, actors or singers on political and social questions,

---

[1] The Greek words in question are of course *sophos* and *sophia*. For the way in which these straddled the meanings of our 'knowledge', 'skill' and 'wisdom', see *The Sophists*, pp. 27 f.

[2] For some interesting passages illustrating Socrates's opinion of such occupations see Schlaifer's article reprinted in Finley, *Slavery*, p. 102, n. 6. It is likely that he distinguished some trades as especially banausic on the ground that they stunted or deformed the body, with a consequential effect on the personality (Xen. *Oec.* 4.2–3). That he believed honest labour was nothing to be ashamed of, even among those of gentle birth, is most strikingly illustrated by his advice to the impoverished Aristarchus and his family in Xen. *Mem.* 2.7.3ff. Yet in *Alc. I* (131b) he calls medicine, physical training, agriculture 'and other crafts' all banausic on the grounds that they do not, in and by themselves, impart self-knowledge or σωφροσύνη.

would have seemed to him pernicious. But at Athens every citizen had an equal right to discuss high policy in the popular Assembly, which was a universal, not a representative body. As Socrates says in the *Protagoras* (319b), in questions requiring technical knowledge— architecture, shipbuilding or the like—the Assembly calls on experts, and shouts down anyone who tries to speak without professional experience, but where the conduct of government is concerned, it is ready to listen to anybody, 'builder, smith, shoemaker, merchant, sea-captain, rich or poor, of good family or none'.

That the shoemaker should stick to his last was not such an un-political statement as it may sound. Everyone, in Socrates's view, was by nature and training fitted for a particular job, and the mind and way of life of a good artisan were inevitably such as to preclude him from acquiring the knowledge, character and powers of judgment which would make him an adequate guide in political affairs. Such a view contravened the whole basis of democracy as then understood at Athens, where the dogma that one man's opinion is as good as another's was acted on so unreservedly that anyone not a slave or a metic might be appointed to office by lot. Politics, said Socrates, was a craft like any other. It needed natural gifts, but above all things study and application.[1] Class came into it accidentally, and by no means exclusively. In Xenophon (*Mem.* 3.6) we find Socrates thoroughly deflating Glaucon, Plato's half-brother, who had political ambitions and the right personal connexions to gratify them, by asking him a few pertinent questions. How can he propose to take a leading part in government when (as quickly proves to be the case) he is ignorant of such essential facts of life as the source of the city's revenues, the amount of its income and ex-penditure, its naval and military strength, the state of its frontier garrisons, or how far it is self-supporting and how far dependent on imports?

However, Glaucon had the contacts and the leisure to put that right if he wished. In general Socrates would have agreed with David Hume that 'poverty and hard labour debase the minds of the common

---

[1] It will be seen that I would slightly modify Popper's statment (*O.S.* 1, 128) that the wisdom needed for ruling was only the peculiarly Socratic wisdom of knowing one's own ignorance. This would be like saying that a doctor would be σοφός if he confessed his ignorance of medicine but continued to treat patients. So much is plain from many passages in the Platonic dialogues, and especially from Xen. *Mem.* 4.2.3–5.

people, and render them unfit for any science or ingenious profession'.[1] In a conversation with Charmides he is said to have described the Assembly as made up of 'dunces and weaklings, fullers, cobblers, joiners, smiths, farmers, merchants, traffickers in the market whose minds are on buying cheap and selling dear . . . men who have never given a thought to public affairs'.[2] Such contempt for the common people was so repugnant to Euripides that he put pure Socratic doctrine into the mouth of a tyrant's lackey, to be refuted by Theseus as the champion of popular power. 'A poor labourer', says Creon's herald (*Suppl.* 420), 'even though he be no simpleton, is by his work made incapable of giving heed to the common good.' Like the writer of *Ecclesiasticus* (ch. xxxviii), Socrates believed of artificers and workmasters that 'each becometh wise in his own work', and no city can become inhabited without them; but like the same writer he would add, 'They shall not be sought for in the council of the people, and in the assembly they shall not mount on high . . . neither shall they declare instruction and judgment.'

The significance of this was not lost on his enemies.

The accuser claimed [writes Xenophon] that he led his associates to treat the established constitution with contempt, declaring that it was folly to appoint the rulers of the city by lot, when no one would be willing to employ a navigator or builder or other technician who had been selected in this way, although the mistakes of such people would have far less disastrous consequences than political mistakes. Arguments like these, the accuser claimed, incited young men to despise the established political order and turned them into violent revolutionaries.[3]

---

[1] See *The Sophists*, p. 128.

[2] Xen. *Mem.* 3.7.6. Since Xenophon himself was no democrat, he may have been inclined to exaggerate Socrates's contempt for the mob. But, as with Plato, one has to account for the devotion of such men to him in the first place.

[3] (a) *Mem.* 1.2.9. Arist. *Rhet.* 1393 b 4 may be a reflection of this passage, as Taylor noted. If so, Taylor's suggestion that ἀθλητάς in the received text of Aristotle should be αὐλητάς is probably right. (See his *VS*, p. 58.)

(b) Most scholars since Cobet have held that 'the accuser' mentioned by Xenophon is Polycrates, writing after Socrates's death (cf. p. 11 above), though Blass believed it was Meletus, the actual prosecutor at his trial. (See Taylor, *VS*, 4 f.) It is claimed that such a political complaint could not have been brought forward at the trial owing to the amnesty declared by the democrats at their restoration, for which see p. 62, n. 1, above and cf. Chroust, *S. M. & M.* 257.

(c) Chroust (*SM & M*, 58) quotes *Dissoi Logoi* 7 as evidence that objection to the lot was only taken over by Socrates from the Sophists, but there is no reason why the writer should not have got it from Socrates, even if his reasons for it are not Socratic. (See *The Sophists*, p. 319.)

No one need accuse Socrates of being anti-democratic, as we now understand democracy, simply because he objected to appointment by lot, for no democracy today, however extreme, would think of resorting to such a bizarre method.[1] Its use at Athens had at least in part a religious motive, being a way of leaving the decision to a god. But Socrates went further, and included popular election in his condemnation. Kings and rulers, he said (according to Xenophon, *Mem.* 3.9.10), are *not those who are chosen by the man in the street* (ὑπὸ τῶν τυχόντων) nor those on whom the lot falls nor those who owe their power to force or trickery, but those who know how to rule.[2] Xenophon describes his classification of the various forms of government thus (*Mem.* 4.6.12):

In his view both monarchy and tyranny were forms of rule, but differed one from the other. The rule of men with their consent and according to the laws of the state was monarchy, but rule over unwilling subjects, not according to law but at the whim of the ruler, was tyranny. A constitution in which the rulers were chosen from among those who fulfilled the requirements of the laws he called an aristocracy, when the qualification for office was property, a plutocracy, and when all the people were eligible, a democracy.

The suggestion in Euripides that Socrates favoured tyranny is monstrously unfair. For him the only tolerable form of government was the rule of law, regarded as a compact entered into voluntarily by all members of the state, whether high or low, and for that reason binding. From this obligation no individual could claim release on a plea of maladministration of the laws by those charged for the time being with giving effect to them, for the reason that such licence, if unchecked, would undermine the framework of law and order which guaranteed and protected the freedom and happiness of the whole body of citizens. The choice before the individual was either to obey the laws, or to get them changed by peaceful persuasion, or else to

---

[1] In speaking of Greek democracy, we are perhaps inclined to forget what a strange method of appointment the lot was. This is rightly emphasized by M. A. Levy in his *Pol. Power in the Anc. World* (p. 92), who calls it 'a method of appointing magistrates which was without precedent and has never since been seriously imitated'. Lesky (*HGL*, 498) more tersely calls it 'an obvious abuse'. On the nature and disadvantages of Athenian democracy see *The Sophists*, pp. 19 f.; for the use of the lot as its 'hallmark', references in Vlastos, Ἴσον. πολ. 3.

[2] Not 'those who know that they do not know how to rule'. Cf. p. 90, n. 1, above.

emigrate. This is made clear in the *Crito* (as explained in *The Sophists*, pp. 143, 146 f.). It is not necessarily a democratic view, for both constitutional monarchy and aristocracy, as defined by Socrates, would fulfil his conditions, and he would probably have favoured the latter. Living under a democracy, his principles made him loyal to its laws, and his native Athens had penetrated too deeply into his bones to make the choice of emigration possible. How could Socrates, of all people, desert the most intellectually alive of all Greek cities where he could meet and argue with men of every shade of opinion, the magnet which attracted *sophistai* like Protagoras, Gorgias, Prodicus and Anaxagoras, the home of Euripides and Aristophanes, the place where he could gather around him a brilliant circle of younger men like Antisthenes and Plato? For preference, he never went outside its walls (*Phaedr.* 230c–d). That being so, he must obey the laws, a course not inconsistent with a profound disapproval of the way the city was governed in his latter days. 'No man can be safe', he says to the representative body of citizens which tried him, 'who genuinely opposes you or any other democracy and tries to prevent many wrongs and illegalities from occurring in the city. A true champion of justice must keep to himself and avoid politics or he will not last long.'[1]

The truth is that, although Socrates might call himself the only true statesman (and one can see what he means), he was not interested in politics as ordinarily understood. He lived and spoke according to certain principles, which brought him into conflict, now with the dictatorial Thirty and again with the restored democracy, and set him apart from all political ambitions. We cannot therefore judge of his political ideas until we have made an examination of his whole philosophy of life, into which they had to be fitted as consequential. It included the conviction that not only wealth but power, reputation and honour were as nothing compared to the well-being of one's soul, that the unexamined life was not worth living because goodness, or the right state of the soul, depended on knowledge, especially self-knowledge, and that to suffer any injury, even death, was better than to commit one, because wrongdoing harmed the soul.

[1] Plato, *Apol.* 31 e–32a. 'Democracy' (Athenian variety) for πλῆθος, as Tredennick translates it, seems a fair rendering.

If ever it was true that the teaching of a philosopher is not to be separated from the whole man, it is true of Socrates, but so far I have tried to convey a sense of personal acquaintance with him before proceeding to more strictly philosophical topics. One may like or dislike him, but at least it is difficult to disagree with the general verdict of his time as he himself summed it up: 'This reputation which I have—it may be true or it may be false, but at any rate the view is held that Socrates is different from the general run of mankind.' This uniqueness above all was what struck his young friends: 'no other man is like him, living or dead; that's the amazing thing'.[1]

ADDITIONAL NOTE: SOME OPINIONS ON SOCRATES'S POLITICAL VIEWS

In 1939 two American scholars, A. D. Winspear and T. Silverberg, published a study of Socrates purporting to apply to him the genetic method which has had considerable success with Plato and Aristotle. They decided that he came from a humble background, as the son of a skilled artisan, and in his younger days was characterized by a rugged honesty, an acceptance of poverty, and a close connexion with the democratic movement, coupled with a devotion to natural science and a materialistic and sceptical outlook. His democratic activity brought him into contact with intellectual and political leaders and so led to a marked improvement in his material and social position. After a transitional period he was won over to the conservatives, surrendered his independence for the flattering approval of the nobility and threw in his lot with a wealthy and aristocratic set which included Alcibiades, Crito, the family of Aristides, Plato (whose 'loathing for democracy' is apparent) and his relatives, and the wealthy manufacturer Cephalus. The accusations concerning Plato's uncle Critias were all too true, and the apologias of Plato and Xenophon worthless: starting as a vigorous democrat, he became a bloodthirsty tyrant under the influence of none other than Socrates himself. The religion of Socrates accorded with his politics, for 'the new gods whom he was accused of introducing were the mystic divinities of the Pythagorean sects—the militant protective deities of international conservatism' (p. 76). (Taylor is brought into the witness box here, although he traced Socrates's Pythagoreanism back to the *Clouds*, whereas in our authors' view Socrates was then in his healthy sceptical stage, and in the

---

[1] Plato, *Apol.* 34e and *Symp.* 221c.

94

Apology 'takes great pains to confuse the issue and to confound the recent suspicion with the earlier attack of Aristophanes', p. 77.) Socrates was now engaged in 'a conspiracy against the democratic constitution of Athens and an intellectual assault on the whole democratic way of life' (p. 84). Even his conduct at the trial of the generals is best interpreted not as a high-minded and courageous action, but 'a move in the incredibly complicated game that was being played by both sides in this hectic period' (p. 67). To make him out an idealist, above the contending factions, was a political ruse to which was directed 'the whole effort of the conservative faction'. As the tradition of idealist philosophy began to find expression, Socrates was caught up in it and 'shared the ascent of philosophy from earth to heaven' (a strange thing to say of the man who in the eyes of posterity 'primus philosophiam devocavit e caelo, et in urbibus collocavit et in domos etiam introduxit'; with Cicero at least, the 'conservative faction' failed in their efforts to get Socrates off the ground).

The character of Plato's *Apology* as an elaborate attempt to throw a veil of idealism over Socrates the political intriguer has evidently escaped Sir Karl Popper. He looks upon the *Apology* and *Crito* as Socrates's 'last will', and concludes from them that 'he showed that a man could die, not only for fate and fame and other grand things of this kind, but also for the freedom of critical thought, and for a self-respect which has nothing to do with self-importance or sentimentality' (*O.S.* 194). It was later that Plato betrayed him, 'just as his uncles had done'. He foisted Pythagorean exclusiveness on him, and in the *Republic* made his most successful attempt to implicate him in his own totalitarian ideas (195 f.). For Socrates was a lover of freedom, a democrat and a humanitarian, whereas the thesis of Popper's book is that 'Plato's political demands are purely totalitarian and anti-humanitarian' (88). He finds the Platonic theory of justice identical with the theory and practice of modern totalitarianism, but, far from being in this the heir of Socrates, Plato is guilty of one of the most heinous intellectual betrayals in history.

These two polar opposites may serve to indicate the twisting and turning to which the evidence can be subjected.[1] Nearest to the truth were surely the older generation of liberal thinkers, or as they have been called 'the Oxford school of neo-idealism', typified by A. E. Taylor and Ernest Barker.[2] Everyone may—perhaps must—be influenced by his own political and social preferences, but these at least were men who put scholarship before

---

[1] I would not be misunderstood as intending by this to put the two on the same level. Between the doctrinaire assertions of the American book and the learning and open-mindedness of Popper there can be no comparison.

[2] Havelock, *Lib. Temp.* 19.

apologetics. It may even have been an advantage that they were not caught up in the reaction against modern Fascism and other forms of totalitarianism. At any rate they cannot be accused of hostility to Socrates, and it was the evidence itself that caused Taylor to write of him (*Socr.* 150): 'It was out of the question that, with all his practical loyalty to the constitution, he should approve of the principle of democracy, the sovereignty of the multitude who have no knowledge of the good, and have never dreamed that such knowledge is a necessary qualification for the direction of their affairs.' And again (151, n. 1): 'His disillusionment as the temper of the Athenian democracy grew narrower and harder in the course of the great war would be all the bitterer that he had grown up in the great "fifty years" before the war, and presumably had hoped and expected very different things.' On p. 58, n. 1, he goes so far as to say that Alcibiades was speaking as a genuine Socratic when he told the Spartans that democracy was 'acknowledged folly' (Thuc. 6.89.5).

Barker's conclusion is simple (*Pol. Th. of P. & A.* 51): 'The anti-democratic trend of his teaching is obvious', and of Plato he says (p. 61): 'Belonging to a family of anti-democratic tendencies, he naturally became a member, somewhere about 407, of the circle which had gathered round Socrates. Here too democracy was out of favour ... Politics was treated as an art: the proper conduct of political affairs was shown to depend on knowledge—a knowledge which neither the democratic assembly itself, nor the officials whom it appointed by the chance of the lot, could be said to possess.'

So far as Socrates had a political standpoint, and so far as it can be disentangled from the aberrations of his ancient admirers and enemies, it is in statements like these that we see him best.

III

PHILOSOPHICAL SIGNIFICANCE

(1) 'PHILOSOPHIA DE CAELO DEVOCATA'

For the Greeks themselves the name of Socrates formed a watershed in the history of their philosophy. The reason they give for this is that he turned men's eyes from the speculations about the nature of the physical world which had been characteristic of the Presocratic period, and concentrated attention on the problems of human life. In the most general terms, his message was that to investigate the origin and ultimate matter of the universe, the composition and motions of the heavenly bodies, the shape of the earth or the causes of natural growth and decay was of far less importance than to understand what it meant to be a human being and for what purpose one was in the world. This estimate of Socrates as a turning-point can be traced to Aristotle, though he does not perhaps give it such incontrovertible support as later writers supposed, and the exaggeratedly schematic view of Greek philosophy which it suggests was the work of the Hellenistic and Graeco-Roman periods. The chief testimonies in Aristotle are these:

(i) In the first chapter of *De partibus animalium* he is asserting the importance of recognizing the formal–final cause as well as the necessary or material. This had not been clear to earlier thinkers because they had no adequate conception of essence ('what it is to be' so-and-so) nor of how to define the real being of anything. Democritus had an inkling of it,[1] 'and in Socrates's time an advance was made as to the method, but the study of nature was given up (ἔληξε), and philosophers turned their attention to practical goodness and political science' (642a 28).

(ii) *Metaph.* 987b 1ff. (and 1078b 17 which repeats it in slightly different words) assigns the change more definitely to Socrates. Aris-

---

[1] For Aristotle on definition before Socrates see vol. II, 483f. (Democritus and the Pythagoreans: for the latter add *Metaph.* A 987a 20.)

totle is explaining Plato's theory of transcendent forms as having arisen out of the problem of how knowledge could be possible in a world which, as the Heracliteans seemed to have demonstrated, was in a perpetual state of flux. This theory he had encountered in his young days.

But when Socrates was busying himself with ethical questions to the complete neglect of nature as a whole, and was seeking in them for the universal and directing the mind for the first time to definitions, Plato, accepting his teaching, came to the conclusion that it applied to something other than the sensible world: the common definition, he reasoned, could not apply to any of the sensibles, since they were always changing.

It will be seen that in both these passages the switch from natural to ethical philosophy comes in by the way. The subject of both is what Aristotle consistently regarded as Socrates's chief contribution to scientific thought, namely his demand for definitions. The first does not even ascribe the switch to Socrates but to philosophers in his time, which is obviously correct. The second does not say that Socrates had never been interested in the study of external nature, but only that he had abandoned it by the time that Plato came into contact with him. Given that Plato was not only old enough to be interested in philosophy but had already been impressed by the difficulties of Heraclitean doctrine, this can hardly have been before his sixty-second year.

The tradition of Socrates as the philosopher who 'brought philosophy down from the skies' became widespread in the Hellenistic period, perhaps under the influence of the Stoic Panaetius,[1] and is familiar to us from Cicero. Its popularity has made it, whatever its historical basis, an important element in the history of thought. After speaking of Pythagoras Cicero says (*Tusc.* 5.4.10):

Ancient philosophy up to Socrates, who was taught by Archelaus the pupil of Anaxagoras, dealt with number and movement, and the source from which all things arise and to which they return; and these early thinkers inquired zealously into the magnitude, intervals and courses of the stars, and all celestial matters. But Socrates first called philosophy down from the sky,

---

[1] So Pohlenz thought (*Die Stoa* 1.194f., 2.10). Panaetius lived *c.* 185–109 B.C.

set it in the cities and even introduced it into homes, and compelled it to consider life and morals, good and evil.

And in the *Academica* (1.4.15):

Socrates I think—indeed it is universally agreed—was the first to divert philosophy from matters which nature herself has wrapped in obscurity, with which all philosophers before him had been concerned, and apply it to ordinary life, directing its inquiries to virtues and vices, and in general to good and evil. Celestial phenomena he regarded as beyond our comprehension, or at any rate, however well we might understand them, as irrelevant to the good life.

One may well wonder where the Sophists come in in all this. In the *Brutus* (8.30–1) Cicero acknowledges that they existed and that Socrates was acting in opposition to them. He introduces them mainly as rhetorical teachers (rhetoric being the subject of the *Brutus*), but sees the moral import of their teaching. As the power of expert oratory came to be recognized, he says, there arose a class of instructors in the art. This was the time when Gorgias, Protagoras, Prodicus, Hippias and many others rose to fame by claiming, arrogantly enough, to teach how speech could make the weaker cause the stronger.

Socrates opposed them [he goes on] and used to refute their instruction by his own subtle brand of argument. His fertile talk gave rise to a succession of accomplished thinkers, and it is claimed that then for the first time philosophy was discovered—not the philosophy of nature, which was older, but this which we are speaking of, whose subject is good and evil, and the life and manners of men.

That Socrates alone brought about the revolution which redirected men's thoughts from nature to human affairs is one of those clichés or over-simplifications of which written history is full. No doubt the assumption (which I hope my own book on the Sophists may have helped to dispel) was that the Sophists did not deserve the name of philosophers. The great tradition running from Socrates through Plato to Aristotle already had the upper hand, and with the notable exception of the Epicureans, most schools, however diverse, liked to think of themselves as the heirs of Socratic thought. In fact the complex causes of the switch of interest from natural science to human affairs were remarkably complex. More interesting now is the much disputed question whether it took place not only in the fifth century at large but in the mind of Socrates himself. Cicero does not deny it any more than Aristotle; indeed by linking Socrates with Archelaus and Anaxagoras he strongly suggests it, and there is much contemporary evidence in its support.

Much of what Cicero says could have been taken from Xenophon, whose contention is, briefly, that on the one hand Socrates was entirely guiltless of the charge of teaching 'what goes on in the heavens and beneath the earth', with all that that implied of atheism and impiety; but on the other hand this was not for want of knowledge: he was himself well versed in such sciences, but disparaged them as being of no practical use. In the first chapter of the *Memorabilia* (11 ff.) we are told that he 'never discussed' nature in general—the origin of the cosmos, or the laws governing celestial phenomena—as most philosophers did. Xenophon gives four reasons why he dismissed all this as folly:[1] (a) It is wrong to neglect the study of human affairs, which concern us much more nearly, so long as knowledge of them is so incomplete;[2] (b) no two scientists agree[3] even on fundamental questions such as whether the sum of things is one or infinitely many, whether everything moves or nothing moves, whether everything comes into existence and decays or nothing does; (c) natural science is of no practical use: studying the laws governing winds, waters and seasons does not give one power over these things; (d) not only are the secrets of the universe unfathomable, but to pry into them is displeasing to the gods.[4]

Xenophon lays great emphasis on the primarily utilitarian character

---

[1] (a)–(c) are in 1.1.12–15 (with (c) repeated at 4.7.5) and (d) in 4.7.6.

[2] Xenophon and Plato agree on Socrates's point of view here. Cf. *Phaedr.* 229e: 'I cannot yet, in the words of the Delphic precept, "know myself", and it seems to me ridiculous to be studying alien matters when still ignorant of this.'

[3] This of course was not original. Cf. Gorgias, *The Sophists*, p. 51.

[4] It was probably from Cicero rather than Xenophon that Milton took the Socratic sentiments which Adam utters in *P.L.* book 8, when he agrees with Raphael

> That not to know at large of things remote
> From use, obscure and subtle, but to know
> That which before us lies in daily life
> Is the prime wisdom; what is more is fume,
> Or emptiness, or fond impertinence,
> And renders us in things that most concern
> Unpractis'd, unprepared, and still to seek.

of Socrates's arguments. In general this was right. Socrates was an intensely practical person, and his equation of the good with what was useful or beneficial comes out as clearly in some of Plato's dialogues.[1] One may suspect, however, that having learned this, Xenophon sometimes made his own choice of examples according to his more commonplace ideas of what was truly beneficial, and that Socrates had other things in mind. Socrates, he says, advised studying geometry so far as it was necessary for measuring a plot of land to be bought or sold, or calculating the profit it would yield. Similarly astronomy should be learned in order to tell the time, the month and the year, in planning a journey, setting a watch and so on. Enough could be picked up from people like night hunters and pilots. 'But he strongly deprecated going so far as to study bodies revolving in different courses, planets and comets, or wearing oneself out in calculating their distances from the earth, their periods and the causes of them. He could see no use in it.' It is in this chapter too (*Mem.* 4. 7. 1–5) that he insists that Socrates knew what he was talking about. In the higher mathematics he was 'not inexperienced', and in the 'useless' parts of astronomy 'not uninstructed'.

All this accords sufficiently with the 'autobiographical' passage in Plato's *Phaedo* (96a ff.) to give good grounds for crediting the latter with some historical truth.[2] Socrates is there made to say that 'when he was young' he developed a passion for natural philosophy in the hope that it would explain the 'why' of things—why they are here, why they ever came into being, why they perish again. He studied the current theories of the origin of life, of physiology, psychology, astronomy and cosmology, but found them all unsatisfying and concluded that he had no aptitude for such subjects. His hopes were again raised by hearing that Anaxagoras had named 'mind' as the first cause, but dashed once more when he found that in its details Anaxagoras's

[1] See pp. 142 ff. below.
[2] It does not however accord with some of the more metaphysical parts of the *Republic*, where Socrates is made to express contempt for the application of mathematics and astronomy to practical ends, and to advocate using them as a means of directing the mind away from the physical world to that of the eternal Forms. See for instance the remarks about geometry at 526d–e, and their context. On a comprehensive view of all the evidence about Socrates, the only reasonable conclusion is that Plato is there reaching out beyond anything that the historical Socrates ever said. Kierkegaard drew attention to the contrast between Xenophon and Plato in this respect (*Irony*, 61 with n.).

system was just another set of physical theories like the rest. The distinctive character of mind as cause was simply ignored, and the explanations alleged were as material and mechanical as if intelligence had no part in them. Since Socrates remained convinced that a thing could only be explained in terms of its function, he gave up natural science after this and turned to entirely different methods of inquiry.

Plato uses this narrative for his own purposes, but it would be strange indeed if it had no basis in fact. To the inherent improbability may be added the congruence of the account with information from Xenophon, and with the equally reasonable supposition that the representation of Socrates in the *Clouds* is a farcical exaggeration of certain known trends of his thought rather than based on nothing at all. At the time of the *Clouds* Plato was a little boy, and may have slipped in the word 'young' about the Socrates of those days, so long before he knew him, even though he was a man of forty-six. Much more probably Aristophanes knew quite well that Socrates's enthusiasm for science had been on the wane for a long time: if he had ever embraced it, that was quite a sufficient handle for comedy,[1] once Aristophanes had decided to make Socrates the collective repository of most of his *bêtes noires*. The statement of Aristotle that the investigation of nature 'ceased' (ἔληξε) in the time of Socrates is an exaggeration. One has only to think of Diogenes of Apollonia, Archelaus (whose association with Socrates is probably historical; see vol. II, 239) and some of the Sophists themselves—Gorgias the pupil of Empedocles, and interested in his theory of pores and effluences, Alcidamas the author of a *Physicus*, Antiphon in the *Truth*, perhaps also Critias.[2] Democritus too was active until after the death of Socrates, though it is a moot point how much his work was known at Athens.

There is thus impressive evidence for a period in the life of Socrates

---

[1] This chronological point unnecessarily troubled Zeller, who is one of those who have seen not a shred of truth in the autobiographical passage of the *Phaedo*. E. Edelstein (*X. u. P. Bild*, 69–73) thought the historicity of the *Phaedo* guaranteed by its agreement with Xenophon.

[2] For Gorgias see Plato, *Meno* 76c; for Alcidamas, D.L. 8.56; for Antiphon, his frr. 23–32, DK; for Critias, Ar. *De an.* 405b 5 (Empedoclean identification of the ψυχή with blood). Diels made this point in *SB Berlin* (1894), but he was probably wrong to build up Polus as a student of physics on the basis of Socrates's ironical σὺ γὰρ τούτων ἔμπειρος at *Gorg.* 465d (p. 357). Some of these, like Gorgias (who laughed at the physical theorists) and Critias, were no doubt mere dabblers; but the theories were certainly continuing to attract interest.

when he was intensely interested in natural science. It would take a lot to shake it, but some have seen it all overthrown—Aristophanes, Xenophon, and Plato himself in the *Phaedo*—by some pleas of Socrates in the *Apology*, a work which all sides in the dispute accept as historical. At 18 b he denies that he is 'a wise man who theorizes about the heavens and has investigated everything beneath the earth, and makes the weaker argument the stronger', and at 23 d he says these are the stock charges hurled at any philosopher whose accusers are at a loss for material. At 19 c he adds,

You have seen it yourselves in the comedy of Aristophanes, someone called Socrates swinging around, declaring that he is treading the air and pouring out a great deal more nonsense about things of which I haven't the slightest understanding. I don't mean to disparage such knowledge ... but the fact is that I take no interest in it. Moreover I can call most of you as witnesses to this, and I beg all who have ever listened to me talking (and there are a great many such) to inform each other by saying whether any of you have ever heard me discourse either much or little on these topics.

There is, then, the evidence that we have previously considered and there is this. It all happened some 2,400 years ago and our information is far from adequate. We cannot hope to know all that lies behind it. But it is reasonable to claim that these words of Socrates cannot annihilate all the rest. Assuming that they were actually used by him in his defence, we need not accuse him of 'lying for the sake of saving his skin'.[1] His study of the natural world may have ended forty years before, and was in any case an inquiry undertaken to satisfy himself. He never taught it publicly nor promulgated any theories of his own,[2] though no doubt he would eagerly debate the current theories with a few chosen friends. When he took to going

---

[1] The phrase about 'lying to save his skin' occurs in almost identical words in Hackforth (*CPA*, 148) and Popper (*OS*, 308). Popper finds that *Apol.* and *Phaedo* flatly contract each other and that only *Apol.* is to be believed. Hackforth also accepts *Apol.* as historical, and goes so far as to say (p. 147): 'It is not the least use to say that Socrates had dropped these pursuits when he found science unsatisfying ... for the language which he uses rules out ... the possibility that at any age whatever he engaged in scientific speculation or research.' Yet rather puzzlingly he can still suppose it 'quite likely that he started with the eager enthusiasm which Plato attributes to him in the famous autobiographical passage of the *Phaedo*' (pp. 152 f.).

[2] The 'intellectual autobiography' of the *Phaedo* is a cento of current theories which even now can be assigned to their authors without difficulty. (See Burnet's notes *ad loc.*) There is no hint that Socrates made any original contribution.

round Athens accosting worthy citizens and questioning them, or talking to any bright young men whom he saw in the palaestra, it was because he had already recognized the futility of the scientists' speculations and the urgent need to know oneself, to find out 'what is pious, what impious; what fine, what ugly; what is just, what is unjust; what is prudence, madness, courage or cowardice; what is a state and what a statesman; what is meant by governing men, and what is a governor'.[1] If these were the questions that he had been pressing on the attention of all and sundry for the last thirty or forty years, can anyone say that his claim of indifference to natural science, made when he was on trial for his life, was falsified by an earlier period of study in it? In any case he had never taken it up for its own sake, or with the same questions in mind as the physical theorists themselves. His question was 'Why?' Why should there be a world like this, and why should we be in it? At first he thought this was what the scientists were asking too, and plunged into their discussions, until he discovered that they were only interested in the question *how* it all came about. Diogenes of Apollonia may have been an exception,[2] and it is noteworthy that in characterizing Socrates as a scientist it is first and foremost the air-theories of Diogenes which Aristophanes puts into his mouth. But Socrates may have already broken with natural science when Diogenes wrote, and while acknowledging his teleological tendency was not likely to be attracted back by a materialistic theory which embodied the directing power in one of the physical elements. Nevertheless, when he became unpopular with those in power, his earlier interest in the subject could be brought up against him like the youthful left-wing escapades of some respected American senator or philosopher today.

Socrates gave up science for ethics, the study of nature for the pursuit of practical principles. But, perhaps because of his early scientific studies, he insisted that ethics itself was a field of exact knowledge calling for the application of rigorous scientific method. For this method Aristotle believed that science would be for ever in

[1] Xen. *Mem.* 1.1.16. So also Aristotle, e.g. *EE* 1216b 4: Socrates used to investigate what is justice, what courage, and so with all the other parts of virtue, because he equated the virtues with knowledge.

[2] See vol. II, p. 362, n. 1.

his debt, while he deplored its exercise in a sphere to which he considered it inappropriate. In Aristotle's eyes (as Gigon has pointed out) Socrates plays a double role in the history of philosophy: he produced a method and a principle indispensable for the proper study and classification of natural phenomena, while at the same time his name marks the end of the scientific and the beginning of the ethical epoch in philosophy.[1] What this method was is the next thing that we have to inquire, only pausing first to note that here at last we have put our finger on the essential difference between Socrates and the Sophists. If the word *philosophy* is taken in its strict sense, as the search for knowledge, the old tradition was justified that he and he alone brought philosophy into human life. That is, he sought to make ethics and politics the subject of a scientific inquiry which should reveal universal laws or truths, in opposition to the scepticism and relativism that had turned all things into matters of opinion and left men's minds at the mercy of the persuader with the smoothest tongue. Even a Protagoras could not escape from this; a Gorgias or a Polus gloried in it.

(2) INDUCTION AND DEFINITION

As I have said,[2] for a thumbnail version of an earlier philosopher's contribution we can generally turn with confidence to Aristotle. Here are no dramatic masterpieces, to tantalize the historian of philosophy as much as they delight the lover of great literature. His bald notes may need elaboration, and possibly modification in the light of his known philosophical assumptions, but their terseness and lucidity make them excellent starting-points for our own study of one of his predecessors. The extent of Socrates's contribution to philosophy, as distinct from Plato's, was probably already a matter of debate in his own time, and his summing-up is this (*Metaph.* 1078b27): 'There are two things which may justly be credited to Socrates, inductive arguments and general definition.' The mention of definition connects the sentence with other passages, already quoted for their bearing on the

---

[1] See Gigon in *Mus. Helv.* 1959, 192. Compare also the interesting remarks of Deman, *Témoignage*, 78 f.: 'Socrate s'est consacré à la recherche morale, mais il a apporté à cette recherche une préoccupation strictement scientifique', etc.

[2] P. 37 above. In the same section will be found what needs to be said about Aristotle's value as a source.

transition from natural to ethical philosophy (p. 97), whose main purport was the methodical advance initiated by Socrates in the comprehension of essence through definition. It is hardly fanciful to detect a note of disappointment in Aristotle's observation that the first man to grasp the importance of these indispensable aids to scientific thinking was the one who abandoned theoretical science for ethics, a subject in which, as he never tires of reminding us in his own ethical writings,[1] scientific accuracy neither can nor should be demanded.

Induction, Aristotle tells us (*Top.* 105a13), is the progress from the particular to the universal, and he illustrates it with an example of Socratic type: if the best navigator is the expert (in Aristotle's words 'the one with knowledge') and the best driver the expert, and so on, we infer that in general the expert (or knowledgeable) is in every occupation the best. Another example might be taken from Plato's *Gorgias* (474d ff.). Socrates gets Polus to agree that bodies are called beautiful (*kala*) because they are either useful or pleasure-giving, and then that the same is true of shapes, colours, sounds, *nomoi* and learning. From this the general conclusion is drawn that if anything is more beautiful than any other it must be either more useful or more pleasant or both. The mind is 'led on' (as the Greek word for induction, *epagōgē*, may signify),[2] from the observation of particular

---

[1] E.g. *EN* 1179b 1: οὐκ ἔστιν ἐν τοῖς πρακτοῖς τέλος τὸ θεωρῆσαι ἕκαστα καὶ γνῶναι, ἀλλὰ μᾶλλον τὸ πράττειν αὐτά. Not to have seen this was in his view a major error on the part of Socrates. Cf. pp. 130 f. below.

[2] The word only becomes technical in Aristotle, and it is difficult to be sure what is the idea behind it. (Cf. however Plato, *Pol.* 278 a.) It often seems to be that suggested above (so Mure in note to O. Tr. of *An. Post.* 71 a 8); e.g. at *Top.* 156a 4, ἐπάγοντα μὲν ἀπὸ τῶν καθ' ἕκαστον ἐπὶ τὸ καθόλου the implicit object of the verb is pretty clearly the interlocutor, and this personal reference is confirmed by the use of the passive at *An. Post.* 81b 2, ἀδύνατον δὲ τὰ καθόλου θεωρῆσαι μὴ δι' ἐπαγωγῆς . . . ἐπαχθῆναι δὲ μὴ ἔχοντας αἴσθησιν ἀδύνατον and 71a21 ἅμα ἐπαγόμενος ἐγνώρισεν. Cicero seems to preserve this meaning when he defines it (in its translation 'inductio') as 'oratio quae rebus non dubiis captat assensionem eius quicum instituta est' (*De inv.* 1.31.51). On the other hand at *Top.* 108b 10, τῇ καθ' ἕκαστα ἐπὶ τῶν ὁμοίων ἐπαγωγῇ τὸ καθόλου ἐστιν ἀξιοῦμεν ἐπάγειν. οὐ γὰρ ῥάδιόν ἐστιν ἐπάγειν μὴ εἰδότας τὰ ὅμοια the verb seems to be used in a dual sense, of *bringing on* or adducing individual instances in order to *bring out*, or make apparent, the universal. The active in ἐπάγειν μὴ εἰδότας contrasts strongly with the passive with μὴ ἔχοντας at 81b 5. So also Cicero shortly after the passage just quoted has 'illud quod inducemus', not 'illum quem'. ἐπάγεσθαι (middle) is so used in the Hippocratic *De fractt.*, which may be slightly later in date than Aristotle. See the passages quoted by Taylor, *VS*, 73. On pp. 112f. he suggests that there may have been a different underlying metaphor. (For a full discussion of this question see Ross, *Analytics*, 481–3.)

instances to grasp a general characteristic shared by all the members of a class. It may be a class of people, things or events. Because the sun has risen with unfailing regularity for thousands of years, we infer not only that it will rise tomorrow but that we can predict the exact time of its rising in any given part of the world. An inductive conclusion may be falsified at any time by a new or newly discovered fact, unless it is made into a truism by refusal to give the name x to anything that has not all the qualities that we have decided to associate with x's. This we do not usually do. The black swans of Australia were not denied the name because hitherto the generalization 'All swans are white' had seemed a safe one. Yet without the constant use of this device of drawing inductions from a limited experience it would be impossible either for laymen to carry on their everyday lives or for scientists to pursue their researches. Since Socrates only employed a rudimentary form of it, with his eye on the good life rather than on logic or scientific method, its full discussion is more appropriate in connexion with Aristotle. Yet it may be said here that, though everyone uses it, with varying degrees of consciousness of what they are doing, logicians are as much concerned today as in the time of Aristotle with the problems that it raises and the obstinate fact that, indispensable as it is to thought and action, it appears to have no perfectly rational justification. Briefly, there are three possibilities:

(*a*) Complete enumeration. The general statement is only made with knowledge of every case falling under it. ('All boys in this school are in the age-group 12–18.') Here it does not seem that any inference has been drawn, but to make the general statement explicitly is a useful step towards drawing further conclusions and combining it with other similar information to make wider generalizations. It is only in these cases that induction can be reduced to valid syllogistic form as Aristotle wished to reduce it.

(*b*) Admission that the conclusion is only probable, and subject to review if a negative instance should be found. ('All schoolboys like holidays.')

(*c*) The claim that the human mind has a faculty of intuition enabling it to 'see' the universal after examination of a sufficient number of individual instances. Complete enumeration, except in certain very limited cases like the one cited above, is impossible at the individual level, but may be possible (or so at least it seemed to Aristotle) at the level of species. Consequently, in treating induction as a part of formal logic, Aristotle operates with species as units. He did however believe in intuition as justifying the initial inductive leap from particulars to the first, or lowest, universal, and in this he was assisted by the belief in specific forms as substantively existing essences, which was a legacy from Socrates through Plato. If specific form is something fixed in nature, it is reasonable to suppose that it may be detected and defined after only a partial examination of the particular instances which share it.

This is to anticipate. To return to Socrates, he was on the one hand at a much earlier, more tentative stage of thought, before logic had been codified and formalized at all, nor was its formalization his aim as it was Aristotle's; but on the other hand, because some form of inductive reasoning, more or less conscious, is a necessity of life, let alone of anything that can be called philosophy, it has been argued that Aristotle was wrong in attributing it in any special way to Socrates. On this it is sufficient to quote Ross:

It would, of course, be as untrue to say that Socrates invented inductive argument as, in Locke's phrase, to suppose that God has been 'so sparing to men to make them barely two-legged creatures, and left it to Aristotle to make them rational'. Professor Taylor can without difficulty produce instances of the use of ἐπάγεσθαι for inductive argument from the early Hippocratic writings. But surely anyone can recognize in Socrates, whether as depicted in the *Memorabilia* or as depicted in what are generally known as the 'Socratic' dialogues of Plato, a careful testing of general opinions by the examination of particular cases that is foreign to the previous schools of Greek philosophy, with which Aristotle is here contrasting Socrates. In this sense the ascription of inductive argument to him is thoroughly justified.

And again:

Aristotle cannot mean that Socrates was the first person who used inductive arguments or gave general definitions, but that he was the first who recognized the importance of them and systematically used the former to get the latter. The inductive arguments referred to are not scientific inductions but arguments from analogy such as we often find Socrates using in the *Memorabilia* and in Plato's 'Socratic' dialogues.[1]

[1] Ross, *Metaph.* 1.xliii and 2.422. The reference is to Taylor's *VS*, 72ff.

Aristotle's own way of describing Socratic arguments is somewhat similar, when he introduces them as a particular mode of persuasion in the *Rhetoric* (1393b4). The use of illustrative examples, he says, resembles induction, which is the starting-point of all reasoning.[1] One variety of it, which Aristotle calls 'the parallel' (παραβολή), is represented by the practice of Socrates, for instance the argument against filling government offices by lot on the ground that no one would use the lot to select athletes for a contest or a steersman from among a crew. The general lesson of these parallels, he adds, is that one ought in every case to choose the man who understands the job.

The nature of analogy, and its relation to induction, is a complex and much-discussed question. Perhaps the most satisfactory course is to refer analogy to the comparison of single cases and reserve induction, as Aristotle did, for the argument which leads from single cases to the universal.[2] Socrates employed both methods, but in the above passage Ross appears to be regarding analogy (as it is often regarded) as an earlier, looser and less systematic form of induction. To keep to induction (as credited by Aristotle to Socrates) for the present, its function is to establish, from a number of observed instances, a general characteristic of a whole class, e.g. of broad-leafed trees that they are deciduous. (The example is Aristotle's.) Although there must be thousands of broad-leafed trees which no one has ever seen, the botanist draws this conclusion with confidence. Induction leads to definition because a definition consists of a collection of these general characteristics, selected with certain requirements in mind:[3]

(*a*) They must be essential to membership of the class, not accidental attributes of certain individuals within it. Many men have blue eyes, but this characteristic has no place in a definition of the species 'man'.

---

[1] Cf. *An. Post.* 100b 3, δῆλον δὴ ὅτι ἡμῖν τὰ πρῶτα ἐπαγωγῇ γνωρίζειν ἀναγκαῖον. This is because all knowledge originates in sensation, and it is induction that enables us to pass beyond the sensation of particulars to apprehension of the universals which provide the premises for syllogism. On *Rhet.* 1393b 4 see also p. 91, n. 3 (*a*) above.

[2] On the relation of induction to analogy see Lloyd, *P. & A.* 172–5 and Robinson, *P.'s Earlier D.* 207, and cf. p. 48, n. 1 above.

[3] These requirements are Aristotle's, based on his own development of Socratic thought including the concept of specific form (εἶδος).

(*b*) They must be collectively sufficient to mark off[1] the class of objects to be defined from all other classes of objects whatsoever. To call man a two-legged living creature is to name characteristics essential to the human race, but they do not constitute a definition, because they do not mark it off from the race of birds.[2] The sum of essential attributes forming the content of the definition was called, among other things, the form (*eidos*) of the class. The use of this word as a technical term of logic is post-Socratic, for there was no science of logic before Plato, and it was only Aristotle who systematized it and gave it anything like a technical vocabulary. But *eidos*, as we shall see, was one of the names used by Socrates for the essential nature that he was seeking to define. In popular use the word commonly designated outward appearance or shape, perhaps particularly of human physique, as being handsome or ugly, 'looking' powerful, weak and so forth. But in both literary and technical (especially medical) language it already meant the peculiar character or essential nature of anything, approximating sometimes to species or class. Thucydides says of the plague (2.50) that 'its *eidos* was beyond description', and in Herodotus the word approaches the meaning of class or species when he speaks (1.94.3) of 'dice, knucklebones, balls and all other *eidea* of playthings'. It is frequent in the medical writings, e.g. *Epidemics* 3.12 (III, 92 L.), 'Many other *eidea* of fevers were widespread, tertian, quartan, nightly, continuous . . .'[3] The use of it by Socrates led to momentous developments when it was taken over by Plato.

(3) RELEVANCE OF INDUCTION AND DEFINITION TO SOCRATES'S ETHICAL AIMS

The interest of Socrates in definitions is one of the best-attested facts about him. Apart from Aristotle, it is insisted on by both Xenophon

[1] This is the primary meaning of ὁρίʒειν (ὁρίʒεσθαι), the verb translated 'define' in Xenophon, Plato and Aristotle, namely to mark off the ὅροι or limits of a field or other territory from those of its neighbour.

[2] There is a story that Plato defined man as a featherless biped, whereupon Diogenes the Cynic produced a plucked chicken and said, 'There is Plato's man for you' (D.L. 6.40).

[3] Taylor's review of the uses of the word in *VS* may be conveniently studied in the summary of Gillespie (*CQ*, 1912, 179f.), where it is followed by a criticism.

(who gives numerous examples besides the general statement, already quoted on p. 104, at *Mem.* 1.1.16) and Plato. But what was his motive? Again our authorities are unanimous, that it was not scientific but practical.[1] Aristotle's bare statement to this effect may be supplemented in particular from Plato. One feature in the thought and speech of his contemporaries seemed to Socrates particularly harmful. Whether in conversation, in political speeches or in the oratory of the law-courts, they made constant use of a great variety of general terms, especially terms descriptive of ethical ideas—justice, temperance, courage, *areté* and so forth. Yet at the same time it was being asserted by Sophists and others that such concepts had no basis in reality. They were not god-given virtues, but only 'by convention', varying from place to place and age to age. Serious thought about the laws of human behaviour had begun with a radical scepticism, which taught that it rested on no fixed principles but each decision must be made empirically and *ad hoc*, based on the expediency of the immediate situation (*kairos*). From this theoretical soil grew the pride of youthful rhetoric in its ability to sway men to or from any course of action by mastery of the persuasive use of words. In such an atmosphere it was not surprising that there was much confusion in the meanings attached to moral terms. Socrates noted this,[2] and disapproved of it. If these terms corresponded to any reality at all, he thought, then one meaning must be true and the others false. If on the other hand the Sophists were right, and their content was purely relative and shifting, it must be wrong to go on using the same words for different things and they ought to go out of use. He himself was convinced that

[1] That the first attempt at systematic inductive methods was made in the context of practical action adds interest to some remarks of the eighteenth-century Dutch mathematician s'Gravesande as paraphrased by E. Cassirer (*Ph. of E.* 61). On the inductive axiom that past experience is a guide to conclusions about the future he said: 'This is not strictly a logical, but a pragmatic axiom; its validity does not lie in the necessity of thought, but in that of action. For all action, all practical relationships with things, would be impossible, if we could not assume that the lessons of former experience will be valid in the future. Scientific prediction does not then involve the syllogistically necessary conclusions of formal logic; it is, nevertheless, a valid and indispensable conclusion by analogy. But we must and can be content with such a conclusion, for that must indeed be true whose denial would imply the negation of all man's empirical existence and all his social life.' On this Cassirer himself comments that 'things have taken a strange turn; the certainty of physics is no longer based on purely logical presuppositions but on a biological and sociological presupposition'.

[2] See the passages from Plato and Xenophon quoted in *The Sophists*, p. 165.

the first alternative was true, and that it was illegitimate and unhelpful for an orator to exhort the people to adopt a certain course of action as being the wisest or most just, or for advocates and jury to debate whether an individual had acted well or badly, justly or unjustly, unless those concerned were agreed upon what wisdom, justice and goodness *are*. If people are not agreed on that, but though using the same words mean different things by them, they will be talking at cross-purposes, and their discussions can make no progress either intellectually or—when ethical terms are in question—morally. Here Socrates was raising for the first time a fundamental question of philosophy, the question by what right we use general terms, including all nouns except proper names, and what is the factual content of such terms, and Aristotle was right to see that this was so. At the same time, as Aristotle also recognized, he did not see it as a logical or ontological question, but simply as an indispensable requirement for what to him was much more important: the discovery of the right way to live.[1]

In Socrates's opinion, then, if order is to be restored to thought on the rights and wrongs of human conduct, the first necessity is to decide what justice, goodness and other virtues are. According to his method, as described by Aristotle and illustrated in Xenophon and Plato (especially but not exclusively the earlier dialogues), the inquiry consists of two stages. The first is to collect instances to which both parties to a discussion agree that the name under consideration may be applied, e.g., if it is piety, to collect instances of agreed pious acts. Secondly, the collected instances are examined in order to discover some common quality in them by virtue of which they bear that name. If they do not share such a common quality, then he claimed it would be improper to go on applying the same word to them all. This common quality, or nexus of common qualities, is their nature, essence

---

[1] This may be what Aristotle had in mind when he said (*Metaph.* 1078b24) that Socrates sought for definitions because he wanted to syllogize, and a definition is the starting-point of a syllogism. Once again he has put it in his own language and seen it as a purely logical process, but Zeller (*Ph. d. Gr.* 129 with n. 2) has pointed to some cases where Socrates is shown using a definition as the basis for further demonstration; and this demonstration is always ethical, to prove that a certain line of conduct should or should not be followed. We must learn to distinguish good from bad, useful from harmful, in order to follow the one and avoid the other (διαλέγοντας κατὰ γένη τὰ μὲν ἀγαθὰ προαιρεῖσθαι τῶν δὲ κακῶν ἀπέχεσθαι Xen. *Mem.* 4.5.11, and cf. 4.1.5).

or 'form'[1] considered as pious. It will provide in fact, if it can be discovered, the definition of piety, abstracted from the accidental properties of time and circumstance which differentiate the individual cases falling under it. As a scientific method this is of course the necessary basis of any study like botany or zoology whose chief task is one of classification. Animals and plants are grouped in genera, species and sub-species according as they exhibit in common certain properties which are regarded by the trained investigator as structural and essential, though often very different from those which strike the eye of the casual observer. As such it was developed by Plato (compare his insistence on classifying according to the *natural* joints or divisions, κατ' ἄρθρα ᾗ πέφυκεν, *Phaedr.* 265 e) and especially appreciated by Aristotle as the first systematic zoologist.

Socrates was not interested in botany or zoology but in his fellow men, and what he wanted to see classified and defined was their actions.

If anyone contradicted him on some point [says Xenophon] without being able to make himself clear, asserting without sufficient proof that so-and-so was wiser, more statesmanlike or braver, or anything of the same kind, he would lead the whole discussion back to the assumed definition.[2] 'You say your man is a better citizen than mine? Then let us consider what we mean by a good citizen.'

---

[1] That logic is not yet a science, but still feeling its way, is well shown by the variety of words and phrases used by Socrates in attempting to get his idea across, in contrast to the firm technical vocabulary of Aristotle. The *Meno* is a treasury of these. Socrates asks for the οὐσία (being, essence, 72b); the ἕν τι εἶδος (single form) which all the instances possess (72c and d); the ἓν κατὰ πάντων, διὰ πάντων, ἐπὶ πᾶσι (the one thing said of them all, running through them all, in them all, 73d, 74a, 75a); τὸ ἐπὶ πᾶσι ταὐτόν (what in them all is the same, 75a); ᾧ ταὐτόν εἰσιν ἅπασαι (that by which they are all the same, 72c); κατὰ ὅλου ἀρετῆς πέρι ὅτι ἐστί (of virtue in general, what it is, 77a); and frequently simply τί ποτ' ἐστί (what it is). Cf. *Lysis* 222b and 223b, *Prot.* 361c, *Laches* 190d, *Charm.* 159a (where the definitions sought are respectively of a friend, of ἀρετή in general, of courage, and of σωφροσύνη).

[2] ἐπὶ τὴν ὑπόθεσιν, *Mem.* 4.6.13. Marchant (Loeb ed.) was surely right to translate the word by 'definition'. The man must be brought to see the underlying assumption of his loosely worded encomium, which is that wisdom, statesmanship and courage have a certain fixed nature and that the subject's behaviour is in accordance with that nature. Only if he can define his standard of reference will his praise have any significance. Similarly at *Euthyphro* 9d, τοῦτο ὑποθέμενος means 'on the definition that you have given' (i.e. of piety, that it is what is pleasing to the gods). Again in the *Meno*, when pressed to inquire whether virtue can be taught before they have decided what it is, Socrates reluctantly agrees on condition that they proceed ἐξ ὑποθέσεως, that is, on a hypothetical *definition*: if virtue is knowledge, then it will be teachable. This use of ὑπόθεσις in both Xenophon and Plato (cf. also *Phaedo* 100b ὑποθέμενος εἶναί τι καλὸν κτλ.) suggests strongly that it was genuinely Socratic, as Ross has pointed out (*Class. Ass. Proc.* 1933, 21).

Who is the good citizen in finance, in war, on an embassy, in debate before the Assembly? From such examples a conclusion could be drawn about good citizenship in general. The fault that he usually had to correct in his interlocutors is that when faced with a question of definition like 'What is courage?' or 'What is piety?' they saw no further than the first stage of the dual process. Some examples are:

Euthyphro, 62d:

What I wanted you to tell me was not one or two of the numerous actions that are pious, but the actual form that we spoke of, which makes them all pious. You did say, didn't you, that impious acts were impious and pious acts pious by reason of a single form? Show me then what the form itself is, so that I can refer to it and use it as a standard, calling an action by you or anyone else pious if it resembles it but not otherwise.

Theaet. 146e:

But the question, Theaetetus, was not what are the objects of science or how many sciences there are. My purpose in asking you was not to count them but to find out what knowledge itself is.

The same point is made in other dialogues (e.g. at *Laches* 191cff.), but the best exposition of the method is in the *Meno*. Without preamble this impetuous young man bursts out with the burning question of the day: 'Can virtue (*areté*) be taught, or how is it acquired?' How can I tell you that, replies Socrates, when I don't even know what it is[1] and have never met anyone who does? Meno is astonished. Has he not met Gorgias, and did not Gorgias know? Here Socrates exhibits a little of his notorious irony. It is Meno who interests him, and whom he wishes to draw out. So he says, 'I'm afraid I'm a forgetful person, and can't say just now what I thought at the time. Probably he did know, and you know his views, so remind me—or tell me yourself if you will. I expect you agree with him.' Meno does, 'so', says Socrates, 'we can leave him out of it, but tell me what *you* say virtue is'. The victim is now in the net, and proceeds to give a string of instances and types of virtue to his own satisfaction, but not to that

---

[1] In the *Protagoras* the question whether virtue can be taught is discussed at length, but there too Socrates returns at the end to what is for him the prior question of definition. They have got themselves into a muddle, he says, and what is needed is 'to make a determined attack on the question what virtue itself is: then we could return to the question whether or not it can be taught' (361c).

of Socrates, who complains that he has been given a swarm of virtues when he only wanted the one thing, virtue. Taking up this metaphor, he gets Meno to agree that if asked what a bee is he would not list and describe different kinds of bee but mention the points in which they were all similar. Can he not do the same for virtue? Meno demurs: virtue does not seem to him to be on the same footing.[1] But under Socrates's guidance, and with specimen definitions of shape and colour to help him, he makes more than one attempt, only to have them shown up as defective by Socrates. This is done by citing counter-instances ('Virtue is the capacity to govern men': 'Then is it virtue in a slave to govern his master?' and so on), because naturally the same inductive process of adducing instances, which can lead to a sound definition, also shows up those that are faulty.[2] Young Meno is easy game, and can only collapse with the complaint that Socrates is a wizard who paralyses his mind and his tongue. But, although he

[1] See 72d, 73a, 74a–b.

[2] I hope it is not simple-minded to say this. Ross (*Class. Ass. Proc.* 1933, 20f.) says Socrates used inductive arguments in two ways: (*a*) to reach the definition of a virtue by agreement, examining cases in order to elicit the general principle common to them; (*b*) destructively, pointing out instances which conform to the proposed definition but are obviously wrong. Robinson (*P.'s Earlier D.* 48) even gives as one reason for his claim that there is no necessary connexion between *epagoge* and definition the fact that 'epagoge is a means to the destruction rather than the establishment of definitions'. But surely the method of arriving at a conclusion is also appropriate for testing it, amending it if necessary, and so getting nearer the truth. The conclusion 'All swans are white' was arrived at by induction, and induction showed it to be inadequate. The result is not destructive, but brings the naturalist nearer to the correct definition of a swan.

It can also be said (with Popper in his *Logic of Sc. Discovery*) that the process of falsifying a generalization is not inductive but deductive; i.e., if I understand the matter correctly, it is an argument of the form: 'The general assumption demands that all *x*'s are *y*; but *a*, which is an *x*, is not *y*; therefore the assumption is false.' This way of putting it is linked to Popper's contention that in science all inferences are deductive: the scientist does not reason from observations to a general hypothesis (which of course can never be *proved* by observation), but first propounds a hypothesis and then tests it as far as possible by observation and experiment. (See also Hare, *Freedom and Reason*, 87f., 92, 109.) It would be rash to become involved at this point in the whole problem of the nature of induction, on which Popper has thrown so much light. But, after reading with some care what he says on the subject in *Conj. and Ref.* ch. 1, I still feel that the initial choice of one theory rather than another must be largely determined by prior observations, even taking into account his remarks about the selectiveness of our observations from early infancy and his claim that the observations which the theory sets out to explain themselves presuppose a framework of theories (p. 47). After all, 'unexpected and unexplained observations' do present themselves (p. 222), and we try to explain them by theory. As excuse for these presumptuous remarks I can only plead the extraordinary interest of Popper's views, which require a book, not a footnote, for their appraisal. To return to the safer ground of history, the process of scientific discovery as Aristotle saw it was from observations to general hypotheses, and in the use of *epagoge* he considered himself to be following Socrates.

himself is in need of the logical lesson that enumeration of instances is not the same as definition of a general concept, his vague feeling that virtue is not something to be defined like a biological species marks him as the pupil of Gorgias and reminds us that Socrates was not only teaching elementary logic but taking his stand on a much bigger question, the universality of value-judgments, in which he was opposed not only by the Sophists but afterwards by Aristotle, who recognized the scientific importance of his method while at the same times denying its applicability in this sphere.[1]

The *Meno* provides an example of the kind of questioning in which Socrates indulged, and which, with its 'numbing' effect that called forth such bitter complaint from Meno, made him so unpopular with all but his friends and sympathizers. We can now give more definite content to the picture of himself which he drew at his trial, going tirelessly round the city, in obedience as he said to the will of Apollo, and questioning one class of citizens after another—poets, politicians, craftsmen—in order to discover wherein lay their claim to wisdom and knowledge. He had one simple criterion. If a man knew anything, he could 'give an account (*logos*)' of it, and in his hands that maid-of-all-work among Greek words takes on the meaning 'definition' or something closely approaching it.[2] To the poets, then, he would put the question 'What is poetry?', to the politicians 'What do you understand by a *politeia*?' or 'You say you will establish a just order of society; now what exactly do you mean by justice?' And the poets would reply, 'Why, when I say poetry I mean the *Iliad* and the *Agamemnon*, and that little thing of my own that I recited at Olympia last month.' Then Socrates would set to work patiently and tirelessly as he did with Meno, pointing out that he had not asked for a list of poems but for a *logos* of the *ousia*—the essential nature—of poetry. What was the common property shared by Homer, Solon, Empedocles, the tragedians, down to the latest paean of Tinnychus that everyone was singing, which made people include them all under

---

[1] See *The Sophists*, pp. 253 f.

[2] Cf. *Laches* 190c οὐκοῦν ὅ γε ἴσμεν, κἂν εἴποιμεν δήπου τί ἐστιν, Xen. *Mem.* 4.6.1 Σωκράτης γὰρ τοὺς μὲν εἰδότας τί ἕκαστον εἴη τῶν ὄντων ἐνόμιζε καὶ τοῖς ἄλλοις ἂν ἐξηγεῖσθαι δύνασθαι. In Plato we find this sense of λόγος fairly well established, e.g. in ὁ τοῦ δικαίου λόγος or λόγος τῆς πολιτείας (*Rep.* 343a, 497c).

one head as poetry rather than calling them history or philosophy or anything else? And when any suggestion of the poets was refuted by the mention of another acknowledged poet who did not fit into their proposed definition, and they went away in a bad temper, Socrates could only sigh and conclude that they must indeed compose their poems in a divine frenzy, as mouthpieces of the god; for if they did it of themselves they would assuredly know what they were doing and could give a *logos* of it. With the craftsmen he was more fortunate. Ask a bronze-worker what he means by the *cire-perdue* method of casting, and he can give you a lucid and adequate answer. Their fault was a lack of modesty in failing to realize that they had not the competence to pronounce with equal ability on matters outside their province.

(4) THE NATURE OF SOCRATIC DEFINITION

The definitions sought by Socrates are sometimes criticized on the ground that they are 'persuasive definitions', a useful term which does not necessarily involve anachronism because it was first coined in the twentieth century.[1] In view of what has been written about this by others, what follows can be little more than a summing-up, and a fairly extensive use of quotation may be excusable. A persuasive definition is one in which the author, instead of simply seeking to clarify the usage of a word and prevent misunderstanding, has argued for that meaning of it of which he himself approves, and which, if adopted, will incline people towards the course of action which he thinks right. He takes a term expressive of value, like goodness, justice or beauty, to which people inevitably react favourably (it has 'emotive force'), and by defining it in a certain way enlists this favourable reaction to further his own moral or aesthetic preferences. 'Persuasive definitions alter the descriptive meaning of a word without disarming its emotive force; hence they are effective instruments of valuational reform.' 'The effect of saying that "the true definition of justice is yz" is to make people . . . apply the evaluative tone of the word "justice" to the thing described by the words yz.'[2]

[1] By C. L. Stevenson. See his article 'Persuasive Definitions' in *Mind*, 1938, or his book *Ethics and Language*.
[2] R. M. Gordon in *J. of Philos.* 1964, 436; R. Robinson, *Definitions*, 166.

Since Socrates's attempts to elicit definitions were concentrated on terms of value, it is very natural that he should fall under suspicion of acting in this way. 'The basic criticism, however', writes R. M. Gordon (*loc. cit.*), 'is not that Socrates surreptitiously *reforms* by offering definitions that are not morally neutral, but that he offers definitions that are not morally neutral.'

It would certainly be difficult to maintain a criticism that Socrates '*surreptitiously* reforms' (to transfer Mr Gordon's italics) by his definitions, whether or not they were morally neutral. It may be assumed at the outset that moral reform was his openly avowed object.[1] 'En cultivant la science il entendait promouvoir la vertu.'[2] But it does not follow that he was guilty of promulgating persuasive definitions. It may of course be true, as Stevenson wrote, that 'to choose a meaning [for justice] is to take sides in a social struggle', and that when theorists have sought to avoid the element of persuasion by defining their terms, 'ironically enough, these very definitions involved that same persuasion; and in a way that veiled and confused it, by making it appear to be purely intellectual analysis' (*loc. cit.* 344). It scarcely needs to be said that Socrates was unaware of the emotive theory of ethical language, although had it been explained to him he would have opposed it on the ground that to say '"this is right" means only "I approve of this"' was to play into the hands of sophistic relativism. Nor could it occur to him that in seeking to discover and define the good for man he might be guilty of the curiously named 'naturalistic fallacy' which, according to G. E. Moore, must inevitably be committed by any definition of 'good'.[3] In view of later advances in ethical theory, it may be claimed that the general question whether

---

[1] It hardly seems necessary to quote evidence, but one might mention that immediately after speaking of his continual search for definitions of moral terms (in *Mem.* 1.1.16, quoted on p. 104 above), Xenophon goes on to say that it was a knowledge of these and similar things which in his opinion would produce fine, liberal characters (καλοὺς κἀγαθούς), and those altogether ignorant of them were little better than slaves. In Plato's *Laches* (190b) he says that, because his two friends want their sons to acquire virtue and have their characters improved, therefore they must find out what virtue is. 'For how can we advise anyone how to acquire something when we have no idea what it is?'

[2] Deman, *Témoignage*, 80.

[3] See for instance *Theories of Ethics*, ed. Philippa Foot, p. 5. She adds that Moore never succeeded in explaining what he meant by a 'natural' property, and it was this difficulty which Stevenson claimed to be removing by his theory of emotive meaning.

an ethical term can be defined other than persuasively is no longer arguable, but, if intention is allowed to be relevant at all, one or two things may be added about Socrates. He was not a dogmatic moralist but an inquirer, who believed that an honest search after the truth about the principles governing human behaviour was most likely, simply because of the better understanding which it would ensure, to lead to an improvement in behaviour itself. It was the Sophists, not Socrates, who were the archpriests of persuasion, and it is to them that we must look for the clearest examples of persuasive definition. 'Justice is obedience to the established laws.' 'Justice is obedience to the dictates of nature, which are often contrary to the established laws.' 'Justice is the right of the stronger.' 'Justice is a device of the weak to frustrate the stronger.' Rhetorical assertions of this kind, thought Socrates, must be replaced by inductively based conclusions if we are to have any hope of finding out what justice or virtue is and living up to it. If the mind was at the mercy of bodily desires and pleasures (according to a Callicles the happiest state for a man to be in), it had little chance of making progress. 'Only the self-controlled can investigate the most important things, and *classifying them according to their kinds* both in discussion and in action choose the good and reject the bad.'[1] The mind must be fresh and keen only because the prerequisite of right action is to replace Sophistic persuasion by understanding of the facts. It would be difficult to improve on Barker's assessment of Socrates in this (*Pol. Thought of P. & A.* 47):

He differed from the Sophists in not attempting to teach new canons of conduct ... He sought to elicit from the ordinary conduct of men a clear conception of the rules by which they already acted. He wished men to analyse carefully the duties of life, and to arrive at a clear conception of their meaning: he did not wish them to bring a new conception, acquired from some other source, and remodel life by its aid.

This is not inconsistent with the addition in the next paragraph:

But it was for no mere intellectual purpose that he craved for definitions: it was always for a moral end.

[1] Xen. *Mem.* 4.5.11. On this passage and the relation between knowledge and self-control or its opposite (ἀκρασία) see further pp. 136 f. below.

Barker cites the analogy of descriptive and prescriptive grammar. (That of the Sophist Protagoras was prescriptive; see *The Sophists*, pp. 219 f., 221.) Prescriptive grammar is misguided, and grammar may be purely descriptive and yet help one to more correct usage: 'Get to know the rules by which you have all along been acting—unknowingly' and therefore imperfectly—and then you will write better Greek.' 'A man who had arrived at a general conception and expressed it in a definition had made explicit the rules on which he had hitherto been unconsciously and imperfectly acting; and his life would be the better for his acting by a known and explicit rule.'

To define something is to express one's understanding not only of what it is but equally, as has been noted (see (*b*), p. 110 above), of what it is not. It is a remedy for confusion, a 'sorting out of things according to their kinds'. So Xenophon, after the sentence just quoted (*Mem.* 4.5.12), says that Socrates derived the Greek word for discussion (διαλέγεσθαι) from a word meaning 'to collect apart',[1] because, properly understood, it was a procedure of joint deliberation among several people for the purpose of arriving at a definition. Underlying the procedure of Socrates is an assumption, or faith, never mentioned because not consciously recognized, that the kinds or classes to which particulars belong, the 'forms' which they possess, have a quasi-substantial nature and hence a stability which enables the essence of each to be grasped, described, and clearly distinguished from all other essences. It is hardly surprising if Socrates did not, in the first, pioneer attempt at such classification, solve at one leap the 'problem of universals' that has plagued philosophers from his day to our own, or arrive at the Wittgensteinian theory of 'family resemblances' which may at last have provided the right answer.[2] But two special circumstances may be mentioned, one common to

---

[1] διαλέγειν. The active is not otherwise in use, and Stenzel (*RE*, 862) notes the suggestion of paradox about the compound (contrast the common συλλέγειν) as a possibly Socratic touch. On this section in Xenophon and the important question of its independence of the *Phaedrus* and relation to that and other passages in Plato, see Stenzel, *RE*, 855–64. The difference between διαλέγειν here (corresponding to διαγιγνώσκειν at 4.1.5) and the διαίρεσις of a later stage of Plato's dialectic was explained by Zeller (*Ph. d. Gr.* 128, n. 4) before Stenzel (860f.). See also Diès, *Autour de P.* 228.

[2] See the claim of Bambrough in 'Universals and Family Resemblances', *Proc. Arist. Soc.* 1960–1; also L. Pompa in *PQ*, 1967.

most Greek thought and the other typically Socratic, as having helped to make his view what it was.

(i) It is probable that the notion of the *eidos* (meaning a natural kind) as something at least quasi-substantial already had a hold on Greek minds.[1] Cf. G. B. Kerferd in *CR*, 1968, 78:

Many of the less satisfactory uses of analogy in Greek thought seem to us to have a false ontological basis—a belief in the existence of natural kinds either at the phenomenal or at the transcendental level. When Plato in the first book of the *Republic* makes Socrates raise the question τοιοῦτος ἄρα ἐστὶν ἑκάτερος αὐτῶν οἷόσπερ ἔοικεν; ['Is each such as that which he resembles?'] (349 d 10) he seems to be appealing to a widely held view that one similarity will be ontologically associated with others.

Such an inherited belief would be of great assistance to Socrates in forming his objective view of moral concepts in opposition to the Sophists, and is perhaps some slight evidence for believing that he came to it from an early study of natural science. It has also an important bearing on the Platonic 'Theory of Ideas', which in its hypostatization of forms, and their separation from particulars, may be seen rather as the culmination of a gradual process than as a radically new and revolutionary doctrine. Scholars dispute for instance whether the use of the phrase 'the *eidos* itself' at *Euthyphro* 6d implies the transcendent forms of the full Platonic theory. Probably not, but its use there in connexion with definition, as in the *Meno* and elsewhere, shows how the Socratic investigations constituted an important stage on the way towards complete hypostatization, the ground for which had already been prepared in the unphilosophical assumptions of Greek thought from which both took their rise.

[1] It is of interest that this use of the word is particularly well attested in medical contexts (as noted on p. 110 above), for the temptation to objectify diseases and their varieties has always been particularly strong for doctors, as Sir H. Cohen pointed out in *Philosophy*, 1952. 'Only in recent times', he wrote, 'has it been widely recognized that, however convenient may be a category of "diseases", they have no separate self-subsistence but are simply abstractions from experience.' Most of us still speak of influenza or malaria as a *thing*, yet we have never met a disease, only sick people; and no two of them repeat the same symptoms exactly. Cohen himself attributed the common mode of thought to a survival from the days when disease was explained as embodied in an evil spirit. 'Even when the spectral origin of the disease was forgotten, the idea of the disease as a clinical entity, a substantial essence with an independent existence, persisted.' The belief, as he remarked, can, by imposing an undue rigidity of treatment, be the reverse of beneficial to the patient. The same fallacy was pointed out much earlier by the French medical writer Cabanis, quoted by Grote, *Plato*, III, 524n.

(ii) More typical of Socrates himself was his teleological outlook, his conviction that to understand the nature of anything was to understand the function or purpose which it was intended to serve. A definition must state not only what we might regard as the essential attributes, but also, and primarily, the *ergon*, or work that the object in question has to perform. Relevant here is not so much the lesson of the natural world (though he was convinced that nature too was providentially designed, Xen. *Mem.* 1.4.4ff., 4.3.3ff.) as his favourite analogy from the crafts—the shoemakers, fullers and cooks, the builders and metal-workers that he so obstinately and tiresomely harped on to illustrate his points (*Gorg.* 491a, Xen. *Mem.* 1.2.37). It is Socratic when Plato in the *Cratylus* (389a–c) makes him say that if a man wants to make a shuttle he must look to the *eidos* of shuttles (the purpose of knowing the *eidos* is always a practical one), and this *eidos*, which he must understand and take as his model, is not simply the shape, or other observable properties, of another shuttle; it is determined by the part which a shuttle has to play in forwarding the work of the weaver. The proper definition of the *eidos* of shuttle does not state its 'form' in the ordinary sense (that it is a piece of wood carved in a certain shape and of certain dimensions), but describes how it is shaped and put together in the way best calculated to perform this task.[1]

(5) THE IGNORANCE OF SOCRATES

But did Socrates positively lay down these all-important definitions of moral virtues, or was his life a continually unsatisfied search for them? It is well known that those dialogues of Plato which have the best claim to be called Socratic tend to lead, ostensibly at least, to a negative conclusion. Possible definitions of the subject of inquiry—courage, temperance, friendship, knowledge, *areté*—are put forward, examined and rejected as faulty, with Socrates sometimes taking the blame for failure on himself. Even Xenophon, who in accordance both with his own temperament and his apologetic purpose shows us a much more positive Socrates, represents him far more often as con-

---

[1] That for Socrates everything, from a horse to a knife, has its own ἔργον and therefore its own ἀρετή or distinctive excellence, has been noted in *The Sophists*, p. 90, n. 1.

sidering, or investigating (σκοπῶν), together with his friends, the nature of this or that virtue than positively stating what it is.[1] Although he turned others away from idleness and vice and implanted in them a desire for goodness, he never professed to teach but achieved his effect by example, manifesting his own goodness both in his actions and in 'the excellence of his conversation about virtue and human affairs in general' (*Mem.* 1.2.3, 18). Xenophon mentions a current criticism that Socrates exhorted men to goodness but was incompetent to show them the way to it, a criticism illustrated by the complaint in the Platonic dialogue *Clitophon* that Socrates continually preaches righteousness, like a god from his platform in a tragedy, but either does not know or declines to divulge the nature of this righteousness that he is always praising to the skies. To counter this criticism Xenophon simply refers, first, to his questioning and refutation of those who thought they knew everything, and secondly to his 'daily conversations' with his companions, as evidence that he did make men better (*ibid.* 1.4.1). To Euthydemus, indeed (*ibid.* 4.2.40), he did 'explain most simply and clearly what knowledge he considered most necessary and what practices were best'; but, Xenophon continues, his aim was not to make men cleverer, more efficient, or more skilled in speaking, but to implant *sophrosyné*.

Some other inquiries into the nature of this or that as recorded by Xenophon (e.g. of graphic art at *Mem.* 3.10 and of leisure at 3.9.9) have the tentative and exploratory character which we know from Plato, and we may fairly quote against him many passages in his own work, as well as other authorities, when, exceptionally and notably in *Mem.* 4, ch. 6, he claims to give a string of examples of Socratic definitions of such things as piety, justice, goodness, beauty and courage. They are not all in substance false to Socratic teaching,[2] but the stylized and neatly rounded arguments in which they are embodied certainly falsify the Socratic method.[3] Xenophon does not

---

[1] *Mem.* 1.1.16, 4.6.1 (σκοπῶν τί ἕκαστον εἴη τῶν ὄντων), 3.9.9 and elsewhere.

[2] E.g. the utilitarian conceptions of goodness and beauty as τὸ ὠφέλιμον and τὸ χρήσιμον, pp. 142 f. below.

[3] Ritter (*Sokr.* 45 f.) regarded these definitions, which he found 'extremely inept', as unintelligent borrowings from Plato. Anyone who has been subjected to a telephone call from a reporter and then read the result in print will suspect that he has an inkling of the way in which the neat little conversations were constructed.

actually mention Socrates's well-known confession of his own ignorance (Zeller, *Ph. d. Gr.* 118, n. 1), but he does show him disclaiming the part of a teacher, preferring to make his friends companions in investigation, and emphasizing the importance of self-knowledge and of not supposing that one knows what one does not (*ibid.* 3.9.6).[1] Aristotle gives us the general statement that 'it was the practice of Socrates to ask questions but not to give answers, for he confessed that he did not know' (*Soph. el.* 183b6–8), and Aeschines (p. 75 above) and Plato provide examples as from his own mouth. Most illuminating is that in the *Theaetetus*, where it is connected with the metaphor of midwifery.

I am so far like the midwife, that I cannot give birth to wisdom; and the common reproach is true, that though I question others, I can myself bring nothing to light because there is no wisdom in me. The reason is this: heaven constrains me to serve as a midwife, but has debarred me from giving birth. So of myself I have no sort of wisdom, nor has any discovery ever been born to me as the child of my soul. Those who frequent my company at first appear, some of them, quite unintelligent; but, as we go further with our discussions, all who are favoured by heaven make progress at a rate that seems surprising to others as well as to themselves, although it is clear that they have never learned anything from me; the many admirable truths they bring to birth have been discovered by themselves from within.[2]

The metaphor of intellectual conception and birth-pangs, as the result of *eros*, recurs in the *Symposium* (206cff.) and the *Republic* (490b), where the lover of knowledge is said to 'have intercourse with' reality, to 'bring forth' intelligence and truth, and so to find release from 'travail'. Elsewhere the intercourse is of mind with mind, and Socrates claims that, like other midwives, he combines with his maieutic skill that of a matchmaker (*Theaet.* 151b) and even of a pander (Xen. *Symp.* 3.10). The close connexion of all this with his profession of ignorance, and its extension beyond Plato, leave no room for doubt that the whole complex is genuinely Socratic.[3]

[1] Cicero's claim (*Brutus* 85.292) to find Socratic irony in Xenophon as well as in Plato and Aeschines is not entirely unjustified. Cf. p. 17 above.

[2] *Theaet.* 150c–d, trans. Cornford. Many other examples of the profession of ignorance could of course be cited. Some references are collected by Deman, *Témoignage*, 64, to which it is worth adding *Charm.* 165b.

[3] The midwife figure itself occurs only in Plato, which made Dorothy Tarrant (*CQ*, 1938, 172) suspect that it might have been his invention, and Robinson (*PED*, 83) state dogmatically that he invented it 'long after Socrates' death'. Among others, however, Stenzel (*PMD*, 4) accepted

Intellectual Midwifery

In plain terms, the maieutic method based on the professed barrenness of the midwife meant getting the patient, or pupil, to make a general statement, usually, though not always, in the form of saying 'what x is' (and often, as in the case of Theaetetus and Meno, after rejecting as inadequate a random enumeration of examples), and by discussion showing that it is in some way defective. The pupil then proposes another, which will improve on the previous one and so bring him nearer the truth. Yet a third may be required, and even the last to be suggested often breaks down and the dialogue ends with a confession of failure, but at the same time on a note of hope. Thus Socrates makes Theaetetus abandon successively the notions that knowledge is (*a*) sensation, (*b*) true belief, (*c*) true belief plus explanation or account (*logos*). This exhausts the tale of Theaetetus's embryo thoughts, but, says Socrates, if he conceives again his offspring will be all the better for the scrutiny of these, and if he does not, he will be a better man for the knowledge of his own ignorance.

This method could do much for a chosen pupil like Theaetetus, if not necessarily in the production of new discoveries, at least as a mental catharsis. Every one of Theaetetus's attempts to discover the nature of knowledge proves to be a 'phantom' or 'wind-egg' (as R. Robinson points out, *PED*, 84), and no doubt the merit of the Socratic method lay rather in weeding out confused and ill-thought-out ideas than in bringing new ones to light. Nevertheless mathematical knowledge, in which young Theaetetus was already expert, was of the *a priori* kind which does 'come out of oneself' and can be explicated by the Socratic or an analogous method; and for Socrates and Plato ethical truths had the same timeless and eternal value.[1] To those for whom the method was unsuited, either youths whose minds 'have

---

it as historical, and there is no good reason to do otherwise. In the *Theaet.* Socrates develops the figure by speaking of the 'miscarriage' of thoughts, and this recurs in the mouth of one of Socrates's disciples in the *Clouds* of Aristophanes (*v.* 137; on this parallel however see Peipers, *Erkenntnistheorie*, 714 f.). Cf. p. 77, n. 1 above.

[1] See my Penguin edition of the *Prot.* and *Meno*, 109 f. In the one clear instance of Socrates's 'drawing out of' a pupil, by question and answer, a correct positive conclusion, namely the experiment on Meno's slave, the problem set is mathematical, and the inference is then drawn that, if it can be solved in this way, so can the problem of defining ἀρετή. Unfortunately for the maieutic method, this cannot be taken as a valid example of it as explained in the *Theaet.* since Socrates himself (and Meno) did know the answer that he was trying to elicit. That was necessary if Meno was to see the point of the experiment.

not conceived at all' or older men whose thoughts were already formed, it was only 'Socrates's usual affectation, shamming ignorance and doing anything rather than answer a question', 'his old game of never giving a positive answer himself, but taking up everyone else's answer and refuting it'. This is the *eironeia* which makes Thrasymachus so angry (*Rep.* 337a), and if we translate it 'irony' we water it down unduly. In the fifth century it was a term of abuse meaning plainly deceit or swindling, as in the *Wasps* (174) and the *Clouds* of Aristophanes, where it appears (at *v.* 449) in a list of villainous qualities along with imposture and all sorts of blackguardly conduct. In Plato's *Laws* (908e) it is used of the worst type of atheist who hypocritically pretends to religion. In Aristotle it is still a form of untruthfulness, and therefore blameable, but specialized into mock-modesty and regarded as preferable to boasting. He quotes Socrates as an example, and the softening down of the word may well have been an effect of the Socratic literature.[1] In Plato it retains its bad sense, in the mouth either of a bitter opponent like Thrasymachus or of one pretending to be angry at the way in which Socrates deceives everyone as to his real character (Alcibiades at *Symp.* 216e, 218d). It is not used for the gentle irony which he employs with his young friends when he puts himself on a level with them and says 'Come now, let's look into this, you and I, for I don't know any more about it than you do'.

The accusation of *eironeia* is also brought against Socrates (though the word is not used) in Xenophon. When he is threatened by the Thirty, Charicles objects to his conduct in 'asking questions when he knows the answers' (*Mem.* 1.2.36), and Hippias (*ibid.* 4.4.9) tells him that he is 'always mocking at others, questioning and refuting everybody but never willing to submit to examination or reveal his own opinion about anything'. It is true that Socrates preferred to ask questions of others, though occasionally in a Platonic dialogue he

---

[1] Arist. *EN* 1127b 22ff. On εἴρων and its derivatives see O. Ribbeck in *Rh. Mus.* 1876 and R. Stark, *Rh. Mus.* 1953, 79ff. Ribbeck describes it as 'ein derber, volkstümlicher Ausdruck, ja um es gerade herauszusagen, ein Schimpfwort'. In modern times 'Socratic irony' is sometimes taken in a much wider sense, in which it was the subject of Kierkegaard's book and of an attractive chapter by Friedländer (*Plato*, Eng. tr. 1, ch. 7). A more strictly scholarly account is in Zeller, *Ph. d. Gr.* 124–6. In Theophrastus (*Char.* 1) the εἴρων is still a man who will praise you to your face and attack you behind your back, and such characters are 'more to be avoided than vipers'.

offers his interlocutor the choice of roles.[1] But the accusation of *eironeia* in the full sense, involving deliberate deceit, can scarcely be maintained. We should not dismiss his profession of ignorance as altogether insincere. His mission was not to impart any body of positive doctrine, but to bring home to men their intellectual need, and then invite them to join with him in the search for truth by the dialectical method of question and answer. He claimed, for instance, that the knowledge necessary for the acquisition of virtue must comprise the discovery of the function of human life as such. Of any other teacher one would naturally expect that he would go on to expound what was this ultimate end or aim, but one may doubt whether it is to be found in the records of any teaching which can reasonably be attributed to Socrates. This, we may assume, was one of the chief reasons which made the more positive Plato feel it his duty not only to reproduce what Socrates said but also to go further and bring out what he thought were its implications. The essence of the Socratic method, the elenchus, is to convince the interlocutor that, whereas he thought he knew something, in fact he does not. Meno complained that its first effect was comparable to an electric shock: the mind went numb. This comparison with the electric sting-ray, said Socrates, would only be valid if the fish itself were in a state of numbness when it inflicts its shock; if he reduces others to doubt, it is only because he is in doubt himself, and this is precisely what Meno has heard from others (*Meno* 79e–80a). Not everyone, it seems, accused Socrates of the *eironeia* of asking questions when he knew the answers perfectly well. No doubt some irony (in the English sense) is present in his words to Meno. He knew that he saw more clearly than his companion what was needful. But he had no cut-and-dried system of knowledge to hand over, nor did he believe that knowledge handed over in this way, even if he possessed it to give, would do a man any good. In the controlled experiment on Meno's slave, undertaken to convince Meno of the value of being reduced to a confession of ignorance, Socrates demonstrates that, even when the teacher knows

[1] *Gorg.* 462b, *Prot.* 338c–d. The results are interesting, in the one case a speech for whose length Socrates very properly thinks an apology is due to Polus (465e), and in the other a brilliant parody of a Sophistic ἐπίδειξις whose solemn approval by such an authority as Hippias must have amused him.

the answer, it is sound educational method not to tell it to the pupil at once but to lead him to discover it step by step through the successive destruction of answers which are plausible but wrong.

Of the many attempts to sum up the aims and achievements of the Socratic conversations, this short one of Hackforth's is one of the best (*Philosophy*, 1933, p. 265):

Two points in particular should be noticed with regard to these conversations: first, that although the primary object is to convince the interlocutor of his own ignorance, yet, since the definitions suggested are always those shared by him with general opinion, or at least some large body of general opinion, the effect, or secondary object, is to show the unsatisfactoriness of commonly received ideas on matters of conduct; secondly, that since many of the definitions are the outcome of Socrates's own suggestions—in some cases actually formulated by him—and yet are found no less than those of his interlocutor to be untenable, Socrates has no ready-made system of ethics to impart. This is, of course, what we should expect from his disclaiming the office of a teacher; he is a fellow-searcher only. Yet it would be wrong to suppose that the results of such conversations are purely negative. For one thing, the discussion commonly reveals an element of truth in each definition;[1] for another, the interlocutor is helped by the lesson of intellectual honesty,[2] is shown an ideal of knowledge unattained, and a method whereby he may progressively attain, or at least approximate, thereto. Thirdly, the suggestion underlying the apparent failure of the discussions is that the whole problem of conduct can only be solved when viewed as a whole: the several 'virtues' cannot be defined nor understood nor possessed in isolation from one another, for they are all different applications of a single knowledge—the knowledge of good and evil.

[1] Versényi goes further (*Socr. Hum.* 118). The aporetic end of a dialogue, he says, 'does not mean that the dialogues contain nothing positive since, in the first place, there is hardly a dialogue that does not arrive at solutions to the problems discussed. These conclusions are negated at the end merely to prevent the student from uncritically accepting them instead of going through reflection that would make them his own.' This, I believe, goes too far. There is more truth in his continuation: 'In the second place, what is positive here is not so much something contained in the written word itself as something that takes place in the learner's soul, namely that he does in fact search for and acquire knowledge.' The question of positive content in Plato's early, 'Socratic' dialogues is also discussed by R. Dieterle in his Freiburg dissertation (1966), *Platons Laches u. Charmides: Unters. ʒ. elenktisch-aporetisch. Struktur d. plat. Frühdialoge.* See the review by Easterling in *CR*, 1968.

[2] Since this article was written, some critics might cavil at the words 'intellectual honesty'. Fallacies are certainly committed in the Socratic dialogues of Plato, and it is a debated point how far either Plato or his master were unaware of them and how far Socrates may have used them deliberately in what he believed to be a good cause.

'In contrasting Socrates with the Sophists', wrote Ernest Barker (*Pol. Thought of P. & A.* 46), 'we must remember that in many respects he was one of them.' In many respects, yes, but in the words 'an ideal of knowledge unattained' Hackforth has put his finger on one of the vital differences between them. His identification with them by his contemporaries was indeed excusable. They held that knowledge (as opposed to shifting opinion) was impossible, for there were no stable and indisputable objects to be known. He demonstrated to everybody that what they called their knowledge was not knowledge at all. Superficially alike, the two statements were fundamentally different, for that of Socrates was based on an unshakeable conviction that knowledge *was* in principle attainable, but that, if there was to be any hope of attaining it, the debris of confused and misleading ideas which filled most men's minds must first be cleared away. Only then could the positive search for knowledge begin. Once his companion had understood the right way to the goal (the *method* in its Greek sense), he was ready to seek it with him, and philosophy was summed up for him in this idea of the 'common search',[1] a conception of the purpose of discussion directly contrary to the sophistic idea of it as a contest aiming at the overthrow of an opponent. Neither knew the truth yet, but if only the other could be persuaded of this, they might set out together with some hope of finding it, or at least approaching it more closely, for the man who has rid his mind of a false conception is already nearer the truth. To be a Socratic is not to follow any system of philosophical doctrine. It implies first and foremost an attitude of mind, an intellectual humility easily mistaken for arrogance, since the true Socratic is convinced of the ignorance not only of himself but of all mankind.

[1] Contrast, in the *Prot.*, Socrates's plea of σύν τε δύ' ἐρχομένω (348d) with Protagoras's reference to ἀγῶνες λόγων at 335a. Some of the many references in both Plato and Xenophon to his habit of κοινῇ ζητεῖν, συζητεῖν, κοινῇ βουλεύεσθαι etc. are collected by Zeller, *Ph. d. Gr.* 118, n. 3. See also the references to κοινὴ σκέψις at *Charm.* 158d, *Crito* 48d, and μετὰ σοῦ σκέψασθαι καὶ συζητῆσαι at *Meno* 80d, and on the agonistic character of sophistic debate *The Sophists*, p. 43.

(6) VIRTUE IS KNOWLEDGE

Three fundamental theses of Socrates are so closely related as to form scarcely separable parts of a single whole. They are: virtue is knowledge; its converse, that wrongdoing can only be due to ignorance and must therefore be considered involuntary; and 'care of the soul' as the primary condition of living well. As far as possible, something will be said about each in turn.

The Socratic paradox (as it is usually called) that virtue is knowledge bears directly on the characteristically fifth-century controversy over the method of acquiring it, whether by teaching or otherwise; and for this reason it has been necessary to say something about it elsewhere. It puts Socrates squarely among his contemporaries, the great Sophists with whom he was crossing swords when Plato was unborn or an infant. In the same place[1] I noted the wide sense of *areté* in earlier and current use (e.g. 'the *areté* of carpentry or any other craft'), which must have made the 'paradox' less paradoxical in his own time, and also makes it essential to remember that, if we use the English word 'virtue', it is only as a counter to stand for the Greek expression.[2]

Once again let us start from Aristotle, about whose general value as a source enough has been said already. In this case much of what he says can be traced back to the Platonic dialogues, but he has not on this account confused Socrates with Plato. That is plain from the undoubtedly genuine references, and is stated explicitly if we may take the following passage from the *Magna Moralia* (as we surely may) to represent Aristotle's opinion. In a brief historical survey the writer mentions first Pythagoras, then Socrates, then Plato, distinguishing the last two thus:[3]

[1] *The Sophists*, pp. 257 f., 252, and for the question in general ch. x as a whole. Cf. also *ibid.* p. 25.

[2] The Greek habit of using 'knowledge' (ἐπιστήμη, ἐπίστασθαι and words of kindred meaning), to denote practical skill or trained ability, and of 'explaining character or behaviour in terms of knowledge', has often been remarked on. See Dodds, *Gks. & Irrat.* 16 f., and cf. his *Gorgias*, 218; Snell, *Ausdrücke*, and *Philol.* 1948, 132. Adam on *Rep.* 382a notes the moral connotation of words like ἀμαθής, ἀπαίδευτος, ἀγνώμων, and remarks that 'the identification of ignorance and vice is in harmony with popular Greek psychology'.

[3] 1182a 20. In general I have been sparing of quotation from the *MM*, owing to the widespread view that it is a product of the Peripatos after Aristotle's death.

The effect of his [*sc.* Socrates's] making the virtues into branches of knowledge was to eliminate the irrational part of the soul, and with it emotion and moral character. So his treatment of virtue was in this respect mistaken. After him Plato, rightly enough, divided the soul into the rational and irrational parts and explained the appropriate virtues of each.

This is valuable information, comparable to what Aristotle tells us about the difference between the Socratic and Platonic treatment of universals, and justifies a belief that what he has taken from Plato as Socratic is genuinely so. It excludes the 'Socrates' of the *Republic* and many other dialogues, and is supported, as we shall see, by Xenophon. At the same time, in his concise and more advanced terminology Aristotle presents us with the 'virtue-is-knowledge' doctrine in its most uncompromising form, in order to point out its shortcomings and contrast it with his own. We may look at it in this form first, and afterwards consider whether its intellectual severity needs any mitigation if we are to get at the mind of Socrates himself.

Aristotle repeats several times that Socrates said or thought that 'the virtues are sciences' or a single virtue (courage) 'is a science'.[1] This he interpreted as an unqualified intellectualism, reached by analogy with pure science and with the practical arts. So *EE* 1216 b 2 ff.:

Socrates believed that knowledge of virtue was the final aim, and he inquired what justice is, and what courage and every other kind of virtue. This was reasonable in view of his conviction that all the virtues were sciences, so that to know justice was at the same time to be just; for as soon as we have learned geometry and architecture we are architects and geometricians. For this reason he inquired what virtue is, but not how or from what it is acquired.

Aristotle comments that this is true of the theoretical sciences but not of the productive, in which knowledge is only a means to a further end, e.g. health in medicine, law and order in political science. Therefore to know what virtue is matters less than to know what conditions will produce it, 'for we do not want to know what courage or justice

---

[1] *EN* 1144b28 Σ. μὲν οὖν λόγους τὰς ἀρετὰς ᾤετο εἶναι· ἐπιστήμας γὰρ εἶναι πάσας; 1144b19, φρονήσεις ᾤετο εἶναι πάσας τὰς ἀρετάς; 1116b4, ὁ Σ. ᾤήθη ἐπιστήμην εἶναι τὴν ἀνδρείαν (also *EE* 1230a7). From the first passage, and *EE* 1246b33 καὶ ὀρθὸν τὸ Σωκρατικὸν ὅτι οὐδὲν ἰσχυρότερον φρονήσεως, ὅτι δὲ ἐπιστήμην ἔφη, οὐκ ὀρθῶς, Joël inferred (*E. & X. S.* 1.211) that Socrates called the virtues ἐπιστῆμαι but not λόγοι or φρονήσεις. Such a rigid terminology seems to be refuted by both Plato's and Aristotle's usage. For the former, see O'Brien, *Socr. Parad.* 79, n. 58, and for the latter p. 132, n. 3, below. Cf. also p. 181, n. 3.

is, but to *be* brave or just, just as we wish to be healthy rather than to know what health is'. This antithesis is one to make Socrates turn in his grave; 'for', he would protest, 'how can I know how virtue is acquired when I don't even know what it is?'[1] Aristotle on the other hand lays it down as his general policy for an ethical treatise (*EN* 1103b26): 'The present study does not aim at theoretical knowledge as others do, for the object of our inquiry is not to know what goodness is but to become good.' Even if one were to agree with Socrates that knowledge of the nature of courage or justice is a necessary precondition of becoming brave or just,[2] it would be difficult to concede that it is a sufficient one. Elsewhere (1144b18) Aristotle himself admits that Socrates was partly right: right in saying that reason[3] was a *sine qua non* of virtue, but wrong in identifying the two.

In Plato's *Protagoras*, as part of an argument for the unity of virtue, Socrates tries to maintain that courage, like any other virtue, is knowledge, because in any dangerous enterprise—diving in a confined space, cavalry engagements, light-armed combat—the trained expert will show more courage than the ignorant. Thus courage is knowledge of what is and what is not to be feared.[4] In an obvious reference to this passage, Aristotle asserted that its claim is the opposite of the truth.[5] Some may be cowards but face what appear to others to be dangers because they know them not to be dangers at all, e.g. in war there are many false alarms which the trained and experienced soldier can recognize as such; but in general those who face dangers owing to experience are not really brave. Those who are skilled at climbing masts, he says, are confident not because they know what is to be feared but because they know what aids are available to them in dangers. The example is similar to Socrates's of

---

[1] *Meno* 71a, *Prot.* 360e–361a, *Laches* 190b.

[2] It is curious that Aristotle, in his irritation against Socrates, should go so far as to speak of knowing what goodness or health is and being good or healthy as alternatives, instead of saying only that Socrates's demand does not go far enough. In his own philosophy any practitioner must first have complete in his mind the εἶδος of what he wishes to produce—health if he is a doctor, a house if he is an architect or builder. Only then does he start to produce it. Thus the formal cause pre-exists in art as well as nature. See *Metaph.* 1032a 32–1032b 14.

[3] φρόνησις at 1144b 18, λόγος at b 29. In this book of the *EN* Aristotle has given his own technical sense to φρόνησις, but Socrates must have used these terms for what at other times he called knowledge. Cf. p. 131, n. 1, above. The cobbler who knows his trade is φρόνιμος at it (*Alc. I* 125a).

[4] 349e–350a, 360d.   [5] *EE* 1230a 6, and cf. *EN* 1116b 4.

the divers, and he would hardly have considered it to invalidate his point. In fact however he was arguing at a different level, as he shows at a later stage (354a–b). Courage is not to be considered in isolation, because all virtue is one, to be summed up as the knowledge of what is ultimately good or evil. At this level death itself may not be an evil to be feared, if one knows that it may result in a greater amount of good, for instance the freedom of one's country. The paradoxical nature of the doctrine appears in a comparison with the superficially similar words of Pericles in the funeral oration (Thuc. 2.40.3): some are made bold by ignorance, he says, but the bravest are those who recognize most clearly what things are fearful and what enjoyable, and are not by this knowledge deterred from dangers. By this high but orthodox standard, men face physical dangers although they know them to be fearful; according to Socrates, they face them in the knowledge that what may happen to them is not an evil at all, if it is more beneficial than cowardice to the real self, the *psyche*.

Aristotle's chief objection to the doctrine is that which would occur to most people, namely that it makes no allowance for weakness of will, lack of self-control, 'incontinence', the effect of appetite or passion.[1] In book 7 of the *Ethics* (*EN* 1145b25) he makes it the starting-point of his own discussion of the right use of these terms, and once again begins with a reference to the *Protagoras*, where the question was raised (at 352b–c) whether knowledge, when it is present, can be 'hauled around like a slave by the passions'. 'Socrates', he continues, 'was totally opposed to this idea, on the ground that there is no such thing as incontinence: when a man acts contrary to what is best, he does not judge it to be so, but acts in ignorance.' So put, says Aristotle bluntly, the doctrine is in plain contradiction to experience; and most of us have to agree with Medea (as Euripides and Ovid depict her) that it is possible to see and approve the better course but follow the worse. Aristotle's own solution, cast in a form to deal most gently with the paradox, is reached through his more advanced technique of analysis. A crude dichotomy between knowledge and ignorance is not enough. Knowledge can be actual or

---

[1] ἀκρασία, usually translated 'incontinence', but more literally 'lack of mastery' over one's passions or lower nature; and πάθος, emotion, passion.

potential (i.e. acquired but not consciously present, as in sleep or drunkenness), universal or particular. After considerable discussion (not relevant here), he concludes that the wrongdoer may know the universal rule, but this is not the efficient cause of a particular action, which is motivated by particular knowledge (i.e. that this present action, in my individual circumstances, is or is not contrary to the rule and therefore wrong). It is this kind of knowledge which is overcome (banished from consciousness, rendered merely potential) by the temptation of pleasure, fear, etc.; but such immediate awareness of particulars is a matter of sense-perception only, and ought not, according to Aristotle's epistemology, to be called knowledge.[1] Thus by the application of Aristotelian distinctions of which Socrates never dreamed, something of his paradox can be saved: 'Because the last term (i.e. the particular)[2] is not a universal nor equally an object of knowledge with the universal, even what Socrates sought to establish seems to come about; for there is no incontinence when knowledge in the full sense is present, nor is it *that* knowledge which is "hauled about" by passion, but perceptual knowledge.' (1147b14.)

Plato contains many passages which support the interpretation of Socrates's dictum as over-intellectual and neglectful of moral weakness. When Aristotle says that in his view to understand the nature of justice was at the same time to be just, he was simply echoing the *Gorgias*, where this conclusion is drawn from an analogy with the practical arts: to 'learn justice' is to be just and will inevitably lead to just action (460b). In the *Laches* Socrates leads the search for a definition of courage, first to knowledge of what is or is not to be feared, and then to include the knowledge of all good and all evil things. This however would make courage identical with virtue as a whole, and Socrates ostensibly writes off the argument as a failure because they had begun by agreeing that it was only a part of it. In fact it has led to precisely what he believed to be the truth and endeavoured to demonstrate in the *Protagoras*. In the *Meno* (87cff.)

---

[1] Knowledge (ἐπιστήμη) must be demonstrable, and can only be of the universal. See *EN* 1139b18ff., 1140b30ff. (ἡ ἐπιστήμη περὶ τῶν καθόλου ἐστὶν ὑπόληψις... μετὰ λόγου γὰρ ἡ ἐπιστήμη), and for a full account of its acquisition *An. Post.* 2, ch. 19.

[2] τὸ ἔσχατον has the double sense of the last (i.e. least inclusive) term of a syllogism (*An. Pr.* 25b33) and also the particular, which being ἄτομον (indivisible) comes last in the downward process of analysis from *summa genera*. (See Bonitz, index 289b39ff.)

he argues that virtue is knowledge on the ground that it must be held to be something good, i.e. always beneficial, never harmful, and all other so-called good things in life (health, wealth, and even a so-called virtue like courage if it is a thoughtless boldness, divorced from knowledge) may bring harm as well as good unless they are wisely and prudently used. Here again the argument is artfully contrived to stimulate thought by being led to ostensible breakdown. If virtue is knowledge, it can be taught, but a search for possible teachers (including the Sophists, who are somewhat lightly dismissed as a doubtful case) reveals none, so the deductive argument is wrecked on the shores of experience. A final suggestion is made, that 'right opinion', which comes to a man not by teaching but in some mysterious manner comparable to the gift of prophecy, may be as good a guide to action as knowledge, so long as it is present; its only fault is its fickleness. Once again the conclusion is that they do not yet know 'what virtue is in and by itself', and are therefore in no position to say how it is acquired.

Xenophon too bears out the intellectualism of Socratic ethics: 'Socrates said that justice and all the rest of virtue was knowledge' (*Mem.* 3.9.5),[1] and the same point is somewhat crudely developed in dialogue form at 4.6.6: no one who knows what he ought to do can think he ought not to do it, and no one acts otherwise than as he thinks he ought to act. In other places, however, Xenophon gives high praise not only to the continence of Socrates's own life but to his continual commendation, in his teaching, of the virtue of self-control—*enkrateia*, the opposite of that *akrasia*, or incontinence, which according to Aristotle was on his assumptions an impossibility.[2] This brings up the question whether the 'paradox' in fact represents such a one-sided view of morality as Aristotle made out. To Joël the solution was simple (*E. u. X. S.* 237): Aristotle, Plato's *Protagoras*, and Xenophon when he says Socrates believed virtue to be knowledge, are giving the genuine Socratic view; Xenophon when he makes Socrates preach self-control and condemn incontinence is giving his own. But it was scarcely as simple as that.

---

[1] Or 'skill acquired by learning', σοφία (*The Sophists*, pp. 27 f.). For its equation with knowledge cf. also *Mem.* 4.6.7 ὃ ἄρα ἐπίσταται ἕκαστος, τοῦτο καὶ σοφός ἐστιν, and Plato, *Prot.* 350d.

[2] See e.g. *Mem.* 1.5, 2.1, 4.5.

To start with Xenophon, his Socrates claims indeed that complete understanding of what is good will inevitably be reflected in action, but deplores *akrasia*, a yielding to the temptations of sensuality, greed or ambition, as the greatest obstacle to such understanding: 'Don't you agree that *akrasia* keeps men from wisdom (*sophia*) and drives them to its opposite? It prevents them from paying attention to, and properly learning, the things that are profitable by drawing them away to pleasures, and often so stuns their perception of good and evil[1] that they choose the worse instead of the better' (*Mem.* 4.5.6). This leads, later in the same conversation (4.5.11), to the assertion that the man of uncontrolled passions is as ignorant and stupid as a beast, because only the self-controlled are in a position 'to investigate the most important things, and classifying them according to their kinds, both in discussion and in action to choose the good and reject the bad'. Here the notions of moral self-control and the acquisition of knowledge are brought together in a way which involves no contradiction.[2] A teacher of mathematics would hardly be inconsistent in warning a weak-willed pupil that a life of drunkenness and debauchery is not conducive to success even in a purely intellectual pursuit. Some degree of moral discipline is a necessary prerequisite of all knowledge,[3] but most of all when what is sought is an understanding of relative values, in which a mind dulled and confused by unthinking indulgence in sensual pleasure will be especially at sea. It must also be remembered that Socrates's constant analogy for virtue was not theoretical science but art or craft (*techné*), mastery of which calls for both knowledge and practice. At *Mem.* 3.9. 1–3 Xenophon claims to give his answer to the question whether

---

[1] So Marchant (Loeb ed.) renders αἰσθανομένους ἐκπλήξασα, on the analogy of παύειν with participle. This gives a sense more obviously in keeping with the 'virtue is knowledge' doctrine, but I doubt if it can be paralleled. Simeterre (*Vertu-science*, 53, n. 72) more plausibly assumes it means that, *although* they perceive good and bad, yet, 'comme frappés d'égarement', they choose the bad, and he cites it as one of the rare passages that appear to contradict the 'virtue is knowledge' doctrine. But he adds that αἰσθάνεσθαι is not the same as knowing or possessing σοφία (3.9.5), and it is plain from the words προσέχειν τε τοῖς ὠφελοῦσι καὶ καταμανθάνειν αὐτὰ κωλύει that Xenophon has the doctrine in mind and intends no contradiction of it.

[2] On the 'inner connexion between διαιρεῖν and προαιρεῖσθαι' cf. the remarks of Stenzel in his *RE* article, 863 f.

[3] As Aristotle agreed: intemperance distorts one's medical or grammatical knowledge (*EE* 1246b27).

courage is natural or can be learned. It remains on the level of Xenophon's comprehension—there is no progress towards the unification of virtue in a single knowledge of good and evil—but so far as it goes it agrees with *Protagoras* 350a (pp. 132 f. above). Nature, says Socrates, plays a part, 'but courage is increased in every man's nature by learning and practice'. Soldiers will fight more bravely if they are using weapons and tactics in which they have been thoroughly trained rather than those with which they are unfamiliar. So too on a higher level in the *Gorgias* (509 d ff.), no one wishes to do wrong, but unwillingness is not enough; one needs a certain power, an art, and only by learning and practising this *techné* will he avoid wrongdoing. In the acquisition of *areté* Socrates did not deny a place to any of the three factors commonly recognized in the fifth century: natural gifts, learning, and practice.[1] Yet his view of the case was still original. Knowledge, in and by itself, of the nature of virtue was sufficient to make a man virtuous; but there was little chance of his learning the truth of it if he had not subjected his body to the negative discipline of resisting sensual indulgence and his mind to the practice of dialectic, the art of discriminating and defining.

Socrates's constant representation of *areté*, the art of good living, as the supreme art or craft, does then detract somewhat from Aristotle's criticism of him for treating it as if it were a theoretical science in which knowledge is the sole and final objective.[2] Although in the productive and practical arts the purpose is fulfilled in the product and not solely in the knowledge or skill itself, there is something in the argument that a skilled carpenter or weaver will inevitably turn out good work; to reduce his handiwork deliberately to the faulty level of a beginner's would be impossible for him. At the same time,

[1] For other examples in Xenophon see O'Brien, *Socr. Parad.* 146 n., and compare his whole note 27, from p. 144. On pp. 136–8 (n. 21) he discusses the qualifications to be made to the purely intellectualist interpretation of the definition of virtue as knowledge. When he speaks of Plato's doctrine that 'virtue is *not knowledge alone, but* knowledge (or right opinion) built on natural endowment and long training', one might well ask whether Plato believed that there was any other kind of knowledge. The selection and education of the guardians in the *Republic* suggest that he did not. Pp. 147 f. state rather differently the way in which the virtues are 'not knowledge alone', bringing out more clearly one of the Platonic modifications of Socratic doctrine.

[2] Simeterre puts it well (*Vertu-science*, 71): 'Dans les techniques, et quelles qu'elles soient, on ne devient maître qu'après un long apprentissage, un sévère entraînement. On ne s'en dispense pas dans l'art difficile de la vertu.'

no one would claim that a simple analogy between this and moral action provides a complete, mature ethical theory. Socrates was the initiator of a revolution, and the first step in a philosophic revolution has two characteristics: it is so rooted in the traditions of its time that its full effects are only gradually realized,[1] and it is presented in a simple and absolute form, leaving to future thinkers the job of providing the necessary qualifications and provisos. The tradition in which Socrates was caught up was that of the Sophists, and his teaching would have been impossible without theirs, much of which he accepted. They based their lives on the conviction that *areté* could be taught, and he concluded that therefore it must be knowledge. Like them he upheld, as we shall see, the principle of utility and was impressed by what they said about the relativity of the good. Antiphon emphasized the need to be master of one's passions as a precondition of choosing the better and avoiding the worse, nor was his advocacy of 'enlightened self-interest' without its appeal for Socrates.[2]

As for the sublime simplicity of Socrates's dictum, that certainly owed much to his own remarkable character. As Joël epigrammatically expressed it, 'in the strength of his character lay the weakness of his philosophy'.[3] But it also reflects the pioneer character of his thought. His was the first attempt to apply philosophical method to ethics, and Aristotle showed perspicacity in giving generous recognition to the value of his achievement for the advance of logic, while deprecating its immediate and universal application to moral theory and practice. Socrates, it may be said, with his 'Virtue is knowledge', did for ethics what Parmenides did for ontology with the assertion that 'what is, is'. Both turned philosophy in an entirely new direction, and both left to their successors the task of refining a simple statement by examining and analysing the concepts underlying its terms, the use of which as single terms had hitherto concealed from consciousness a variety of meanings. Both stated as an absolute and universal truth something which needed to be said, which the advance of philosophy would never refute, but to which it would assign its due place as part of a

[1] See the quotation from T. S. Kuhn on p. 32 above.

[2] See also *The Sophists*, ch. x.

[3] *E. u. X. S.* 1.256: 'Die Stärke des Charakters wird zur Schwäche der Philosophie.' See *The Sophists*, p. 258.

larger whole.[1] That is why it seemed worth mentioning Aristotle's refinements (pp. 131 ff. above), as an example of this process at work. 'Virtue is knowledge.' But what sort of knowledge? Actual, potential, universal, particular? And is knowledge the whole of virtue, or an essential integrating element in it?

If Socrates held virtue to be knowledge, whether or not he believed that either he or any man had acquired it, he must have had some conception of the object of that knowledge. Though a single object, it had two aspects. In one aspect it was knowledge of the end and aim of human life, which embraced and transcended all partial ends and individual arts such as those aiming at health, physical safety, wealth, political power and so on. These may or may not make for the best and happiest life, for they are all instrumental to further ends, and it depends how they are used. Secondly, the knowledge required is self-knowledge. We have seen that Socrates's conception of a definition is teleological (p. 122 above): to know the nature of anything is to know its function. If we could understand our own nature, therefore, we should know what is the right and natural goal of our life, and this is the knowledge which would give us the *areté* that we are seeking.

(7) ALL WRONGDOING IS INVOLUNTARY: SOCRATES A DETERMINIST?

If virtue is knowledge, and to know the good is to do it, wickedness is due to ignorance and therefore, strictly speaking, involuntary. This corollary made a deep impression on Plato, and in spite of his more advanced psychology he retained it as his own up to the end. If in his earlier works he attributes it to Socrates, he repeats it later in dialogues where Socrates is not even nominally the speaker. In the *Timaeus* the statement that 'no one is voluntarily wicked' is connected with a remarkable theory that all vices have their origin in somatic disorders,

[1] Joël is good on this, e.g. on p. 222 where he speaks of 'the general historical law that every new truth is at first accepted absolutely before its individuality and relativity are recognized'; and p. 249: 'Every beginning is one-sided, and Socrates marks the beginning of *Geistesphilosophie*.' One may however, while admitting the rationalistic bias of Socrates, differ from him over the extent to which Xenophon has distorted it. Simeterre's conclusion on this is sound (*Vertu-science*, 54): with his practical inclinations, he may have exaggerated the role of ἄσκησις and μελέτη, but if he has not maintained his master's thesis at every point, he has not failed to give us the essentials.

and in the *Laws* it is repeated on the more Socratic ground that no man will deliberately harm his most precious possession, which is his soul. In the *Protagoras* Socrates himself says: 'My own opinion is more or less this: no wise man believes that anyone sins willingly or willingly perpetrates any base or evil act; they know very well that every base or evil action is committed involuntarily.' In the *Meno*, an argument making a wickedly sophistical use of ambiguity is used to demonstrate that 'no one wishes evil', on the ground that 'to desire and obtain evil things' is a recipe for unhappiness, so that anyone who ostensibly wishes evil must be presumed to be ignorant that it is evil. The *Republic* asserts that, whether one considers pleasure, reputation or profit, the man who commends justice speaks the truth, while the man who disparages it (does not lie, but) speaks in ignorance. He must therefore be gently persuaded, for his error is not voluntary.[1]

Plato, then, maintained the paradox at all periods,[2] but Aristotle opposed it on the grounds that it makes men no longer masters of their own actions. 'It is irrational to suppose that a man who acts unjustly does not wish to be unjust or a man who acts dissolutely to be dissolute.' 'Wickedness *is* voluntary, or else we shall have to quarrel with what we have just said and deny that a man is the author and begetter of his actions.'[3] This criticism of the doctrine as deterministic is put most clearly in the *Magna Moralia*, and has been repeated in modern times. *MM* 1187a7 expresses it thus:

Socrates claimed that it is not in our power to be worthy or worthless men. If, he said, you were to ask anyone whether he would like to be just or unjust, no one would choose injustice, and it is the same with courage and cowardice and the other virtues. Evidently any who are vicious will not be vicious voluntarily. Neither, in consequence, will they be voluntarily virtuous.

Karl Joël was one who took this as a complete description of Socratic ethics, which he therefore regarded as primitively deterministic.

---

[1] *Tim.* 86d, *Laws* 731c and 860d, *Prot.* 345d, *Meno* 78a, *Rep.* 589c. Related are *Soph.* 228c, *Phileb.* 22b.

[2] Joël, as we have seen, rejected Xenophon's account on the grounds that it allowed for ἀκρασία, which on the Socratic paradox is impossible. But if we wish to pick on every apparent inconsistency, we can say equally that Plato himself denied that according to Socrates it is impossible to do wrong willingly. At *Crito* 49a he asks οὐδενὶ τρόπῳ φαμὲν ἑκόντας ἀδικητέον εἶναι; and what would be the point of asking this question if voluntary wrongdoing were impossible anyway?

[3] *EN* 1114a11, 1113b16.

All wrong action is involuntary. Whether we are good or bad does not depend on ourselves. No one wills unrighteousness, cowardice etc., but only righteousness etc. (*MM* 1187a). On this basis it would be nonsensical to exhort to virtue. The will as such cannot be improved, because it is entirely unfree, in bondage to the reason. (*E. u. X. S.* 266.)

That the beginning of psychology should be as primitive as the beginning of physical science (*ibid.* 227) is, as he says, natural enough; but what he is doing is to force this nascent psychology into the categories appropriate to a maturer stage. To say that if no one is voluntarily bad then no one is voluntarily good may seem an obvious inference, but it is nevertheless an inference drawn by Aristotle or his follower, not by Socrates.[1] Not for him the searching analysis, which we find in Aristotle, of the interrelated concepts of desire, wish, deliberation, choice, voluntary and involuntary, nor of the status of an act committed involuntarily but arising out of a condition brought on by voluntary action in the past. What Socrates did, as Aristotle frankly acknowledges, was to initiate the whole discussion out of which such analysis sprang. To Socrates the matter appeared thus. No man with full knowledge of his own and his fellows' nature, and of the consequences of his acts, would make a wrong choice of action. But what man has such knowledge? Neither himself nor anyone known to him. His awareness of this laid on him the obligation to make it clear to others, and having convinced them both of their ignorance and of the paramount need of knowledge, to persuade them to shun those ways of life which were an impediment to discovery and accept the help of his maieutic powers. As Joël himself goes on to say, he did not seek to prove (better, to discover) that virtue is good—that was a truism—but what virtue is. And he urged others to do the same. This *was* an exhortation to acquire virtue, in the only way in which Socrates thought it could be acquired.

NOTE. One of the best short expositions of the essence of Socraticism is Ritter's on pp. 54–7 of his *Sokrates*, where he states and answers four objections to the doctrine that virtue is knowledge. The fourth is that such intel-

---

[1] I think it is plain that the author of the *MM* has heard no more attributed to Socrates than that no one would choose to be unjust. The addition of the word σπουδαίους at line 7, and the conclusion ὥστε δῆλον ὅτι οὐδὲ σπουδαῖοι, are his own.

lectual determinism destroys the point of moral precept and the recognition of any strict or absolute duty. The gist of his answer is worth repeating to supplement the one above. True, he says, a man in possession of full knowledge would have no duty in the sense of a command laid on him by a higher authority which he must recognize, and it would be superfluous to demand moral action from him. Where there is natural necessity there is no duty. But in Socrates's (and Plato's) belief, imperfect and limited humanity is incapable of such complete insight. σοφία is for God, only φιλοσοφία for men.[1] Their search for wisdom is above all a search for self-knowledge. This cannot be taken for granted, but remains a duty, because the necessity of seeking knowledge is not always recognized, being in conflict with the urge towards pleasure and honour. It can only be maintained, in the face of many temptations, by an optimistic belief in its overriding value. Nevertheless the duty of self-examination may be felt so deeply that it sums up all duties in itself, and in content and importance does not fall below any of the fundamental moral demands that have ever been made or could be made.

(8) THE GOOD AND THE USEFUL

In *Republic* I (336c–d) Thrasymachus opens his attack by challenging Socrates to say what he means by justice or right conduct: 'And don't tell me that it is the necessary or the beneficial or the helpful or the profitable or the advantageous, but speak plainly and precisely, for if you give me such nonsensical answers I won't stand it.' Socrates was famous for this utilitarian approach to goodness and virtue.[2] At 339b he agrees that he believes justice to be something advantageous. In the *Hippias Major* he says: 'Let us postulate that whatever is useful is beautiful (or fine, *kalon*).'[3] In the *Gorgias* (474d) all things fine—bodies, colours, shapes, sounds, habits or pursuits—are so called either in view of their usefulness for some specific purpose or because they give pleasure. In the *Meno* (87d–e) he argues that, if *areté* is what makes

---

[1] Cf. *Apol.* 23a–b: Apollo revealed to Socrates the inadequacy of human wisdom and laid on him the task of bringing it home to others; Xen. *Mem.* 1.3.2: he prayed for no specific thing, because the gods know best what things are good.

[2] The terms used to connote utility include ὠφέλιμον, χρήσιμον, συμφέρον, λυσιτελοῦν. With the *Rep.* passage cf. *Clitophon* 409c.

[3] P. 68 above. The beauty competition in Xenophon's *Symp.* (described just before) is fought on the same arguments. The close connexion of καλόν with ἀγαθόν, and of both with usefulness for practical ends, has been remarked on in *The Sophists*, pp. 170 f. A good example of their identification by Socrates in Xen. *Mem.* 3.8.5.

us good, it must be something advantageous or useful, since all good things are useful. Many things normally considered such—health,[1] strength, wealth—may in certain circumstances lead to harm. What we have to find is something always, unfailingly advantageous. Sometimes goodness is coupled with pleasure as well as usefulness, as in the *Protagoras* (358b): 'All actions aimed at this end, namely a pleasant and painless life, must be fine actions, that is, good and beneficial. If then the pleasant is the good . . .' The knowledge and wisdom necessary for a good life consist in acquiring an 'art of measurement' which will reveal the real, as opposed to the apparent, magnitude of pleasures. As with physical objects, they may deceive by appearing larger when close at hand, smaller when distant. If we are able to judge their actual measurements, we shall ensure not only a momentary, fleeting pleasure which may be followed by unhappiness, but the maximum of pleasure and minimum of pain throughout our lives. In the metric art, or hedonic calculus, lies salvation, since it 'cancels the effect of the immediate impression and by revealing the true state of affairs causes the soul to have peace and to abide in the truth, thus saving our life' (*Prot.* 356d–e).

The utilitarian conception of good is certainly Socratic. Xenophon makes him say, just before his identification of justice and the rest of virtue with knowledge (*Mem.* 3.9.4): 'All men, I believe, choose from the various courses open to them the one which they think will be most advantageous to them, and follow that.' An important consequence is that goodness is relative to a desired end. This is especially emphasized by Xenophon in two conversations, with Aristippus and Euthydemus.[2] Aristippus was a hedonist in the vulgar sense of indulging excessively in food, drink and sex, and had already been rebuked by Socrates for his unwisdom. He hopes to get his own back by asking Socrates if he knows of anything good, and then, when Socrates gives any of the usual answers and names some one thing commonly thought to be good, showing that in certain circumstances it can be bad. Socrates however counters by asking whether he is to name something good for a fever, or for ophthalmia, or for hunger or what, 'because if you are asking me whether I know of something good which is not the good *of*

---

[1] In Xenophon (*Mem.* 4.2.32) Socrates gives an example of circumstances in which the sick may have an advantage over the healthy.
[2] *Mem.* 3.8.1–7, 4.6.8–9.

anything, I neither know nor want to know'. Similarly with what is beautiful (*kalon*), Socrates knows plenty of beautiful things, all unlike one another. 'How can what is beautiful be unlike what is beautiful?' In the way that a beautiful (fine) wrestler is unlike a beautiful runner, a shield, beautiful for protection, differs from a javelin which is beautiful for its swift and powerful motion. The answer is the same for good and beautiful because what is good in relation to anything is beautiful in relation to the same thing. *Areté* is expressly mentioned as an example. The question whether in that case a dung-basket is beautiful leaves Socrates unperturbed. 'Of course, and a golden shield is ugly if the one is well made for its special work and the other badly.' Since everything has its own limited province of usefulness, everything may be said to be both good and bad, beautiful and ugly: what is good for hunger is often bad for fever, a build that is beautiful for wrestling is often ugly for running, 'for all things are good and beautiful in relation to the purposes for which they are well adapted'.

The conversation with Euthydemus follows the same lines. The good is nothing but the useful, and what is useful to one man may be hurtful to another. Beauty is similarly related to function. What is useful is beautiful in relation to that for which it is useful, and it is impossible to mention anything—body, utensil or whatever—which is beautiful for *all* purposes.

In these conversations Socrates is making exactly the same point that Protagoras makes in Plato's dialogue, that nothing is good or bad, beneficial or harmful, *in abstracto*, but only in relation to a particular object. (*The Sophists*, pp. 166 f.) Similarly in the *Phaedrus* (*ibid.* p. 187, n. 3) he asks how anyone can call himself a doctor because he knows the effect of certain drugs and treatments, if he has no idea which of them is appropriate to a particular patient with a particular illness, at what stage they should be applied or for how long. Socrates did not scorn empiricism in the ordinary exigencies of life, he was as alive as any Sophist to the folly of imposing rigid rules indiscriminately, and one of the most indisputably Socratic tenets is that the goodness of anything lies in its fitness to perform its proper function. But once the importance of calculation is admitted, and hence the need for knowledge if pleasures are to be chosen with discrimination (and even a Callicles is forced to admit in the end that there are bad pleasures as well as good, because some are beneficial and others harmful, *Gorg.* 499 b–d), Socrates is able to proceed, by apparently common-sense arguments, to stand common sense on its head. According to Xenophon (*Mem.* 4.8.6), when on trial for his life he could claim that no one had lived a better, or a pleasanter, more enjoyable life than he; for they live best who make the best effort to become as good as possible, and most pleasantly they who are most conscious that they are improving. Good (= useful or needful) things can obviously be arranged in a hierarchy: the right arms and equipment give soldiers the means to fight well; over and above this, the right strategy and tactics are needed if their fighting is to be effective; if this has brought victory, that only leaves further aims, and the means to them, undecided, for which a yet higher wisdom and knowledge are required. How is the former enemy to be treated, and how is the country to be so ordered that the fruits of victory are a peaceful, prosperous and happy life?[1] Every art—strategy, medicine, politics and the rest—has its own particular aim, to which particular means are relative. This is 'the good' for it—victory, or health, or power over one's fellows. But at the end of each there is always a further aim. Victory may turn sour on the victors, restored health may mean only the continuation of an unhappy life, political power may be frustrating. 'Men think of the practically useful as that helping them to get what they want, but it is more useful to know what is worth wanting.'[2] Thrasymachus and Clitophon were right to be annoyed when they asked in what consisted human excellence, righteousness or good conduct, and were put off with the answer that it was 'the useful'; for this was an answer without content. *What* is useful, *what* will further the ends of human life? The doctor as such, the general as such, know what they want to achieve—in the one case health, in the other victory —and this guides them in their choice of implements and means. But when it comes to the aim of human existence, the good life which the *areté* that we are seeking is to ensure, one cannot name any single, material thing. Any that could be mentioned might be misused, and

---

[1] This particular example is invented, not taken from a Socratic conversation; but it is essentially Socratic.

[2] Gouldner, *Enter Plato*, 182, which I quote to draw attention to his sensible remarks on this and the following page.

(as Versényi has pointed out, *Socr. Hum.* 76f.) would in any case be a particular instance incapable of universality. What is wanted is 'that quality, characteristic mark, or formal structure that all good things, no matter how relative, particular and materially different, must share if they are to be good at all'.

Socrates agreed with the Sophists that different specific, or subordinate, activities had their different ends or 'goods', calling for different means to acquire them. On the other hand he deplored the extreme, individualistic relativism which said that whatever any man thought right was right for him. The ends, and so the means, were objectively determined, and the expert would attain them while the ignorant would not. Hence his insistence on 'leading the discussion back to the definition'. To decide who is the better citizen, one must inquire what is the function of a good citizen.[1] First he is considered in separate aspects: who is the good citizen in economic matters, in war, in debate and so forth? From these instances (as dozens of examples show) must be extracted the *eidos* common to them all, which would turn out to be knowledge—in this case knowledge of what a *polis* is and for what end it was constituted. Where Socrates went beyond the Sophists was in seeing the need for this formal definition. Yet he could never have satisfied a Thrasymachus, for seeing the need did not mean that he could fulfil it easily or quickly. Indeed he was only too well aware that the search was long and difficult, if not endless. It might take a lifetime, but it would be a lifetime well spent, for 'the unexamined life is not the life for a human being' (*Apol.* 38a). He laid no claim to the knowledge which was virtue, but only a certain insight into the right way to look for it. The clue lay in the close connexion between essence and function, between what a thing is and what it is *for*. One cannot know what a shuttle is without understanding the work of the weaver and what he is trying to make. To know what a cook or a doctor or a general is is to know his job, and leads to a knowledge of the particular *areté* which will enable him to perform it. If therefore we want to learn what is *areté* as such, the supreme or universal excellence which will enable us all, whatever our craft, profession or standing, to live the span of human life in the best possible way, we must first know ourselves, for

[1] This is Xenophon's example at *Mem.* 4.6.13 ff., quoted on pp. 113 f. above.

with that self-knowledge will come the knowledge of our chief end. Pursued to this extreme, the doctrine which started out as utilitarian and even selfish may end in such an apparently unpractical conclusion as that it is better to suffer wrong than to inflict it, and having done a wrong, better to be punished for it than to escape. For the real self, which is to be 'benefited', turns out to be the *psyche*, and this is only harmed by the commission of wrongful acts, and improved by chastisement.[1]

(9) SELF-KNOWLEDGE AND 'CARE OF THE SOUL'

One of Socrates's most insistent exhortations to his fellow-citizens was that they should look after—care for, tend—their souls (τῆς ψυχῆς ἐπιμελεῖσθαι). In the *Apology* he says (29 d):

I will not cease from philosophy and from exhorting you, and declaring the truth to every one of you I meet, saying in the words I am accustomed to use: 'My good friend . . . are you not ashamed of caring for money and how to get as much of it as you can, and for honour and reputation, and not caring or taking thought for wisdom and truth and for your *psyche*, and how to make it as good as possible?'

And at 30a:

I go about doing nothing else but urging you, young and old alike, not to care for your bodies or for money sooner than, or as much as, for your *psyche*, and how to make it as good as you can.

The original word *psyche* avoids the overtones which the English translation 'soul' has acquired through centuries of use in a Christian context. As Socrates understood it, the effort that he demanded of his fellows was philosophic and intellectual rather than religious, though the *psyche* did not lack religious associations in and before his time. Burnet went so far as to say that 'not only had the word *psyche* never been used in this way, but the existence of what Socrates called by that name had never been realized'.[2] To make good this statement called for

---

[1] Plato, *Gorg.* 469b, 509c, 477a. Such doctrine was not to be produced on every occasion, nor in answer to every kind of question. In judging conversations like that with Aristippus, it is important not to forget what Grote pointed out (*Plato*, III, 538): 'The real Socrates, since he talked incessantly and with everyone, must have known how to diversify his conversation and adapt it to each listener.'

[2] 'Socratic Doctrine of the Soul', *Ess. & Add.* 140. The above translations from the *Apology* are his.

an inquiry into the history of the word which he proceeded to make, as others have also done. By the fifth century it had certainly acquired remarkably complex associations. There was still the Homeric conception of it as the breath-soul which was a worthless thing without the body and had no connexion with thought or emotion. There was the primitive ghost-*psyche* which could be summoned back to prophesy and to help or take vengeance on the living. There was the *psyche* of the mystery-religions, akin to the divine and capable of a blessed life after death if the necessary rites or practices had been observed, with the addition, among the Pythagoreans, of the pursuit of *philosophia*. *Psyche* could mean courage, and 'of a good *psyche*' (εὔψυχος) brave, or it could mean bare life, so that 'to love one's *psyche*' was to cling to life in a cowardly way,[1] and swooning was a temporary loss of *psyche* (λιποψυχία). Both in the Orphic and in the Ionian-scientific tradition this life-substance was a portion of the surrounding air or *aither* enclosed in a body, and would fly off to rejoin it at death. This, though material, was the divine element and seems to have been associated with the power of thought,[2] as the *psyche* also is in Sophocles when Creon says that only power reveals the *psyche*, thought and mind of a man (*Ant.* 175–7). Here it verges on character, and it is used in moral contexts also. Pindar speaks of 'keeping one's *psyche* from unrighteousness',[3] and Sophocles of 'a well-disposed *psyche* with righteous thoughts'.[4] The law of homicide demanded forfeiture of 'the

---

[1] In the very speech in which he exhorts the Athenians to 'care for their *psyche*' in an entirely different sense, Socrates can also use φιλοψυχία in this sense of a clinging to mere life (*Apol.* 37c). ἔμψυχος is of course a common word for living or animate.

[2] Although in Eur. *Hel.* 1014 the subject is νοῦς, and in *Suppl.* 533 πνεῦμα, both seem identical with the ψυχαί of the Potidaea epitaph. See Guthrie, *Gks. & Gods*, 262f., and cf. the phrase ὅσ' ἔστ' ἔμψυχα καὶ γνώμην ἔχει at *Medea*, 230. At fr. 839.9ff. the aetherial part is nameless.

[3] *Ol.* 2.70. This might be said to be in an Orphic setting, since the passage deals with transmigration and the blessedness awaiting those who have lived three righteous lives in succession.

[4] Fr. 97 N. Since this is a little inconvenient for Burnet's argument, he can only say that it 'goes rather beyond its [the *psyche*'s] ordinary range' (p. 154), and he is similarly impelled to play down the significance of Soph. *Phil.* 55 and 1013 (p. 156). It must be said, however, that *psyche* is sometimes used as a synonym for a person, even redundantly or periphrastically, as when Electra, clasping the urn which she supposes to contain the ashes of Orestes, calls it ψυχῆς 'Ορέστου λοιπόν—'all that is left of Orestes' (Soph. *El.* 1127). This should warn us not to give too much weight to the word in lines like ἀρκεῖν γὰρ οἶμαι... μίαν ψυχὴν τάδ' ἐκτίνουσαν ἢν εὔνους παρῇ or when Clytemnestra calls Orestes τῆς ἐμῆς ψυχῆς γεγώς—'my own offspring' (*ibid.* 775). Perhaps it has little more weight at *Ph.* 55, where 'to deceive the *psyche* of Philoctetes' means simply to deceive Philoctetes, though it is arguable that the periphrasis would hardly have been possible here if it had not been natural to associate the *psyche* with the mind.

psyche which did or planned the deed', combining the senses of life and the power of thought and deliberation.[1] When Aristophanes calls the school of Socrates 'a home of clever *psychai*', this may of course be a satirical allusion to his own use of the word (*Clouds*, 94).

These examples, many of them taken from Burnet's own collection, may make us hesitate to go the whole way with him in his belief that no one before Socrates had ever said 'that there is something in us which is capable of attaining wisdom, that this same thing is capable of attaining goodness and righteousness, and that it was called "soul" (ψυχή)'. More to the point is his observation (p. 158) that we do not dispose of Socrates's claim to originality by observing that his conception of the soul was reached by combining certain features of existing beliefs: 'the power of transfusing the apparently disparate is exactly what is meant by originality'. Nor does Burnet even mention what is perhaps the most distinctive feature of the Socratic doctrine, namely the description of the relationship of soul to body in terms of the craftsman analogy: soul is to body as the user to the used, the workman to his tool.

In brief, what Socrates thought about the human *psyche* was that it was the true self. The living man *is* the *psyche*, and the body (which for the Homeric heroes and those still brought up on Homer took such decided preference over it) is only the set of tools or instruments of which he makes use in order to live. A craftsman can only do good work if he is in command of his tools and can guide them as he wishes, an accomplishment which demands knowledge and practice. Similarly life can only be lived well if the *psyche* is in command of (ἄρχει) the body.[2] It meant purely and simply the intelligence,[3] which in a properly

---

[1] ἡ δράσασα καὶ βουλεύσασα ψυχή, Antiphon Tetr. Γ. α. 7. This is quoted by Burnet (154 f.), who passes somewhat lightly over the evident power of the *psyche* to initiate and plan an action.

[2] Thus the later, Stoic epithet for the intelligence, τὸ ἡγεμονικόν, perpetuates the genuine Socratic idea. It is foreshadowed by the ἡγεμονοῦν of Plato, *Tim.* 41 c. Cf. also the use of τὸ ἡγούμενον by Aristotle, *EN* 1113 a6.

[3] Socrates's language is not completely consistent on this point. At *Alc. I* 133 b he speaks of τοῦτον αὐτῆς τὸν τόπον ἐν ᾧ ἐγγίγνεται ἡ ψυχῆς ἀρετή, σοφία and immediately after of τῆς ψυχῆς . . . τοῦτο περὶ οὗ τὸ εἰδέναι τε καὶ φρονεῖν ἐστιν. This language is construed by Jowett's editors (1, 601 n. 1) as expressing 'the view of reason as an innermost self *within* the human soul', a view which they call 'characteristic of the last phase of Plato's thought (*Philebus*, *Timaeus*)'. It is, I am sure, no more than a momentary concession to the common view of ψυχή as the seat of life. For Socrates throughout the dialogue, but especially when he describes the ψυχή as that which is to be cherished because its function is to govern the body, it is the mind, as indeed it is when he calls it that whose ἀρετή is σοφία, for a thing is rightly defined with

ordered life is in complete control of the senses and emotions. Its proper virtue is wisdom (σοφία) and thought (τὸ φρονεῖν), and to improve the *psyche* is to take thought for wisdom (φρόνησις) and truth (*Apol.* 29 d, p. 147 above). This identification of the *psyche* with the self and the self with the reason might be said to have roots both in Ionian scientific thought and in Pythagoreanism, yet there was certainly novelty in Socrates's development of it,[1] apart from the fact that the ordinary Athenian, whom he particularly wished to persuade, was not in the habit of letting his life be ruled by either of these influences. The arguments leading to this conception of the soul have the familiar Socratic ring, and make clear its intimate connexion with his other fundamental conception, that of knowledge, and in particular self-knowledge, as the prerequisite of the good life. They are best set forth in the *First Alcibiades*, a dialogue which, whether or not Plato wrote it, was aptly described by Burnet as 'designed as a sort of introduction to Socratic philosophy for beginners'.[2]

Alcibiades, still under twenty, has ambitions to be a leader of men, both in politics and war. He ought then to have some understanding of such concepts as right and wrong, expedient and inexpedient. Socrates first gets him to contradict himself on these subjects, thus proving that he did not know their meaning although he thought he did. He next points out that it is not ignorance that matters, but ignorance that you are ignorant. Alcibiades does not know how to fly any more than he knows how to govern justly or for the good of the Athenians, but since he is aware of his ignorance he will not try, and no harm will be done.

reference to its ἀρετή. (In his analogy, the eye which wishes to see *itself* must look to the seat (τόπος) of its ἀρετή.) There is no contradiction between the view of the soul in the *Alc.* and that at *Apol.* 29 d: to care for the ψυχή is to care for φρόνησις and ἀλήθεια.

[1] It may be that in some respects Democritus came close to the Socratic position, in spite of the inclusion of soul in his all-embracing materialism. Vlastos has claimed that he 'would advise men, exactly as did Socrates, to care for their souls' (*Philos. Rev.* 1945, 578 ff.). Yet there are legitimate doubts about the genuineness of his ethical fragments, as well as about the relative dates of his writings and Socrates's dialectical activity, and I can add nothing to what I have said in vol. II, 489 ff. On the constitution of the soul in Democritus, see the index *s.v.* 'atomists: soul'.

[2] *Ess. & Add.* 139. Cf. D. Tarrant in *CQ*, 1938, 167: 'an able exposition of the Socratic method of ἔλεγχος and induction. The personality of Socrates is . . . again drawn on familiar lines.' In antiquity the dialogue was universally accepted as Plato's, but its authorship has been doubted in modern times, especially by German critics, against whom it was stoutly defended by its Budé editor Croiset in 1920. More recently its authenticity has been upheld by A. Motte in *L'Ant. Class.* (1961). See also the appraisal by R. Weil in *L'Inf. Litt.* (1964), and the references given by the revisers of Jowett's *Dialogues of Plato*, vol. I, 601 n. I.

Again (a favourite illustration), there is no harm in his knowing nothing of seamanship if he is content to be a passenger and leave the steering to the skilled helmsman, but there may be disaster if he thinks himself capable of taking over the helm.

Socrates next gets Alcibiades to agree that for success in life it is necessary to care for, or take pains over, oneself (ἐπιμελεῖσθαι ἑαυτοῦ), to improve and train oneself, and goes on to demonstrate that you cannot tend and improve a thing unless you know its nature. As always, he is trying to 'lead the discussion back to a definition' (p. 113 above). 'Knowing how' for Socrates must be preceded by 'knowing what', a lesson that the Sophists had failed to learn. First he draws a distinction between tending a thing itself and tending something that belongs to it. These are generally the subjects of different skills. To tend the foot is the job of the trainer (or doctor or chiropodist); to tend what belongs to the foot—i.e. shoes—belongs to the cobbler. Now such things as wealth and reputation are not ourselves but things belonging to us, and therefore to augment these externals—which many regard as a proper aim in life—is not to look after ourselves at all, and the art of tending ourselves is a different one. What is this art? Well, can anyone make a good shoe or mend one if he does not know what a shoe is and what it is intended to do? No. One must understand the nature and purpose of anything before one can make, mend or look after it properly. So in life, we cannot acquire an art of self-improvement unless we first understand what we ourselves are. Our first duty, therefore, is to obey the Delphic command, 'Know thyself', 'for once we know ourselves, we may learn how to care for ourselves, but otherwise we never shall'.[1]

How do we come by this knowledge of our real selves?[2] It is reached by means of a further distinction, between the user of anything and what he uses. Alcibiades is first made to admit that the two are always distinct: he and Socrates are people, conversing by means of *logoi*, and

---

[1] 128b–129a, 124a. Commendation of the Delphic precept occurs again in Plato at *Phaedrus*, 229e, and in Xenophon at *Mem.* 4.2.24 and 3.9.6, where not knowing oneself is equated with not knowing one's own ignorance, a folly which in the *Alcibiades* has already been exposed. Plut. *Adv. Col.* 1118c quotes Aristotle as saying that it was the starting-point of Socrates's inquiries into the nature of man. (ἀπορίας ταύτης there refers to the question τί ἄνθρωπός ἐστι, though this is not made clear by the passage as printed in the fragments of Aristotle by Rose (fr. 1) or Ross (*De phil.* fr. 1).)   [2] τί ποτ' ἐσμὲν αὐτοί, 129b.

the *logoi* they use are different from themselves. A shoemaker is distinct from his knife and awl, a musician from his instrument. But we can go further. A shoemaker, we say, or any other craftsman, uses not only his tools but also his hands and eyes. We may generalize this and say that the body as a whole is something which a man uses to carry out his purposes, his legs to take him where he wants to go, and so on. And if we agree that such a statement is meaningful, we must agree that in speaking of a man we mean something different from his body—that, in fact, which makes use of the body as its instrument. There is nothing that this can be except the *psyche*, which uses and controls (ἄρχει) the body.[1] Therefore he who said 'know thyself' was in fact bidding us know our *psyche* (130e). Going back to the earlier distinction, to know the body is to know something that belongs to oneself, as a shoe to a foot, but not one's real self; and likewise to look after the body is not to look after one's real self. To know oneself is at once an intellectual and a moral insight, for it is to know that the *psyche*, not the body, is intended by nature or God (cf. 124c) to be the ruling element: to know oneself is to be self-controlled (*sophron*, 131b, and 133c). This may throw some further light on our earlier discussions of Socratic intellectualism (pp. 135 ff. above). It is at this point, too, that Socrates makes use of the argument to oppose the prevailing sexual standards: he himself may be correctly described as a lover of Alcibiades, because he loves his *psyche*; those who love his body love not Alcibiades, but only something belonging to him (p. 75 above).

All of this is familiar Socratic doctrine, the elements of which can be found repeated many times in the Socratic writings, but are so presented here as to bring out their interrelations in a single continuous argument. We are not surprised therefore when, after establishing that to know ourselves is to know the *psyche* and not the body, he goes on to say that if we want to know what the *psyche* is, we must look 'particularly at that part of it in which its virtue resides', and adds at once that this virtue of the *psyche* is wisdom (*sophia*). To know what something is is to know what it is *for*, and we have already discovered that

---

[1] It is difficult to understand what was in Jaeger's mind when he wrote (*Paideia*, II, 43) that 'in his [Socrates's] thought, there is no opposition between psychical and physical man'. The body is as extraneous to the man himself, his *psyche*, as the saw is to the carpenter.

this *ergon* or function of the soul is to rule, govern or control. That virtue is knowledge is true right through the scale of human occupations. The virtue of a shoemaker is knowledge, of what shoes are for and how to make them; the virtue of a doctor is knowledge, of the body and how to tend it. And the virtue of a complete man both as an individual and as a social being is knowledge of the moral and statesmanlike virtues—justice, courage and the rest—which all ambitious Athenian politicians carelessly claimed to understand, but of the nature of which it was Socrates's painful duty to point out that they (and himself no less) were so far ignorant.[1] Here we have the whole train of thought that lay behind the exhortation in the *Apology* to care for the *psyche* and for wisdom and truth, rather than for money or reputation, which it would have been inappropriate, or rather impossible, to unfold in a speech before the judges at his trial.

(10) RELIGIOUS BELIEFS OF SOCRATES: IS THE SOUL IMMORTAL?

The next point made in the *Alcibiades* comes rather unexpectedly to a modern reader, but is introduced by Socrates without preamble: 'Can we mention', he asks (133c), 'anything more divine about the soul than what is concerned with knowledge and thought? Then this aspect of it[2] resembles God, and it is by looking toward that and understanding all that is divine—God and wisdom—that a man will most fully know himself.' God, he goes on, reflects the nature of *psyche* more clearly and brightly than anything in our own souls, and we may therefore use him as a mirror for human nature too, if what we are looking for is the *areté* of the soul, and this is the best way to see and understand

[1] In describing the first serious attempt in history to define the meaning of the word 'good', I have not thought it helpful or fair to compare it directly with the ideas of the twentieth century A.D., as set forth in a book like R. M. Hare's *Language of Morals*. But one outstanding difference between the two may be noted. On p. 100 of that book Professor Hare speaks of certain words which he calls 'functional words', and the example he gives is a Socratic one: 'We do not know what a carpenter is until we know what a carpenter is supposed to do.' But the extrapolation from this kind of case to man in general is no longer allowed: '"man" in "good man" is not normally a functional word, and never so when moral commendation is being given' (p. 145). The point is elaborated in his essay reprinted in the Foot collection, pp. 78–82.

[2] τοῦτο αὐτῆς. As often, one envies the elusiveness which the omission of the noun makes possible for a Greek. It is by no means certain that 'part' is the best word to supply. τόπος at 133b is metaphorical, and carried over from the example of the eye. If pressed for a noun, the writer might well have suggested δύναμις.

153

ourselves.[1] With this passage in mind, Jowett's editors (1. 601 n. 1) say that in the *Alcibiades* 'the religious spirit is more positive than in Plato's earlier dialogues', and give this as a reason for supposing it a later and possibly spurious work. But the religious references in the *Apology* are equally positive, and the conception of a divine mind as a universal and purer counterpart of our own was common in the fifth century and is attributed to Socrates by Xenophon. In Plato's *Apology* Socrates says that it would be wrong to disobey God's commands through fear of death (28 e), and that, fond as he is of the Athenians, he will obey God rather than them (29 d), that God has sent him to the city for its good (30 d–e), and that the fortunes of the good are not neglected by the gods (41 d). He claims that it is 'not permitted (θεμιτόν)' for a better man to be harmed by a worse (30 d), and the forbidding agent is clearly not human but divine. Both *Apology* and *Euthyphro* mention his serious acceptance of the 'divine sign', which he regarded as a voice from God. How far one is justified in translating ὁ θεός simply as 'God' is a difficult question. At 29 d Socrates presumably has chiefly in mind Apollo and his oracle, and at 41 d he speaks of 'the gods' in the plural. Yet in some cases he seems to have advanced beyond the popular theology to the notion of a single divine power, for which 'God' is the least misleading modern equivalent. In any case it cannot be said that the religious language of the *Apology* is less 'positive' than that of the *Alcibiades*, and we certainly have no right to say that it is used in a different spirit.

Closest to the thought of the *Alcibiades* about God and the soul is the passage in Xenophon (*Mem.* 1.4.17) where Socrates says to Aristodemus: 'Just consider that your own mind within you controls your body as it will. So you must believe that the wisdom in the whole universe disposes all things according to its pleasure.' This supreme being appears at 4.3.13, in contrast to 'the other gods', as 'he who co-ordinates and holds together the whole cosmos', and a little further on

[1] The sentences about using God as a mirror are omitted from our manuscripts of the dialogue, but were read by Eusebius and other ancient authors. They are restored by Burnet in the Oxford text and in Jowett's translation, and are obviously necessary to complete the rather elaborate analogy with mirrors and the eye which Plato is drawing. Croiset's objection (Budé ed. 110 n. 1) that they only repeat what has gone before is misleading, nor is his claim convincing that their content has a Neoplatonic tinge.

in the same chapter the *psyche* of man is described as that which 'more than anything else that is human partakes of the divine'. The resemblance of the language here to that reported of Anaximenes, who compared the universal breath or air to the human soul, which is also air, and holds us together (vol. 1, 131), reminds us how old is this connexion between human and universal soul. The intellectual character of the universal soul as divine *mind*, and its creative role, were emphasized in Socrates's own lifetime by Anaxagoras and Diogenes of Apollonia, and considering its possibilities for spiritualization it is not surprising that he should have taken over the belief and adapted it to his own teaching. At 1.4.8 he claims it is absurd that wisdom should 'by some lucky chance' reside in the tiny portions of matter which form our bodies, and yet 'all the huge and infinitely numerous bodies' in the universe should have achieved the regularity and order which they display without any thought at all.[1] His criticism of Anaxagoras was not that he made Mind the moving force behind the whole universe, but that having done so, he ignored it, and explained the cosmic phenomena by mechanical causes which seemed to have no relation whatsoever to intelligence.

The mentions of a god who is the supreme wisdom in the world, as our minds are in us, are associated with an insistence on his loving care for mankind. At 1.4.5 this being is 'he who created man from the beginning', and Socrates points out in detail how our own parts are designed to serve our ends, and at 4.3.10 how the lower animals too exist for the sake of man. God cares for men (as also in Plato's *Apology*, 41 d), takes thought for them, loves them, assists them, as well as being their creator.[2] All this excludes the supposition that Socrates merely shared the vague pantheism of contemporary intellectuals. He uses 'God' or 'the gods' indifferently, but with a bias towards the former, and we have seen mention of a supreme governor of the universe contrasted with lesser gods. In so far as he genuinely believed in the gods of popular polytheism (and Xenophon was emphatic in defending him against charges of neglecting their cult), he probably thought of them

---

[1] A similar argument is used in Plato's *Philebus* (29b–30b), a late dialogue which nevertheless has Socrates as its chief speaker. The idea behind it certainly goes back to the fifth century.

[2] See the phrases collected by Zeller, *Ph. d. Gr.* 178 n. 3.

as different manifestations of the one supreme spirit. This was the position of many thinking men, and an apparently indifferent use of 'the god', 'the gods' and 'the divine' (neuter) is characteristic of the age. 'If you make trial of the gods by serving them', says Xenophon's Socrates (*Mem.* 1.4.18), 'and see whether they will give you counsel in the things which are hidden from men, you will discover that the divine is such, and so great, that at one and the same time it sees and hears everything and is everywhere and takes care of everything.' The words 'in the things hidden from men' are a reminder that Socrates deprecated resort to oracles as a substitute for thought. In matters where the gods have given men the power to judge for themselves, they emphatically ought to take the trouble to learn what is necessary and make up their own minds: to trouble the gods about such things is contrary to true religion (ἀθέμιτα: see *Mem.* 1.1.9). To sum up, Socrates believed in a god who was the supreme Mind, responsible for the ordering of the universe and at the same time the creator of men. Men moreover had a special relation with him in that their own minds, which controlled their bodies as God controlled the physical movements of the universe, were, though less perfect than the mind of God, of the same nature, and worked on the same principles. In fact, if one looked only to the *areté* of the human soul and disregarded its shortcomings, the two were identical. Whether or not because of this relationship, God had a special regard for man, and had designed both man's own body and the rest of nature for his benefit.

These religious views are amply attested for Socrates, and they create a presumption that he believed the soul to persist after death in a manner more satisfying than the shadowy and witless existence of the Homeric dead; but in deference to many scholars who have thought him to be agnostic on this point, it must be looked at further. To call the soul, or mind, the divine part of man does not by itself imply personal, individual survival. The hope of the mystic was to lose his individuality by being caught up into the one all-pervading spirit, and this absorption was probably the expectation of all, mystics or natural philosophers, who believed in the airy (and ultimately aetherial) nature of the *psyche* and in the *aither* as a living and 'governing' element in the

universe. For believers in transmigration like the Orphics and Pythagoreans, individual survival, carrying with it rewards and punishments
for the kind of life lived on earth, was the fate only of those who were
still caught in the wheel and destined for reincarnation. The final goal
was again reabsorption.[1] In one form or another—through the
mysteries, the philosophers, and superstitions of a primitive antiquity—
this belief would be fairly widespread in the fifth century, and is probably behind Euripides's lines about the mind of the dead 'plunging
immortal into the immortal *aither*' (*Hel.* 1014ff.).

That is one reason for caution in using the reference in the *Alcibiades*
to the soul as divine as evidence that Socrates believed in personal
immortality. Another is the doubt expressed by some scholars concerning the date of the dialogue. Even if intended as 'an introduction to
Socratic philosophy' it might, if not written before the middle of the
fourth century, include in all innocence something that was not
Socratic. For the closest parallel to its statement of the divinity of the
human reason, put briefly and soberly with none of the language about
initiation, rebirth and so on which Plato adopted from the mystery-
religions, we have to look to Aristotle. In the tenth book of the *Ethics*
he argues that the best and highest form of human life would consist in
the uninterrupted exercise of the reason; 'but', he goes on (1177b27),
'it is not by virtue of our humanity that we can live this life, but in so
far as there is something of the divine in us'. A little later on, in
exact agreement with the *Alcibiades*, he says that nevertheless this divine
faculty of reason is above all others a man's true self (1178a7). If the
Alcibiades was written, as some think, about the time of Plato's death
and Aristotle's maturity, the addition might be very natural. It might
indeed be supposed (as Plato did suppose) that the soul's independence
of the body, and hence its immortality, were the natural consequence of
the sharp dualism of soul and body that is maintained in the main part
of the dialogue, the thoroughly Socratic argument that the body is not
the real man but only an instrument of which the man (that is, the
psyche) makes use. But we cannot yet say for certain that Socrates drew
that conclusion.

It is safer to turn first to the *Apology*, the most certainly Socratic of

[1] See vol. 1, especially 480f. and 466 with n. 2.

all Plato's works.[1] There Socrates says in several places what he thinks about death. On no other subject is it truer to say that everyone has his own Socrates. Some read into these passages agnosticism, others religious faith in a future life. First of all the text must speak for itself. At 28e he says it would be shameful if, after facing death in battle at the command of the state, he should now through fear of death disobey the god's command to philosophize by examining himself and others.

To fear death is only an instance of thinking oneself wise when one is not; for it is to think one knows what one does not know. No one in fact knows whether death may not even be the greatest of all good things for man, yet men fear it as if they knew well that it was the greatest evil ... This perhaps is the point in which I am different from the rest of men, and if I could make any claim to be wiser than another, it is in this, that just as I have no full knowledge about the things in Hades, so also I am aware of my ignorance. This however I do know, that it is both evil and base to do wrong and disobey a better, be he god or man. Therefore I shall never fear nor run away from something which for all I know may be good, but rather from evils which I know to be evils.

After the death-sentence Socrates addresses a few words to those who had voted for his acquittal. First he tells them of the silence of his divine sign or voice (p. 83 above), which means that 'what has

---

[1] Concerning the historicity of the *Apol.* every shade of opinion has been held (see Ehnmark in *Eranos*, 1946, 106 ff. for this, especially in its bearing on the question of immortality), but few have been found to deny its essential faithfulness to the Socratic philosophy. Admittedly a special case has been made of the third speech (38 c ff.), delivered after sentence has been passed, but even a sceptic like Wilamowitz agreed that in composing it 'Plato must have carefully avoided saying anything that Socrates himself could not have said' (Ehnmark, *loc. cit.* 108). There is really no good reason to separate this speech from the rest, and about the whole the most reasonable supposition is that Plato (who makes a point of mentioning his own presence at the trial: 34a, 38b), while doubtless polishing up and reducing to better order what Socrates actually said, has not falsified the facts or the spirit of his remarks. At the very most, he will have gone no further than Thucydides in reporting speeches in his history, some of which he had only heard at second hand. See *The Sophists*, p. 85. In Plato's case we must take into account that he was present himself and that the occasion was the final crisis in the life of the man whom he admired most in all the world. It is sufficient guarantee that he has given the substance of what Socrates said, and that, if anything has been added by way of vindicating Socrates's memory, it will be in keeping with his real character and views.

If it is still denied that we can know for certain whether Socrates himself used the opportunity of his trial to make such a complete *apologia pro vita sua*, we can only reply that it would have been an entirely reasonable thing for him to do, and that in any case the account of his life and beliefs which Plato gives us is true to the real man.

happened to me must be something good, and those of us who think death is an evil cannot be right'. He continues (40c):

Looking at it another way we may also feel a strong hope that it is good. Death is one of two things. Either the dead man is as if he no longer exists, and has no sensations at all; or else as men say it is a change and migration of the soul from here to another place. If we have no sensation, but death is like a sleep in which the sleeper has not even a dream, then it must be a wonderful boon; for if a man had to pick out the night in which he slept so soundly that he did not even dream, and setting beside it the other nights and days of his life, to compare them with that night and say how many better and pleasanter days and nights he had spent, I truly believe that not only an ordinary man but even the Great King himself would find them easy to count. If then that is death, I count it a gain, for in this way the whole of time will seem no more than a single night.

If on the other hand death is a sort of migration to another place, and the common tales are true that all the dead are there, what finer thing could there be than this? Would it not be a good journey that takes one to Hades, away from these self-styled judges here, to find the true judges who are said to dispense justice there—Minos, Rhadamanthys, Aeacus, Triptolemus and other demigods who were just in their own lives? Or what would not one of you give to meet Orpheus and Musaeus and Hesiod and Homer? I myself would have a wonderful time there, with Palamedes and Ajax son of Telamon and any other of the ancients who had met his death as the result of an unjust verdict, comparing my experiences with theirs. There would be some pleasure in that. Best of all, I could examine and interrogate the inhabitants of Hades as I do the people here, to find out which of them is wise, and which thinks he is though he is not. What would not a man give to question the leader of the great army at Troy, or Odysseus or Sisyphus or thousands more whom one might mention, both men and women? It would be an infinite happiness to consort and converse with them and examine them— and at any rate they don't put people to death for it there! For among the advantages which those in Hades have over us is the fact that they are immortal for the rest of time, if what we are told is true.

And you too, my friends, must face death with good hope, convinced of the truth of this one thing, that no evil can happen to a good man either in life or in death, nor are his fortunes neglected by the gods.

Then there is the final sentence of the whole *Apology*:

Now the time is up and we must go, I to death and you to life; but which of us is going to the better fate is known to none, except it be to God.

It is only by reading such passages as this at length that one can catch something of the flavour of the man, which was at least as much of an influence on his friends and posterity as any positive doctrine that he had to teach. Indeed, as these same passages show, with such a naturally undogmatic person it is not always easy to say what he did teach, and the majority who like and admire him tend to see in his language whatever they themselves believe. The agnostic greets him as a kindred spirit because he has said that to claim knowledge of what happens after death is to claim to know what one does not know: he states possible alternatives and leaves them open. The religious-minded is impressed by the fact that whenever he mentions death it is to say that it is something good. In this speech, it is true, he entertains the possibility that it may be either a new life, in which one will meet the great men of the past, or a dreamless sleep, and professes to see good in both. But one would not expect him to assert his innermost convictions in a public speech, in which indeed he treats the matter with a certain amount of humour, as when he imagines himself carrying on in the next world the inquisitorial activities which had made him so unpopular in this. One may feel with Taylor that 'it requires a singularly dull and tasteless reader not to see that his own sympathies are with the hope of a blessed immortality' (*VS*, 31). Hints of his own belief appear rather in statements like 'the fortunes of a good man are not neglected by the gods'. The man who believed that the souls of the righteous are in the hand of God, it may be said, is unlikely to have believed that death means utter extinction. The nature of death, he concludes, is unknown *except it be to God*; and that exception, one might argue, makes all the difference.

My own reading of the *Apology* inclines me to this second interpretation, but there is too much to be said on both sides for the question to be resolved on the basis of these passages alone. They must be taken with other considerations. It would be unusual, to put it no higher, for anyone with Socrates's views both about man as the supreme object of the care and solicitude of God, for whose sake the rest of creation exists (and for this one may cite both Plato's *Apology* and Xenophon as quoted on p. 155 above), and about the nature and importance of the human soul, to hold at the same time that physical death was the end and the soul perished with the body. A belief in the independence of the soul, and its indifference to the fate of the body, goes naturally with that sharp distinction between them which we find drawn not only in the *Alcibiades* but in the *Apology* and elsewhere in the more indubitably Socratic parts of Plato. Always for Socrates they were two different things, with the *psyche* (that is, the rational faculty) superior and the body only its sometimes refractory instrument. Hence the supreme importance of 'tendance of the *psyche*' (i.e. the training of the mind), and although Socrates saw this as issuing primarily in the living of a practically good life on earth, he most probably thought that just as it was of an altogether superior nature to the body, so also it outlived it.

Of course if one took the *Phaedo* as a mere continuation of the *Apology*, relating what Socrates said to his intimate friends on the day of his death with as much fidelity as the *Apology* employs in telling what he said before the five hundred judges at his trial, there would be no question about it; for there Socrates does maintain that the *psyche* not only is distinct from, and superior to, the body, but differs from it as the eternal from the temporal. It would, however, be here too a 'dull and tasteless reader' who did not sense the entirely different character of the two works, the intellectual modesty of the one and the human simplicity of its alternatives—either a dreamless sleep or a new life much like this one—and the elaborate combination in the other of mystical language about reincarnation with metaphysical argument about the soul's relation to the eternal Forms. As to this, I have already expressed the view (pp. 33 f. above) that if Socrates had not felt confident of personal immortality, it would have been impossible for Plato to have written an account of his last conversation and death, however imaginative in its details, of which the whole purpose was to instil such confidence. In marked contrast to the *Apology*, he tells us that he himself was not present, and he has felt free to support the simple, unproved faith of his friend with the kind of arguments that appealed to his more speculative nature. Even so, there are many touches of the well-remembered Socrates, not only in the perfect calm and steadfastness with which he goes to meet his death. Surely Socratic is the 'quiet laugh' with which he replies to Crito's request as to how they should bury him: 'Any way you please, provided you can catch me', with the explanation that the dead body which they will shortly see is something quite different from Socrates, the person now talking to them. The *Apology*, though innocent of any theories of reincarnation, speaks of death as a 'change of abode for the soul from here to another place' and 'like going to another country', and this language is exactly paralleled in the *Phaedo*.[1] In the *Phaedo* also Socrates repeats his hope of meeting among the dead with better men than those now living (63b). Even the Socratic profession of ignorance and posing of alternatives is not forgotten there (91b): 'If what I say is true, it is indeed well to believe it; but if there is nothing for a man when he has died, at least I shall be less troublesome to the company than if I were bemoaning my fate.' That however was before the final arguments, after which the Platonic Socrates takes over, and when he has described a possible course of events for the soul both in and out of the body, claims that even if one cannot be positive on such a matter, yet something like it must be true 'because the soul has been clearly shown to be (φαίνεται οὖσα) immortal' (114d). Plato thinks he has proved what Socrates only believed, the fact of the soul's immortality, but when it comes to the details of its fate he remembers again how the undogmatic Socrates, the knower of his own ignorance, used to speak. Something like his *mythos* must be true, 'for it is fitting, and it is worth taking a chance on believing that it is so—the risk is a good one —and one should repeat such things to oneself like a charm, which is why I have spun out the story at such length'. The reason, as always with Socrates, is practical: belief in the scheme of transmigration which he has outlined, with promotion to better lives for the good and *vice versa*, will encourage a man to think little of bodily pleasures, to pursue knowledge and 'deck the *psyche* with her proper adornments, self-control, justice, courage, freedom and truth' (114d–e).

The *Phaedo* is a dialogue inspired by Socrates, but in certain important ways going beyond him. To claim to separate the Socratic from the Platonic will seem to many presumptuous, but one can only follow

[1] Cf. *Apol.* 40c, μετοίκησις τῇ ψυχῇ τοῦ τόπου τοῦ ἐνθένδε εἰς ἄλλον τόπον with *Phaedo*, 117c, τὴν μετοίκησιν τὴν ἐνθένδε ἐκεῖσε, and 40e, εἰ δ' αὖ οἷον ἀποδημῆσαί ἐστιν ὁ θάνατος ἐνθένδε εἰς ἄλλον τόπον, with 61e, where Socrates speaks of himself as μέλλοντα ἐκεῖσε ἀποδημεῖν. (ἀποδημία also at 67b.) On the relations between the *Apol.* and *Phaedo* see also Ehnmark in *Eranos*, 1946.

one's own best judgment and leave the verdict to others. I have already given a character sketch of Socrates based on what seemed the most trustworthy evidence, and it is to this impression of his personality as a whole that we must turn for the answer to a question like this.[1] He seems to have been a man who, as Aristotle said, applied the whole of his remarkable intellectual powers to the solution of questions of practical conduct. In higher matters I would suggest that he was guided by a simple religious faith. Certain problems were in principle soluble by human effort. To trouble the gods with these was lazy and stupid. But there would always be truths beyond the scope of human explanation, and for these one must trust the word of the gods, whether given by oracles or through other channels.[2] There was no irony in the way he talked of his divine sign: he put himself unreservedly in the hands of what he sincerely believed to be an inspiration from heaven. He possessed the religious virtue of humility (which in others also has sometimes been taken for arrogance), and with it, despite his ceaseless questioning of everything in the human sphere, of unquestioning belief. There is nothing impossible or unprecedented in the union of a keen and penetrating insight in human affairs, and an unerring eye for humbug, with a simple religious piety. He cannot have laid such emphasis on the 'care' of the *psyche* as the real man, without believing that as it was both truly human and had some share in the divine nature, so also it was the lasting part of us, and that the treatment accorded it in this life would affect its nature and fortunes in the next (*Phaedo*, 63c). The difference between him and Plato is that whereas he was content to believe in immortality as the humbler and less theologically minded Christian does, as an article of simple faith, Plato felt the need to support it with arguments which might at least strengthen the fearful,

---

[1] It is obviously theoretically possible that parallels between *Apol.* and *Phaedo* are due to the Platonic character of the former rather than to Socratic elements in the latter. Only this feeling of personal acquaintance with an integral character, Socrates, enables one to reject such an—as I see it—incredible hypothesis.

[2] Xen. *Mem.* 1.1.6–9, especially 9: τοὺς δὲ μηδὲν τῶν τοιούτων οἰομένους εἶναι δαιμόνιον, ἀλλὰ πάντα τῆς ἀνθρωπίνης γνώμης δαιμονᾶν· ἔφη. Hackforth put it well (*CPA*, 96): 'He was, I think, content and wisely content not to attempt an explicit reconciliation of reason with faith; not out of indifference, nor in a spirit of complacent, condescending toleration of traditional belief, but rather because he possessed that rare wisdom which knows that, while no bounds may properly be set to the activity of human reason—that the ἀνεξέταστος βίος is οὐ βιωτὸς ἀνθρώπῳ—yet ἡ ἀνθρωπίνη σοφία ὀλίγου τινὸς ἀξία ἐστὶ καὶ οὐδενός.'

if not convert the unbelieving. He sought to promote the immortality of the soul from religious belief to philosophical doctrine.

This however involves in the end an essential change of attitude. Once focus attention on the *psyche* to the extent necessary for a proof of its immortality, and one is inevitably, if insensibly, led to the attitude which Plato adopts in the *Phaedo*, of contempt for this life and a fixation on the other. Life becomes something that the philosopher will long to escape from, and while it lasts, he will regard it as practice, or training, for death; that is to say, as death is the release of soul from body, so he will hold the body in contempt (ὀλιγωρεῖν 68c), and keep the soul as pure from the taint of its senses and desires as is possible in this life.[1] One becomes immersed in Orphic and Pythagorean notions of the body as a tomb or prison for the soul, and this life as a kind of purgatory, from which the philosopher's eyes should be averted to gaze on the bliss of the world beyond. This attitude of Plato's I would venture to call essentially un-Socratic. One remark in Burnet's essay on the Socratic doctrine of the soul is profoundly true, but difficult to reconcile with his fixed idea that the *Phaedo* contains nothing but pure Socratic doctrine. 'It does not seem, then', he wrote, 'that this [belief in immortality] formed the ordinary theme of his discourse. What he did preach as the one thing needful for the soul was that it should strive after wisdom and goodness' (p. 159). These twin goals must be brought back to their Greek originals: *sophia*, the knowledge and skill essential for all good craftsmanship, from shoemaking to moral and political science; and *areté*, the excellence which meant being good *at* something, in this case living to the utmost of one's powers. Socrates saw his proper place not 'practising for death' in philosophic retirement (however Callicles might sneer), but thrashing out practical questions with the political and rhetorical teachers of Athens in her heyday, as well as instilling a proper sense of values into his younger friends in gymnasium or palaestra.

[1] See especially in the *Phaedo*, 61b–c, 64a, 67c–e.

(11) THE LEGACY OF SOCRATES

Even systematic philosophers, whose ideas are perpetuated in voluminous writings, have been differently understood by their followers.
This was even more certain to happen with Socrates, who taught by
word of mouth and insisted that his only advantage over others was the
knowledge of his own ignorance. His service to philosophy was the
same as that which he claimed to have performed for the Athenian
people, namely to be a gadfly which provoked and stung them into
fresh activity. Much of his influence was due not to anything that he
said at all, but to the magnetic effect of his personality and the example
of his life and death, to the consistency and integrity with which he
followed his own conscience rather than adopting any belief or legal
enactment simply because it was accepted or enjoined, while un-
questioningly admitting the right of the state, to which he owed
parents, education, and lifelong protection, to deal with him as it
thought fit if he could not persuade it otherwise. Inevitably, therefore,
in the years following his death, the most diverse philosophers and
schools could claim to be following in his footsteps though some at
least of them may appear to us to be highly un-Socratic in their
conclusions. Here was an inspiring talker, of outstanding intellect and,
for his time at least, a unique power of logical discrimination, who was
prepared to devote all his time to an examination of human conduct,
in the conviction that life was not a meaningless chaos or the heartless
jest of an unfeeling higher power but had a definite direction and purpose. Nothing therefore was more important for himself or for others
than to ask themselves continually what was the good for man and
what the peculiarly human *areté* or excellence which would enable him
to attain that good. But it is essential to remember that, as we have seen
already, Socrates himself never claimed to have the answer to these
questions. He wished to counter those Sophists and others who saw
the best life as one of self-indulgence or tyrannical power, those whom
Plato's Callicles represents when he identifies the good with pleasure.
It must be true, for instance, to say that the orator who pleases the
demos may do them much harm, and that the one who aims at their

good may have to say some very unpalatable things; and though pleasure in itself may be *a* good thing, such statements as these would be impossible if pleasure and good were identical. How was he to show that such Sophists were wrong?

To a large extent he tried to do it by meeting them on their own ground. Granted that self-interest is paramount, and our object is to maximize our own enjoyment, success demands that it be enlightened self-interest. Unreflecting pursuit of the pleasure of the moment may lead to future misery. This is the thin end of the Socratic wedge. Everyone admitted it, but it follows that actions pleasant in themselves may lead to great harm, even if the meaning of harm is still restricted to what is painful. Hence pleasure cannot be itself the end of life. If we want a word to be the equivalent of 'good' (ἀγαθόν) and explain it, we must try another. Socrates himself suggested 'useful' or 'beneficial'. The good must be something which always benefits, never harms. Acts which in themselves give pleasure may now be referred to this as a higher standard. We may ask, still maintaining our attitude of pure self-interest, 'Will it be for my ultimate benefit to act thus?' Having got as far as this, it was easy for him to show that we cannot live the best life without knowledge or wisdom. We have seen how this is necessary to acquire the 'art of measurement' whereby we can calculate the course of action which will in the long term give us the maximum of pleasure and the minimum of pain. In the *Protagoras*, where to the dismay of some of his admirers he apparently champions the cause of pleasure as the good, he gets Protagoras first to agree that the pleasure on which we base our calculations must be in the future as well as the present, and finally to include under 'pleasure' everything that in other dialogues (e.g. *Meno*) he describes as 'beneficial'. All this is carefully excluded when in the *Gorgias* he argues *against* the equivalence of pleasure with the good. 'Pleasures' in the *Protagoras* include most of what in modern speech comes under the heading of 'values', with at least as much emphasis on spiritual values as on any others.

So it turned out that on a nominally hard-headed and even individualistically utilitarian basis one can, with Socrates for a guide, achieve at least as high and altruistic a code of morals as most people are ever likely to aspire to. It was not, as we know, the sum total of his teaching, which included the belief that the real self is the rational and moral *psyche*, and that therefore the true meaning of 'benefiting oneself' was benefiting one's *psyche*, which could only be harmed by a life of unpunished wrongdoing. I would add myself that in calculating the future benefit or harm likely to accrue from a course of action, he would include the treatment of the soul by the divine power in a future life. All this was an inspiration to his followers, but not a sufficient answer to moral sceptics, because it left open the question of what was in fact the ultimate end and purpose of human life. Advocacy of 'the beneficial' as the criterion of action leaves undecided the nature of the benefit which the doer hopes to receive. Socrates, the reverse of a hedonist by nature, had used the hedonistic argument, pressed to a logical conclusion, to turn the tables on the hedonists themselves, but this expedient had its limitations. It left open the question: 'Beneficial for what?' A man might still take even physical pleasure as his ultimate aim, provided he proceeded with just enough caution to ensure that the pleasures of the day did not interfere with those of the morrow. Or he might choose power. The attainment of this may well necessitate, as the biography of some dictators shows, a curtailment of pleasures in the ordinary sense, even a life of strict personal asceticism. The hedonic calculus provides no answer to this, and if Socrates says, 'But you are ignoring the effect on your *psyche* and what will happen to it after death', communication breaks down, as Plato showed in the *Gorgias*; for what he relies on is simply not believed by the adversary, nor is there any means of convincing him of what is to some extent an act of faith. (Cf. *Theaet.* 177 a.)

In one way, then, the aim of Socrates's immediate followers and their schools was to give content to the 'good' which he had set them to seek but himself left undetermined. On the side of method, he bequeathed to them the negative virtues of elenchus or refutation, the dispeller of false pretensions to knowledge, and a sense of the supreme importance of agreeing upon the meaning of words, working towards definitions by means of dialectic or discussion. His insistence on definitions was noted by such widely different characters as Plato and Xenophon, and could lead, according to temperament, to a form of linguistic philosophy on the one hand and, on the other, to philosophic realism when Plato hypostatized the objects of definition and gave them independent existence.[1] Similarly his dialectical and elenctic skill could either be used constructively or lose itself in a somewhat barren eristic. In the eyes of Grote, Socrates himself was the supreme eristic,[2] and certainly his arguments, as they appear in Plato, were sometimes of a rather dubious nature; but at least his aim was not personal victory in a Sophistic contest, but the elucidation of the truth. Otherwise his life would have taken a different course, and he might have died a natural death.

As for the various answers which his pupils gave to the unanswered question of the good for man, one or two of these may be made the subject of a short concluding section before we turn, in the next volume, to the one who, whatever we may think of his faithfulness to their master's teaching, was one of the most universal thinkers of all time. The others, so far as our knowledge goes, seem to have seized on one aspect of Socrates and developed it at the expense of the rest. Plato, however much he may have built on to Socraticism in the way of positive doctrine, shows himself aware of its true spirit when his Socrates says that education does not mean handing over knowledge ready made, nor conferring on the mind a capacity that it did not have before, as sight might be given to a blind eye. The eye of the mind is not blind, but in most people it is looking the wrong way. To educate is to convert or turn it round so that it looks in the right direction (*Rep.* 518b–d).

[1] Perhaps the man who came nearest to the aims of Socrates in his search for the meanings of words was not a Greek at all, but a contemporary in a distant land who knew nothing of him. It was said of Confucius (*Analects*, 13.3) that when asked what he would do first if he were given charge of the administration of a country, he replied: 'It would certainly be to correct language' (World's Classics translation). His hearers were surprised, so he explained that if language is not correct, then what is said is not what is meant; if what is said is not what is meant, what ought to be done remains undone; if this remains undone, morals and arts deteriorate, justice goes astray, and the people stand about in helpless confusion. With this may be compared the words given to Socrates by Plato, *Phaedo*, 115e: 'You may be sure, my dear Cebes, that inaccurate language is not only in itself a mistake: it implants evil in men's souls' (trans. Bluck).

[2] See especially his *Plato*, III, 479, where he says that although the Megarians acquired the name of eristics, they 'cannot possibly have surpassed Socrates, and probably did not equal him, in the refutative elenchus . . . No one of these Megarics probably ever enunciated so sweeping a negative programme, or declared so emphatically his own inability to communicate positive instruction, as Socrates in the Platonic Apology. A person more thoroughly eristic than Socrates never lived.'

(12) THE IMMEDIATE FOLLOWERS OF SOCRATES

To know who were the closest followers or friends of Socrates, we can hardly do better than look at the list of those whom Plato is careful to mention by name in the *Phaedo* (59b) as present with him in his last hours in the prison, or whose absence Plato felt must be accounted for. Phaedo the narrator was said to be a native of Elis.[1] The Athenians present included Apollodorus, Critobulus and his father Crito, Hermogenes, Epigenes, Aeschines, Antisthenes, Ctesippus and Menexenus. From other city-states there were Simmias, Cebes and Phaedondes from Thebes, Euclides and Terpsion from Megara. Aristippus and Cleombrotus were said to be absent in Aegina, and Plato himself was ill.[2] Simmias and Cebes, disciples of the Pythagorean Philolaus, of course play a large part in the *Phaedo*'s discussions of immortality, and Crito, Hermogenes, Ctesippus, Menexenus and Euclides appear also in other Platonic dialogues. Echecrates of Phlius, to whom Phaedo is telling the story, was also a pupil of Philolaus, which adds to the Pythagorean atmosphere of the dialogue.[3] All except Aeschines, Phaedo, Ctesippus and Cleombrotus occur in Xenophon as companions of Socrates. Of some, little or nothing is known. Aeschines we have already met as a writer of Socratic dialogues (p. 11), but the only companions of whom we know anything as philosophers are Antisthenes, Euclides and Aristippus, each of whom was the reputed founder of a school which maintained the particular aspect of Socraticism that

[1] Grote (*Plato*, III, 503 note *m*) opined that the historical circumstances of his capture and sale into slavery at Athens (D.L. 2.105) could only be explained on the assumption that 'Eleian' was a mistake for 'Melian'—a suggestion which Mary Renault used to dramatic effect in her novel *The Last of the Wine*. See however von Fritz in *RE*, xxxviii. Halbb. 1538 (also for everything known or conjectured about Phaedo).

[2] I had never paid much attention to this (though, as Burnet says *ad loc.*, 'many strange things have been written' about it) until an able colleague in a different subject said in a letter that Plato's conduct in deserting Socrates in his last hours, however unwell he might be, was to him unforgivable. In the context it is certainly a remarkable statement, and it might be interesting to speculate on why Plato inserted it. To judge him unfavourably on it would be manifestly unfair, since not only do we owe our knowledge of the circumstance solely to Plato himself but the whole of the *Phaedo*, to say nothing of other dialogues, reveals beyond doubt the reality and strength of his devotion to Socrates. His feelings may have been so intense that he could not bear the prospect of witnessing the actual death of 'the best, wisest and most righteous man that he knew'. He could have made his farewell earlier to an understanding Socrates. But since we have absolutely nothing to go on but his own four words, all such guesses at motivation are idle.

[3] For references see Bluck's *Phaedo*, 34 ff.

appealed to him. Of the opinions of these men themselves, Plato must have been well aware, but their successors can only have been active from the time of Aristotle onwards. It seems appropriate therefore to say something here about those who, like Plato, were personal friends of Socrates, and to leave a full discussion of their 'schools'—the Cynic, Cyrenaic and Megarian—to a later stage.

Each one seems to have taken a single feature of the conversations, or personal example, of Socrates, and carried it to extremes as representing for him the 'true' spirit of his teaching, while ignoring the rest as irrelevant. Antisthenes has been considered in *The Sophists*.[1] For him what mattered about Socrates was that he was indifferent to worldly possessions and pleasures and proclaimed the supremacy of virtue. Following his example, Diogenes and the Cynics adopted an extreme asceticism and cult of poverty, with the ragged cloak,[2] staff and beggar's wallet as their badge together with a complete disregard of appearances and (perhaps a curious corollary of the cult of virtue) a deliberate flouting of accepted standards of decency in public behaviour. Not for them the occasional careful toilet in compliment to a friend and host, nor the pleasures of the *symposion* into which Socrates could throw himself with wholehearted enjoyment.

At the opposite extreme, at least on a superficial view, was *Aristippus*. Well might St Augustine marvel that these 'two noble philosophers, both of them in Athens and both Socratics, should find the meaning of life in such different, indeed irreconcilable goals' (*Civ. Dei*, 18.41). Aristippus, a native of Cyrene (whence the name of his followers, Cyrenaics), was said to have been brought to Athens by the fame of Socrates. He taught as a Sophist, the first of Socrates's pupils, it was said, to charge fees, and made sufficient reputation to be invited to the court of Dionysius[3] where he was said to have much enjoyed the luxurious life. An anecdote told by Diogenes Laertius (2.83) makes

---

[1] See especially pp. 304–11.

[2] This at least was Socratic. See p. 69 with n. 2 above. But Socrates wore it not from pride, but only because he had more important things than a new cloak to think about. His reported rebuke to Antisthenes (D.L. 2.36), who adjusted his cloak to show the rents, is true to character: 'I can see your vanity through your cloak.'

[3] No doubt the elder, as a scholiast on Lucian says (fr. 37 B Mannebach). See Grote (reference in next note).

him older than the Socratic Aeschines. Probably he was a little older than Plato, and Diodorus (15.76) speaks of him as still alive in 366. It may be assumed that he returned to Cyrene to end his days, where his daughter Arētē and grandson Aristippus (the 'mother-taught'), together with other Cyreneans, developed his hedonistic views and became known as the Cyrenaic school.[1]

Most of the evidence for his views is very late, and does not always distinguish clearly between Aristippus himself and later modifications by his followers, who after Epicurus were concerned to maintain certain differences from the rival conception of hedonism.[2] We also encounter him, however, in Xenophon and Aristotle, who are free from the possibility of such confusion, and with whom therefore we must start. In a passage of the *Metaphysics* Aristotle is arguing that not all forms of cause are to be looked for in every subject, e.g. in unchangeable things like the objects of mathematics there is no place for a cause of motion nor for goodness as a principle. He continues (996a29):

Therefore in mathematics nothing is proved by this kind of cause, nor is any demonstration made on the grounds that so-and-so is better or worse. Nothing of this kind is ever mentioned at all. For this reason certain Sophists, for instance Aristippus, disparaged mathematics because the other arts, even the vulgar ones like carpentry and cobbling, spoke always in terms of better or worse, whereas mathematics took no account of good and bad.[3]

According to Aristotle's Greek commentator, Aristippus went to the length of making this an argument for the non-existence of the objects

---

[1] For the above details about Aristippus see D.L. 65 f. etc. (frr. 1–8 Mannebach), and on his relations with Dionysius I, Grote's *Plato*, III, 549 note s. Mannebach (*A. et Cyr. Frr.* 89) would put the date of his death at c. 355. For Arētē and Aristippus Μητροδίδακτος D.L. 2.72 and 83, Aristocles (second century A.D.) *ap.* Eus. *P.E.* 14.18.

[2] C. J. Classen in *Hermes* 1958 aims at separating Aristippus from the Cyrenaics, but perhaps goes too far. It is difficult to maintain, on whatever grounds, that when D. L. describes the Cyrenaics at 2.86 as οἱ ἐπὶ τῆς ἀγωγῆς τῆς 'Αριστίππου μείναντες this *cannot* be interpreted as intended to mean that they kept to the teaching of Aristippus (p. 184). Mannebach (*A. et Cyr. Frr.* 86) says only that the word ἀγωγή signifies nothing more definite than 'vivendi quandam aut philosophandi rationem in universum'. Though Cyrenaicism as a whole is being reserved for later treatment, readers may like to have the following references to some of the literature on them and Aristippus. Texts are collected and commented on by E. Mannebach, *A. et Cyr. Frr.* (1961) and G. Giannantoni, *I Cirenaici* (1958). (My own references are to Mannebach's ed.) Otherwise one might select Grote's account in his *Plato*, III, 530–60, and Stenzel's article *Kyrenaiker* in the *RE*. (Natorp's on Aristippus is somewhat outdated.)

[3] These critics of mathematics occur again, unnamed, at 1078a33. The only other mention of Aristippus in Aristotle concerns his rebuke to Plato and has already been mentioned (p. 36, n. 2).

of mathematics, on the premise that 'everything that exists works for some good or fine end'.[1] He may well have claimed to find the germ of this curious ontological argument in Socrates, to judge from passages like Plato, *Rep.* 352 d ff.

We have already looked (pp. 143 f.) at conversations between Socrates and Aristippus in Xenophon in which Socrates avoided a trap by insisting on the relativity of 'good' to the particular end in view. On another occasion (*Mem.* 2. 1) Socrates tried to pin Aristippus down to a choice of two types of life. There are those fit to govern others, who must have trained themselves to be courageous, enduring of hardships, physically fit and in full command of their appetites; and those lacking in these qualities, who are fit only to be subject to the rule of others, liable at any time to be robbed, enslaved or subjected to any other indignity or suffering. Aristippus replied that neither rule nor slavery appealed to him, but in his opinion there was a third, middle way: the road to happiness lay through freedom, which was certainly not the lot of a ruler or commander, with all the risks and hard work that it entailed. He wished only to pass through life as easily and pleasantly as possible, and thought that he could achieve this by not identifying himself with any particular state but being 'everywhere an alien (*xenos*)'.[2] It is in criticism of this predilection for the life of ease and pleasure that Socrates repeats the allegory of Prodicus about the choice of Heracles (*The Sophists*, pp. 277 f.).

We need not here go into the question (not always very meaningful) whether the companion of Socrates or his grandson of the same name should be regarded as the founder of the Cyrenaic school. Different views have been held, and one can hardly go beyond the judicious verdict of Mannebach (p. 88) that the grandson built the doctrine on foundations laid by his grandfather. (But see p. 174, n. 1 below.) So far as the sources allow us to differentiate between Aristippus and later

---

[1] Pseudo-Alex. *In Metaph.* 1078a31, fr. 154 A in M. εἰ γὰρ πᾶν, φησὶν ὁ ᾿Α., ὃν ἀγαθοῦ ἢ καλοῦ ἕνεκεν ἐργάζεται, τὰ δὲ μαθηματικὰ οὔτε καλοῦ οὔτε ἀγαθοῦ στοχάζεται, τὰ μαθηματικὰ ἄρα οὔκ εἰσιν.

[2] Aristippus is sometimes cited as the originator of the Cynic and Stoic κοσμοπολίτης. Perhaps the practical effect was much the same, but in form at least there is a difference between belonging everywhere and belonging nowhere, being πολίτης and being ξένος. Antisthenes, if not his followers, is actually said to have been opposed to Aristippus (as in most other things) in believing that the wise man ought to take part in government (Aug. *Civ. Dei*, 18.41, Aristippus fr. 231 M.).

modifications of his views, they supplement but do not contradict the information in Xenophon and Aristotle. Much is in the form of anecdote and repartee, including the kind of floating saying that is attributed to others also. They show that mixture of a kind of cockney wit with sheer boorish rudeness which also characterized Diogenes the Cynic. The one thing that some of Socrates's younger friends do not seem to have learned from him is urbanity, and if Aristippus really criticized an expression of Plato's because 'Socrates never spoke like that' (p. 36, n. 2 above), it was a case of pot and kettle if not of mote and beam. At the court of Dionysius he seems to have had the position of the licensed jester and parasite who in medieval times could speak to the king with an effrontery that would not be tolerated in an ordinary courtier. One example will suffice. When he asked for money Dionysius replied: 'But you said the wise man would never be in want.' 'Give me the money and then we will go into that.' Dionysius gave it, whereupon Aristippus replied, 'You see, I am not in want'.[1] He is generally represented as living a life of luxury and unrestrained pleasure, fond of rich food, drink, fine clothes, scents and women (frr. 72–83). As to ownership of wealth and possessions, he is said on the one hand to have asserted that, unlike shoes, one's property could never be too large for comfort (Stobaeus, fr. 67), and on the other to have advised his friends to limit their possessions to what they could save, with their own lives, from a shipwreck (fr. 9 A, B, D and E). No doubt he saw the advantage of enjoying the bounty of a tyrant rather than undergoing the toil of amassing one's own fortune and the responsibilities of looking after it. He was also said to have accepted the risks involved in such a course, and while he enjoyed wearing fine purple, to be willing to put up with rags if he had to (frr. 30–4). One pleasant story about him, told by a commentator on Horace, is reminiscent of Socrates's rebuke to Antisthenes (p. 170, n. 2 above). One day at the baths he took Diogenes's old cloak and left his own purple one behind. Diogenes followed him out without it, demanding the return of his own, whereat Aristippus chided him for caring so much about his reputation that he would rather go cold than put on a purple cloak (fr. 32c).

[1] D.L. 2.82, fr. 45 M. The story has more point in the Greek, where ἀπορεῖν means both to be in want and to be at a loss.

Diogenes Laertius (2.83–5) gives a long list of titles of writings by Aristippus, which lends some colour to Grote's suspicions of those who claim that he was a mere voluptuary, and that anything like a doctrine came from his grandson.[1] They may however have consisted largely of isolated apophthegms. That consideration apart, from the scattered late sources one may reasonably credit Aristippus the Socratic with the following views. Only practical principles of conduct should be studied, not mathematics (as we have seen) nor the physical world, for it was not knowable, nor, if it were, would the knowledge serve any useful purpose (fr. 145). Pleasure was the end at which the *psyche* should aim (frr. 156, 157, 161), and this hedonism was of the strictest sort. Pleasure was confined to bodily pleasure (frr. 181–3) and consequently to the pleasure of the moment: neither the anticipation of future nor the recollection of past pleasures could be called pleasure (frr. 207–9: in Mannebach's opinion Aelian in fr. 208 is beyond doubt preserving Aristippus's own words). Such pleasures of course are in any case mental rather than physical, but Aristippus had another reason, based on his theory that pleasure and pain were motions, the one smooth and the other rough, or, as it is also put, 'he showed that the *telos* (end or aim, i.e. in his case pleasure) is smooth motion spreading to the senses' (frr. 193 and following). These motions, though caused by and therefore contemporary with the bodily events, are communicated to the *psyche* (otherwise, presumably, we could not be conscious of them), and 'the motion of the *psyche* dies away with time' (fr. 209). It was in this glorification of bodily pleasures and insistence that pleasure consisted in motion that the followers of Aristippus were most at odds with the hedonism of Epicurus, who exalted the pleasures of the mind and the static or stable pleasures equated simply with absence of pain.

Like his teacher Socrates, Aristippus believed that a man should be

---

[1] Grote, *Plato*, III, 549 note *r*. The case for the younger Aristippus as founder of the school rests on a single statement of Aristocles (*ap.* Eus. *P.E.* 14.18, divided in M. between frr. 155, 163 and 201) that the elder said nothing clear about the τέλος but only that the substance of happiness lay potentially in pleasure. The younger σαφῶς ὡρίσατο τὸ τέλος εἶναι τὸ ἡδέως ζῆν, ἡδονὴν ἐντάττων τὴν κατὰ κίνησιν. This is not much to go on, especially as (*a*) Aristocles has just referred to the elder Aristippus as ὁ τὴν καλουμένην Κυρηναϊκὴν συστησάμενος αἵρεσιν, and (*b*) the doctrine that pleasure is a motion is one of the few that can with some confidence be ascribed to the elder. See Mannebach's note to fr. 193. Other late testimonies definitely refer to the Socratic Aristippus as founder of the school. See frr. 125, 126 A–C, 132 *et al.* On the existence and probable nature of Aristippus's writings see Mannebach on fr. 121, pp. 76ff.

master of himself, and never allow himself to be mastered, or overcome, by pleasures. But whereas to Socrates this seemed to entail of necessity the leading of a temperate life, the pupil drew no such conclusion. His view as reported (fr. 45, from Stobaeus) was that to be the master of pleasures meant not to refrain from them but to enjoy them without being at their mercy, just as to be master of a ship or a horse does not mean to make no use of it but to guide it where one will. For all his purple and his scents, he could claim that he had as much self-control as Diogenes, for just as, if a man had a body impervious to fire, he could safely commit himself to the flames of Etna, so the man with the proper attitude to pleasure could plunge into it without being burned or wasted (fr. 56).[1] Ancient writers loved to quote his retort on being reproached for his association with the famous courtesan Lais: 'I possess Lais, she does not possess me' (frr. 57 A–G). In conformity with this he enjoyed in full measure the pleasures that were at hand or easily procurable, but saw no reason to exert himself to gain pleasures the acquisition of which involved hard work or effort (frr. 54 A and B).

In spite of some modern opinion, it is scarcely rash to attribute also to Aristippus a sceptical theory of knowledge which agrees well with the ethic of immediate sensual pleasure to which, in his eyes, it must have been subordinate.[2] It is summed up in the sentence 'only of the

---

[1] One is reminded of the late J. L. Austin's comment on taking two portions of a favourite sweet of which there are only enough portions to allow one for each of the company: 'I am tempted to help myself to two segments and do so, thus succumbing to temptation ... But do I lose control of myself? ... Not a bit of it. We often succumb to temptation with calm and even with finesse.' This argument, from his Presidential Address to the Aristotelian Society (1956, pp. 24f.), is quoted and criticized by Gellner in *Words and Things* (Pelican ed. 1968), 242.

[2] To be strict, Eusebius attributed it to οἱ κατ' Ἀ. (or κατ' Ἀ. τὸν Κυρηναῖον) λέγοντες, and Aristocles to ἔνιοι τῶν ἐκ τῆς Κυρήνης (frr. 211 A and B, 212). Cicero and Sextus (frr. 213 A–C, 217) speak of the Cyrenaics, and D.L. (2.92) of 'those who maintained the ἀγωγή of Aristippus (*sc.* the Socratic) and were called Cyrenaics'. In another place (fr. 210) Aristocles refers a statement of similar meaning to the grandson, but on the difficulty of distinguishing the two from this source see p. 174, n. 1. Judging by what has been seen of them already, Eusebius and his source Aristocles, when they use the name Aristippus unqualified, are more likely to have meant the Socratic than the Μητροδίδακτος. Nevertheless what I have said above goes against the most recent scholarship. Mannebach (pp. 114–17) conjectures that the sceptical theory of knowledge was taught by the younger Aristippus, who however did not originate it but learned it from Pyrrho, an idea which, as he frankly notes, Pohlenz regarded as 'not within the bounds of probability'. The trouble is that supporters of the opposite view have relied heavily on a belief that certain passages in Plato are directed against Aristippus, a belief which, not being susceptible of proof, is not taken into account here. If certainty is impossible, at least the sceptical theory is in complete harmony with Aristippus's form of hedonism and was probably set forth in some of his fairly numerous writings.

feelings can we be certain'.[1] Sextus (*Math.* 7.190ff., fr. 217), after remarking that the Cyrenaic school, like the Platonic, appears to have had its origin in the teaching of Socrates, explains their view thus. We apprehend without possibility of error our own feelings, affections or sensations, but can know nothing of their causes. We can state incontrovertibly that we have a sensation of sweetness or whiteness but not that this sensation is produced by an object which is sweet or white. 'The affection which takes place in us reveals to us nothing more than itself.' Both he and Plutarch (*Adv. Col.* 1120bff., fr. 218) adduce in this connexion the evidence of pathological states in which honey can produce a sensation of bitterness or an affected eye make everything appear tinged with red, and Sextus adds hallucinations. The affections or sensations are also described (by Cicero, see fr. 213 A) as 'interior motions' (or disturbances, *permotiones intimae*). The theory at once reminds us of Protagoras, and Eusebius (fr. 211 A) speaks of 'those who follow Aristippus in saying that only the feelings convey certainty, and again the followers of Metrodorus and Protagoras who say that one must trust nothing but the bodily sensations'. This does not suggest any great difference,[2] nor is it accurate, seeing that Protagoras applied the same canon to moral concepts like justice (*The Sophists*, pp. 171 ff.). Cicero (*Ac. pr.* 2.46.142, fr. 213 A) tried to distinguish them in this way: 'The judgment of Protagoras is one thing, that that which appears to each man is true for him, and that of the Cyrenaics another, who think that nothing can be judged except the interior motions.' In so far as the tradition can be relied on, the difference amounts to this, that Aristippus and the Cyrenaics were epistemologically more sceptical than Protagoras (i.e. they thought that even less could be known), but ontologically less so, in that they would not go all the way with him in denying the existence of a reality outside ourselves. We simply could not say whether there was one or, if there was, what it was like. This slight modification of Protagoras's doctrine is very likely to have

---

[1] μόνα τὰ πάθη καταληπτά, frr. 211 A and B, 212, and in various paraphrases in the rest of frr. 211–18. πάθη is a wider word than αἰσθήσεις, including (and in some contexts confined to) the emotions, but ancient explanations of the doctrine show it to have rested primarily on sensation for its credibility.

[2] Though admittedly Eusebius later (14.19) quotes Aristocles as calling Metrodorus and Protagoras together τοὺς τὴν ἐναντίαν βαδίζοντας. Protagoras surely differed more from Metrodorus than from Aristippus.

been the work of a Socratic of the generation following Protagoras himself.[1]

Two further notes on Aristippus may be quoted from our late sources. The first (rather dubious perhaps) suggests that he had a Prodicean interest in differentiating between words of similar meaning or form.[2] The second (fr. 227) states that he called it ridiculous to pray and make requests to the divinity: doctors, he said, do not give food or drink to a sick man when he asks for it, but when it is good for him.

All this shows that, although ending up with such different conclusions, especially moral, Aristippus had listened to Socrates and remembered much of what he heard. In his scepticism he might claim that he was only carrying out the Socratic advice to be aware of his own ignorance. Like Socrates he eschewed political activity, though Socrates, far from being 'everywhere an alien', was heart and soul a citizen of Athens and loyal to her laws. Like Socrates too he was interested first and foremost in practical living and deprecated carrying mathematical and physical studies beyond the point at which they ceased to serve practical ends. Themistius was right in numbering him among 'the genuine band of Socrates' in so far as he kept to the study of good and evil and human happiness. (See fr. 143 in M.) Though his chosen goal was different, he echoed Socratic language in maintaining that the *psyche had* its goal or distinctive aim (τέλος τῆς ψυχῆς, fr. 156). With him also the teleological hypothesis applied not only to man but to all existing things, and he used the analogy of the humbler creative occupations to support it. His attitude to prayer went one stage further than Socrates, but is based on his teaching that since the

[1] I.e. Aristippus. Grote (*Plato*, III, 560) thought his doctrine substantially the same as the 'man the measure' of Protagoras, and indeed the difference is not great. Zeller (*Ph. d. Gr.* 350f.) granted that in asserting the subjectivity of all our impressions the two are identical, but saw a difference which I confess I do not find at all clear. The German runs: 'Ihre [*sc.* the Cyrenaics'] Ansicht unterscheidet sich von der seinigen nur dadurch, dass dieselben bestimmter auf die Empfindung unserer Zustände zurückführen, in dieser, nicht in der durch die aüsseren Sinne vermittelten Wahrnehmung, das ursprünglich Gegebene suchen.' He adds in a note that both Cicero and Eusebius (i.e. Aristocles) exaggerate the difference. But today the most favoured view is probably Mannebach's (p. 114) that it 'neither can be demonstrated nor is even probable' that the Cyrenaics were following in Protagoras's footsteps. Here again the argument has been confused by an understandable opposition to those who have tried to prove the contrary by reading Aristippus into Plato.

[2] Frr. 22 A and B. The example given is θάρσος and θράσος.

gods know what is good for us we ought not to pray for specific gifts (Xen. *Mem.* 1.3.2). As for his hedonism, which provides such a contrast both to Socrates's life and to the spirit of his teaching, we must always remember, first that Socrates did not himself answer his own question about the ultimate aim of human life and secondly that, as I have tried to show, what he did say lent itself certainly to a utilitarian, and even to a hedonistic, interpretation. Stenzel put it (*RE*, 2. Reihe, v. Halbb.887) that the Cyrenaic doctrine of pleasure is not so much (as it had been called) a polar reversal of the Socratic ethic as a narrowing to the individual of a basic Socratic tenet. It might be more accurate to say that though both men had the individual in mind Aristippus left out much of what Socrates said about the nature of the *psyche* and the kind of conduct which would benefit it.

Finally, as justification for giving so much space to one who, it may be thought, exists only on the margin of philosophy, we have Plato. Plato never names Aristippus, and it would be dangerous to follow the older critics in using certain of his dialogues as evidence for Aristippus's views, on the assumption that he is necessarily the target of criticism. But the two were contemporaries and acquaintances, and when one thinks that in the *Theaetetus* Plato criticizes a sceptical theory of knowledge which certainly has affinities with the Cyrenaic, and that the *Philebus* is wholly devoted to discussion of the place of pleasure in the good life, raising such questions as whether pleasure is of the body or the soul, the status of pleasures of anticipation and memory, the relation of pleasure to movement and to the neutral state of absence of pain, it would be equally rash to exclude the possibility that he is replying to a fellow-pupil of Socrates who must have seemed to him to have gone wildly astray. The *Philebus* is universally, and with good reason, agreed to be one of Plato's latest dialogues, belonging to a period in which Socrates is made to hand over the whole conduct of a dialogue to another or else is absent altogether. Yet in the *Philebus* he is back again in the centre of the picture, directing the whole conversation. These are questions to consider when we come to Plato. But the possibility that he is sometimes attacking Aristippus must certainly not be denied *a priori* if we want to see his philosophy, as we should, as arising from the debates that raged in his own time, and in response to which he formulated his problems and produced his own answer to the Socratic question: What is the ultimate aim of human life?

Euclides of Megara (best called by the full Greek form of his name to avoid confusion with his more famous namesake), besides being mentioned by Plato as present during the last hours of Socrates, is made to narrate the conversation which forms the main part of the *Theaetetus*.[1] If a story of Gellius can be relied on (*Noct. Att.* 6.10), his acquaintance with Socrates went back to the Megarian Decree of 432, and the evidence of the *Theaetetus* shows him to have been still alive when Theaetetus was brought back from Corinth dying of wounds and dysentery. This must have been in 369 when Euclides was an old man of eighty or more.[2] After the death of Socrates, Plato and some of his other companions left Athens to stay for a while with Euclides at Megara,[3] and Megara, together with Thebes (or Boeotia) the home of Simmias and Cebes, is mentioned in *Crito* (53b) and *Phaedo* (99a) as a place in which Socrates himself could have found refuge had he chosen to evade the sentence of the Athenians. It is evident therefore that Euclides was an intimate member of the Socratic circle. As to his teaching we are even more at a disadvantage than with Aristippus. Plato never mentions him in a philosophical context, and Aristotle never assigns a doctrine to him by name, but speaks only of 'the Megarians', so that we have to rely solely on much later sources. The names of a number of his pupils are on record, as well as of later members of the school.[4] Among them was Eubulides, famous as the author of certain logical puzzles, including one which has troubled philosophers down to the present century: that, namely, which asks whether the man who says 'I am lying' is speaking the truth or not.

[1] More accurately, he orders a slave to read out the account of it which he had written earlier with the aid of notes made at the time, checked and supplemented by Socrates. Cf. pp. 23 f. above.

[2] He need not have been much older, since like other youths he could well have been attracted into the circle of Socrates at the age of 18 or little more. It has been disputed at which of two battles fought between Athens and Corinth in the manhood of Theaetetus he met his fate, that of 394 or that of 369, but the question was settled beyond reasonable doubt by Eva Sachs, in her monograph *De Theaeteto*, pp. 22 ff. See also von Fritz in *RE*, 2. Reihe, x. Halbb. 1351 f.

[3] D.L. (2.106 and 3.6) states this on the excellent authority of Hermodorus, a friend or pupil (ἑταῖρος) of Plato who wrote a book about him (Simpl. *Phys.* 247.33, 256.32). He added that Plato's age at the time was 28. On the question of the 'tyrants', fear of whom drove Plato and his friends to take this course, see Zeller, *Ph. d. Gr.* 402 n. 2.

[4] For these see e.g. Zeller, *Ph. d. Gr.* 246–8, and cf. *The Sophists*, p. 217.

His date is roughly indicated by the facts that he is said to have been a teacher of Demosthenes and to have made personal attacks on Aristotle.[1] 'The Megarians' as a school of thought are first mentioned in Aristotle, and may not have been recognized as such before his time.[2] It seems certain that they carried philosophy further than Euclides, especially in the development of logic, and it would therefore be unsafe to hold him responsible for a doctrine simply on the ground that it was called 'Megarian'. Six dialogues were ascribed to him (they are named in D.L. 2.108), but their genuineness was doubted by Panaetius the Stoic (*ibid.* 64).

Only one positive doctrine can be safely credited to Euclides, namely the unity of the good. The testimonies are:

(i) Cicero, *Ac. pr.* 2.42.129. Cicero begins somewhat oddly by saying that, 'as I have read', the *princeps* of the *Megaricorum nobilis disciplina* was Xenophanes, followed by Parmenides and Zeno. 'Then', he continues, 'came Euclides, a disciple of Socrates from Megara, after whom they were called Megarians. He said that that alone was good which was one, all alike, and always the same.'

(ii) D.L. 2.106: 'He declared that the good was one, though called by many names, sometimes wisdom, sometimes God, and again mind (*nous*) and so on. Things opposed to the good he rejected, saying that they did not exist.'

(iii) With these one may compare a passage from the history of philosophy of Aristocles quoted by Eusebius (*P.E.* 14.17), which speaks only of the Megarians without mentioning Euclides by name. He ranks them with those who condemned the senses and claimed that only reason was to be trusted. 'So said, in earlier times, Xenophanes, Parmenides, Zeno and Melissus, and later the followers of Stilpo and the Megarians. For this reason the last-named said that what is is one and anything else does not exist,[3] and that nothing comes into being or is destroyed or undergoes any movement whatever.'

[1] On the paradoxes of Eubulides see W. and M. Kneale, *Dev. of Logic*, 114 (and their index *s.v.* 'liar, the' for later attempts to solve it), and Grote, *Plato*, III, 482f. with note *o*. His attacks on Aristotle are mentioned by D.L. 2.108, and Aristocles *ap.* Eus. *P.E.* 15.2, and his connexion with Demosthenes by D.L. *ibid.* and [Plut.] *Vit. orat.* 845c.

[2] *Metaph.* 1046b29. Cf. the remarks of Taylor, *VS*, 19 n. 2.

[3] This is the sense whatever the exact reading, but the reading in Heinichen's (1842) and Gifford's (1903) editions, καὶ τὸ ἕτερον μὴ εἶναι, yields it much more naturally than καὶ τὸ μὴ ὂν ἕτερον εἶναι (Zeller, *Ph. d. Gr.* 261 n. 2), i.e. 'and the non-existent is something else'.

There was thus a tradition, represented by Cicero and Aristocles, which classified the Megarian as a continuation of the Eleatic school. Aristocles has assimilated it wholly to Parmenides by confining its basic dogma to the unity of being, without mention of the good. Nor does he so much as mention Socrates as an influence. Cicero and Diogenes, however, who profess to be speaking of Euclides in person, do bring in his association with Socrates, and the fact that for him the 'one being' was 'the good'. The tendency of older scholarship was to lay stress on the Eleatic element and assume that Euclides had been impressed by Parmenidean arguments before he met Socrates;[1] but the one doctrine which can be credited to him with certainty suggests that his approach was different from the Eleatic.[2] Both were agreed on the unity of what exists, and in this Euclides no doubt owed something to Parmenides; but the Eleatic was a doctrine of being, pure and simple, whereas Euclides, as a follower of Socrates, was concerned with the nature of the good. Assuming that the statement in Diogenes most fully represents his view (for it includes Cicero's version and also accounts for the doctrine of his followers that only one thing exists), what he said about the good was twofold: it is a unity though called by many names, and what is opposed to it—i.e. evil—has no existence. The first is a legitimate deduction from the teaching of Socrates that all virtue, or goodness, can be reduced to the one thing, wisdom or knowledge. Temperance, justice, courage, quickness of mind, memory, and a noble heart, no less than external advantages such as health, strength, physical beauty and wealth—all these (he says in the *Meno*) may be harmful as well as beneficial unless they are allied to, and guided by, knowledge and good sense. But it was agreed that the term 'goodness' ought only to be applied to that which always benefits, never harms, and this one unfailingly beneficial factor turns out to be wisdom.[3]

---

[1] E.g. Natorp, *RE*, VI, 1001; Zeller, *Ph. d. Gr.* 245 n. 3; Robin, *Greek Thought* (Eng. ed. of 1928), 162: 'That he was first attached to the principles of Eleaticism is certain.' If there is anything in the story that he was already consorting with Socrates in 432, this is unlikely.

[2] Cf. von Fritz in *RE*, Suppl. V, 707 ff., to whose discussion my own remarks are much indebted. He calls it the *Grunddogma*, and there is justice in Grote's remark (*Plato*, III, 475) that 'this one doctrine [*sc.* the identity of τὸ ἕν with τὸ ἀγαθόν] is all that we know about Euclides: what consequences he derived from it, or whether any, we do not know'.

[3] *Meno*, 87 e ff. In using terms like knowledge, wisdom and good sense interchangeably, I am only following Socrates's example, who refers to goodness, almost in the same breath, as

Since Socrates was also a devout theist, who believed that God alone had full knowledge of what was good for man, Euclides could suppose that he was still carrying on the spirit of his master's teaching when he said that God too was but another name for the goodness which was knowledge.

In the *Republic* (505 b–c) Plato, through the mouth of Socrates, remarks on the absurdity of those who say that the good is knowledge, and when asked 'Knowledge of what?' can only reply 'Of the good'. This has been thought to be a criticism of Euclides,[1] though the fact that knowledge was for him one of the 'many names' applied to the good hardly justifies the inference. It is in fact a criticism that could with some justice be brought against Socrates himself, and it is followed very shortly by a repetition on Glaucon's part of the familiar complaint that Socrates always refuses to give a positive answer when asked whether goodness is knowledge or pleasure or anything else. After yet another protestation of his own ignorance, and the wrongfulness of talking as if one knows what one does not, he yields to pressure and undertakes to describe, not the good itself (that would be too ambitious), but something that he 'imagines to be the offspring of the good and to resemble it closely'. This turns out to be the sun, and we now have the famous disquisition on the degrees of knowledge, intelligibility and being under the images of the sun, divided line and cave, in the course of which 'the good' is described (at 509b) as 'not identical with being (reality), but beyond and superior to it'. In other words, when the Platonic Socrates is persuaded or bullied into formulating a positive doctrine, we can be sure that we owe it to Plato himself, though he has sufficient recollection of the real Socrates, and sufficient

ἐπιστήμη, φρόνησις and νοῦς; and it will be noticed that the latter two are among the names which according to Euclides are given to the good. Thompson in his *Meno* says that φρόνησις is the mental faculty correlative to ἐπιστήμη, but it too could be used with a dependent genitive (φ. ἀγαθοῦ, *Rep.* 505 b and c), where the only possible English equivalent is 'knowledge'. Nevertheless I think there is a nuance of difference. The knowledge Socrates has in mind is not ἐπιστήμη as commonly used, to mean often no more than technical know-how. It is that 'knowledge of what is and is not to be feared' (*Prot.* 360 d) which sees pain or death as a lesser evil than dishonourable conduct, and this better deserves the name of insight or wisdom which φρόνησις also conveyed.

[1] E.g. by Zeller, *Ph. d. Gr.* 260 n. 1. Cf. Stenzel in *RE*, 2. Reihe, v. Halbb. 876 f. Dümmler and others have thought of the ubiquitous Antisthenes. See Adam *ad loc.*: in his opinion the criticism applies, and was intended to apply, to Plato himself and other disciples of Socrates.

dramatic sense, to make him preface it with the warning that he can only offer an opinion, that unsubstantiated opinion is ugly and blind, and that he will probably make a fool of himself (506 c–d).

The doctrine of Euclides, though we cannot reconstruct it fully, evidently resembled Plato's in so far as it elevated the good to the status of an eternal and unchanging metaphysical principle, but coming more deeply and immediately under Eleatic influence he equated it directly with the One Being of Parmenides and declared that it alone could be said to exist. The doctrine of a plurality of transcendently existing Forms was Plato's own. Even in the *Republic*, however, the good is made superior to the other Forms (objects of knowledge), which are said to owe to it in some unspecified way both their intelligibility and their existence (509 b); and it appears from Aristotle that in his later years Plato equated it with unity ('the One'), to which he granted a higher grade of reality than to the Forms. The Forms themselves were now said, in Aristotle's terms, to have a 'material' as well as a formal component, owing their existence to the combination of the One with the great-and-small; that is, to the imposition of unity and limit on an indefinite continuum.[1] At this later stage the One is itself 'being' or 'existence' (οὐσία), whereas in the *Republic* the single Form of good was explicitly said to be 'not being but beyond being'. In view of this passage in the first book of Aristotle's *Metaphysics*, another in the last book (1091 b 13) which mentions no names is regularly referred to Plato by commentators. It runs: 'Of those who maintain the existence of the unchangeable substances, some identify absolute unity with absolute goodness, but thought that its substance lay chiefly in its unity.'[2] So far as our information from Cicero and Diogenes takes us, this could be a pretty accurate statement of the position of Euclides.[3] Both he and Plato thought deeply about the ontological difficulties bequeathed by Parmenides, and probably had many a friendly discussion about the nature of being and unity and their

---

[1] Ar. *Metaph.* 987 b 20. 'Material' is of course used in the Aristotelian sense, not in that of corporeality.

[2] Literally, they 'say the One itself is the Good itself, but thought that its substance was chiefly the one'.

[3] I do not think (though others may) that the use of the plural, τὰς ἀκινήτους οὐσίας, is an objection to this, especially since οἱ μέν indicates that Aristotle intended the phrase to embrace a wide class of which he is only mentioning a part.

relation to the good which had been the object of Socrates's unending search. No true pupil of Socrates could doubt that it existed, but to more metaphysical natures than his the doctrine of the unity of being created a serious problem.

Parmenides had said that besides the One Being nothing existed, Euclides that nothing existed besides the One Good or, to follow our sources more exactly, nothing *opposed* to it; that is, evil was non-existent. Von Fritz has pointed out (*RE*, Suppl. v, 716) that even this can be seen as a modification of Socratic teaching brought about by turning it (under Eleatic influence) into speculative theory. The corollary of 'virtue is knowledge' is that wickedness is error, for no one knowingly and willingly chooses to do wrong. This robs evil of any status as a positive power opposed to goodness and reduces it to mere intellectual inadequacy or absence of knowledge or, as von Fritz puts it, a 'logical nothing'. Unfortunately however we have no clue to the arguments by which Euclides arrived at his conclusion.

In saying that the good was one, and that what was opposed to the good did not exist, was Euclides maintaining a strict Parmenidean monism, only substituting 'good' for 'being' as the one thing that exists? In view of the scantiness of our information an answer to this question must be partly speculative, but is perhaps worth attempting. I have just hinted at the possibility that 'nothing *opposed* to the good' may not be the same as 'nothing *but* the good', which excludes a neutral class. Again, L. Robin may have been on the right lines in suggesting an analogy with the physical atomism of Leucippus and Democritus.[1] These thought that they were adhering to the Parmenidean canon of the unity of being by equating it with 'the solid' (or 'the full'), irrespective of the fact that this one being was represented by millions of tiny particles dispersed through space (which was 'non-being'). They were one in substance, and only 'the solid' existed. Similarly, in what Robin called a 'logical atomism', the one substance could be 'the good', single, homogeneous and unchanging, but could be dispersed through a plurality of particular things or living creatures as *their*

---

[1] *Gr. Thought*, 163. Since I do not find Robin's language altogether clear (particularly his use of the word 'essences'), I cannot claim to be reproducing his interpretation. I can only say that his comparison with atomism provided a starting-point for my own reconstruction, the conjectural nature of which must be admitted.

substance. To it they would owe their being, as the Forms did for Plato. In spite of differences caused by the interposition of the equally unchanging Forms between the Form of the Good and the changing particulars in the sensible world of becoming, the equation of existence with goodness (what is best is most fully real) would be a fundamental mark of resemblance between the ways in which these two men developed their common inheritance from Socrates.

In addition to his positive doctrine of the good as uniquely existent, two matters of philosophic method are recorded for Euclides by Diogenes (2.107).

(i) He attacked a proof by opposing its conclusions, not its premises. This has reminded scholars, not unreasonably, of the dialectical method of Zeno of Elea,[1] thus providing some further evidence of Eleatic influence on Euclides. The method, usually involving the *reductio ad absurdum* of an opponent's view, was apt to generate heat and be stigmatized as eristic, whence perhaps the anecdote (D.L. 2.30) that Socrates, observing his fondness for eristic arguments, once said to him, 'You will be able to get on with Sophists, Euclides, but not with men'.

(ii) He rejected the argument from parallel cases. The component cases, he said, must be either similar or dissimilar. If they are similar, it is better to deal with the original case itself rather than what resembles it; if dissimilar, the comparison is irrelevant.[2] Here Euclides dares to criticize the use of analogy to which Socrates himself was so much addicted. In interpreting him, we must bear in mind that the word (ὅμοιος) translated 'similar' was ambiguous in Greek, wavering in meaning between similarity and complete identity.[3] If the subject of the argument and the other objects chosen to illustrate it are only instances of the same thing, it is better to draw conclusions from the subject itself than from the others; if the identity is incomplete, the

[1] E.g. Natorp, *RE*, VI, 1002; Robin, *Gr. Thought*, 163. For von Fritz, on the other hand, it corresponded to the usual practice of Socrates (*RE*, Suppl. V, 717), in amusing contrast to Robin, in whose eyes it showed that Euclides had 'abandoned the inductive dialectic of Socrates'. (It looks as if Robin is running this argument and the next together, in the reverse order to D.L.'s, as parts of a single compound argument. I doubt if this is right.)

[2] εἰ μὲν ἐξ ὁμοίων, περὶ αὐτὰ δεῖν μᾶλλον ἢ οἷς ὅμοιά ἐστιν ἀναστρέφεσθαι· εἰ δ' ἐξ ἀνομοίων παρέλκειν τὴν παράθεσιν.

[3] See vol. I, 230 and 305, and cf. the phrase τὸ αὐτὸ καὶ ὅμοιον in Arist. *GC*, 323b11.

comparison introduces an irrelevant factor which may be misleading. Gomperz gives as an example that Euclides would not have deduced the necessity of expert knowledge in statesmanship from analogies with pilots, farmers or doctors, in which partial resemblances go with important differences, but solely from consideration of the facts of political life.[1]

The foregoing account has shown, I hope, that even from the scanty evidence at our disposal we can form some idea of what Euclides took from Socrates and how he modified or developed it; and also of certain resemblances and differences between his version of Socraticism and that of his friend and contemporary Plato. Like Plato he wished to give a theoretical or metaphysical backing to the mainly practical and ethical teaching of Socrates about the good; and both men were convinced that in any such theory the Eleatic doctrine of being had to be taken into account.[2] But whereas Plato accommodated it to a place in a grandiose metaphysical scheme in which the Pythagoreans and Heraclitus also played a part, as well as Socrates and the genius of its author himself, Euclides seems to have clung more closely to both the methods and the results of Parmenides and Zeno. He was even further removed than Plato from the empirical world, and moved in a world of dialectical abstractions and dilemmas depending on the uncompromising use of an 'either–or' dichotomy. There are hints of this in what we are told of the man himself, and it certainly applied to his followers, whose achievements were mainly in the field of logic. Working by means of paradoxes and puzzles, or logical traps, they earned for themselves the name of eristics, but the advances that they made were real and important.

As with Antisthenes and Aristippus, scholars have claimed to detect veiled criticisms of Euclides in a number of dialogues of Plato. (They include the *Euthydemus*, *Republic*, *Parmenides*, *Theaetetus* and *Sophist*.) However, since for every scholar who makes this claim there is another

---

[1] Gomperz, *Gr. Th.* II, 188 f. Von Fritz (*loc. cit.*) thought it more likely that the criticism was aimed at Platonic myths and similes than at the analogical arguments of Socrates. He mentions the ambiguity of the word λόγος (which can include μῦθος), but says nothing about παραβολή, which Aristotle used to denote precisely the Socratic argument from analogy. (See p. 109 above.)

[2] For Plato, see index to vol. II, *s.v.* 'Plato: debt to Parmenides'.

to deny it, it will be best to continue the policy adopted for Aristippus, and deny ourselves the use of Plato as an aid to the reconstruction of his thought. Enough has been said, however, to show the close connexions, both personal and philosophical, between the two, and this should add interest to our study of Plato himself.

BIBLIOGRAPHY

The following list contains full particulars of books or articles mentioned (often with shortened titles) in the next or notes. In addition, a few titles have been included which may be useful for reference although there has not been occasion to mention them in the course of the work, but the list makes no pretensions to completeness. For Socrates, there are the bibliographies in Magalhães-Vilhena's two books and Gigon's commentaries on Xenophon's *Memorabilia*, books I and II, and the useful survey of the state of scholarship by Cornelia de Vogel in *Phronesis*, 1955.

Collections of source-material have been included in the general bibliography under the names of their editors.

The Greek commentators on Aristotle are referred to in the text by page and line in the appropriate volume of the Berlin Academy's edition (*Commentaria in Aristotelem Graeca*, various dates).

ADAM, A. M. 'Socrates, "quantum mutatus ab illo"', *CQ*, 1918, 121–39.

ADAM, J. (ed.). *Platonis Apologia Socratis*. Cambridge, 1910.

ADAM, J. *Platonis Protagoras, with introduction, notes & appendices*. Cambridge, 1921.

ADAM, J. *The Republic of Plato, edited with critical notes, commentary & appendices*. 2 vols., Cambridge, 1926–9. (2nd ed. with introduction by D. A. Rees, 1963.)

AMANDRY, P. *La mantique apollinienne à Delphes: essai sur le fonctionnement de l'oracle*. Paris, 1950.

AMUNDSEN, L. 'Fragment of a Philosophical Text, P. Osl. Inv. 1039', *Symbolae Osloenses*, 1966, 5–20.

ANSCOMBE, G. E. M. and GEACH, P. T. *Three Philosophers*. Ithaca, N.Y. and Oxford, 1961.

ARNIM, H. VON. *Xenophons Memorabilien und Apologie des Sokrates*. Copenhagen, 1923 (Royal Danish Academy of Science, Philos.-Hist. section, no. 8.1).

AYER, A. J. *Philosophical Essays*. London, 1954.

BAILEY, C. *The Greek Atomists and Epicurus*. Oxford, 1928.

BAKER, W. W. 'An apologetic for Xenophon's *Memorabilia*', *CJ*, XII (1916–17), 293–309.

BAMBROUGH, J. R. 'Universals and Family Resemblances', *Proceedings of the Aristotelian Society*, 1960–1, 208–22.

BARKER, E. *Political Thought of Plato and Aristotle*. New York and London, 1959.

BIEBER, M. 'Maske', *RE*, XXVIII. Halbb. (1930), 2070–120.

BLUCK, R. S. *Plato's Meno, edited with Introduction and Commentary*. Cambridge, 1961.

BURKE, J. T. A. 'A Classical Aspect of Hogarth's Theory of Art', *Journal of the Warburg and Courtauld Institutes*, 1943, 151–3.

Bibliography

BURKERT, W. *Weisheit und Wissenschaft: Studien zu Pythagoras, Philolaos und Platon.* Nürnberg, 1962.

BURNET, J. *Plato's Phaedo, edited with introduction and notes.* Oxford, 1911.

BURNET, J. *Greek Philosophy: Part I, Thales to Plato* (all published). London, 1924.

BURNET, J. *Plato's Euthyphro, Apology of Socrates and Crito, edited with notes.* Oxford 1924.

BURNET, J. *Essays and Addresses.* London, 1929.

BURNET, J. *Early Greek Philosophy.* 4th ed., London, 1930.

BURY, J. B. *A History of Greece to the Death of Alexander the Great.* London, 1900. (3rd ed. by R. Meiggs, 1951.)

BURY, R. G. *The Symposium of Plato edited with introduction, critical notes and commentary.* Cambridge (Heffer), 1909.

CALDER, W. M., III. 'Socrates at Amphipolis', *Phronesis*, 1961, 83–5.

CALOGERO, G. 'Gorgias and the Socratic Principle *Nemo sua sponte peccat*', *JHS*, 1957 (1), 12–17.

CAMPBELL, L. *The Theaetetus of Plato, with a revised text and English notes.* Oxford, 1883.

CASSIRER, E. *The Philosophy of the Enlightenment,* transl. F. C. A. Koelln and J. P. Pettegrove. Princeton Univ. Press, 1951. (Beacon Press repr. 1962.)

CHERNISS, H. *Aristotle's Criticism of Presocratic Philosophy.* Baltimore, 1935 (reprinted New York, 1964).

CHROUST, A. H. *Socrates, Man and Myth.* London, 1957.

CLASSEN, C. J. 'Aristippose', *Hermes*, 1958, 182–92.

CLASSEN, C. J. 'The Study of Language among Socrates' Contemporaries', *Proceedings of the African Classical Associations*, 1959, 33–49.

CLOCHÉ, P. 'L'Affaire des Arginusines', *Revue Historique*, 1919, 5–68.

COHEN, SIR H. 'The Status of Brain in the Concept of Mind', *Philosophy*, 1952, 259–72.

CORNFORD, F. M. *The Origin of Attic Comedy.* Cambridge, 1914.

CORNFORD, F. M. 'The Athenian Philosophical Schools', *Cambridge Ancient History,* vol. VI, 1927.

CORNFORD, F. M. *The Republic of Plato, translated with introduction and notes.* Oxford, 1941 (and later reprints).

COULTER, J. A. 'The Relation of the *Apology of Socrates* to Gorgias's *Defense of Palamedes* and Plato's critique of Gorgianic rhetoric', *HSCP*, 1964, 269–303.

CROSSMAN, R. H. S. *Plato Today.* 2nd ed., London, 1959.

DEMAN, T. *Le émoignage d'Aristote sur Socrate.* Paris, 1942.

DEVEREUX, G. 'Greek Pseudo-homosexuality and the Greek Miracle', *Symbolae Osloenses,* 1967, 69–92.

DIELS, H. and KRANZ, W. *Die Fragmente der Vorsokratiker* (Greek and German). 10th ed., 3 vols., Berlin, 1960–1.

DIÈS, A. *Autour de Platon: I. Les voisinages: Socrate. II. Les dialogues—esquisses doctrinales.* Paris, 1927.

DITTENBERGER, W. *Sylloge Inscriptionum Graecarum.* 3rd ed., 4 vols., Leipzig, 1915–21.

DITTMAR, H. *Aischines von Sphettos: Studien zur Literaturgeschichte der Sokratiker.* Berlin, 1912.

DODDS, E. R. *The Greeks and the Irrational.* California Univ. Press, 1951.

DODDS, E. R. *Plato, Gorgias, a Revised Text with Introduction and Commentary.* Oxford, 1959.

DOVER, K. J. 'Eros and Nomos', *BICS*, 1964, 31–42.

Bibliography

DOVER, K. J. *Aristophanes: Clouds, edited with introduction and commentary.* Oxford, 1968.

DREXLER, H. 'Gedanken über den Sokrates der platonischen Apologie', *Emerita*, 1961, 177–201.

DUDLEY, D. R. *A History of Cynicism.* London, 1938.

DUPRÉEL, E. *La Légende socratique et les sources de Platon.* Brussels, 1922.

DUPRÉEL, E. *Les Sophistes.* Neuchâtel, 1948.

EASTERLING, H. J. Review of R. Dieterle's *Platons Laches und Charmides* (Freiburg diss., privately printed, 1966), *CR*, 1968, 236 f.

EDELSTEIN, E. *Xenophontisches und platonisches Bild des Sokrates.* Berlin, 1935.

EHNMARK, E. 'Socrates and the Immortality of the Soul', *Eranos*, 1946, 105–22.

EHRENBERG, V. *Society and Civilisation in Greece and Rome.* Cambridge, Mass. (Harvard Univ. Press), 1964.

ERASMUS, S. 'Richterzahl und Stimmenverhältnisse im Sokratesprozess', *Gymnasium*, 1964, 40–2.

ERBSE, H. 'Sokrates im Schatten der aristophanischen Wolken', *Hermes*, 1954, 385–420.

FERGUSON, A. S. 'The Impiety of Socrates', *CQ*, 1913, 157–75.

FERGUSON, J. 'On the Date of Socrates's Conversion', *Eranos*, 1964, 70–3.

FESTUGIÈRE, A. J. *Epicurus and his Gods*, transl. C. W. Chilton. Oxford (Blackwell), 1955.

FIELD, G. C. 'Aristotle's Account of the Historical Origin of the Theory of Ideas', *CQ*, 1923, 113–24.

FIELD, G. C. 'Socrates and Plato in the Post-Aristotelian Tradition', *CQ*, 1924, 127–36.

FIELD, G. C. *Plato and his Contemporaries.* London, 1930.

FOOT, P. (ed.). *Theories of Ethics.* Oxford, 1967.

FRANKENA, W. K. 'The Naturalistic Fallacy', *Mind*, 1939, 464–77 (reprinted in Foot, *q.v.*).

FRIEDLÄNDER, P. *Plato*, transl. H. Meyerhoff, vol. I, *An Introduction*, London, 1958, vol. II, *The Dialogues, First Period*, 1964 [actually 1965].

FRITZ, K. VON. 'Megariker', *R.E.* Suppl. V (1931), 707–24.

FRITZ, K. VON. 'Theaitetos (2)', *RE*, 2. Reihe, x. Halbb. (1934), 1351–72.

FRITZ, K. VON. 'Antisthenes und Sokrates in Xenophons *Symposion*', *Rheinisches Museum*, 1935, 19–45.

FRITZ, K. VON. 'Phaidon (3)', *RE*, xxxviii. Halbb. (1938), 1538–42.

FRITZ, K. VON. 'Xeniades', *RE*, 2. Reihe, xviii. Halbb. (1967), 1438–40.

GANTAR, K. 'Amicus Sibi I', *Živa Antika*, 1966, 135–75.

GELLNER, E. *Words and Things.* London, 1959 (reprinted by Penguin Books, Harmondsworth, 1968).

GELZER, T. 'Aristophanes und sein Sokrates', *Museum Helveticum*, 1956, 65–93.

GIANNANTONI, G. *I Cirenaici: raccolta delle fonte antiche. Traduzione e studio introduttivo.* Florence, 1958.

GIANNANTONI, G. 'La pritania di Socrate nel 406a. C.', *Rivista critica di storia della filosofia*, 1962, 3–25.

GIGON, O. *Sokrates, sein Bild in Dichtung und Geschichte.* Bern, 1947.

GIGON, O. *Kommentar zum ersten Buch von Xenophons Memorabilien.* Basel, 1953. Ditto, *zum zweiten Buch*, 1956.

GIGON, O. Review of Magalhães-Villhena, *Le problème de Socrate*, *Gnomon*, 1955, 259–66.

Bibliography

GIGON, O. 'Die sokratische "Doxographie" bei Aristoteles', *Museum Helveticum*, 1959, 174–212.

GILLESPIE, C. M. 'The Use of εἶδος and ἰδέα in Hippocrates', *CQ*, 1912, 179–203.

GLADIGOW, B. 'Zum Makarismos des Weisen', *Hermes*, 1967, 404–33.

GOMPERZ, T. *Greek Thinkers: A History of Ancient Philosophy.* 4 vols., London, 1901–12. (Vol. I transl. L. Magnus, vols. II–IV by C. G. Berry.) Re-issued in paperback, London, 1964.

GORDON, R. M. 'Socratic Definitions and Moral Neutrality', *Journal of Philosophy*, 1964, 433–50.

GOULDNER, W. W. *Enter Plato.* London, 1967.

GRANT, SIR A. *The Ethics of Aristotle, Illustrated with Essays and Notes.* 4th ed., 2 vols., London, 1885.

GROTE, G. *Plato and the other Companions of Sokrates.* 3rd ed. 3 vols., London, 1875.

GRUBE, G. M. A. *Plato's Thought.* London, 1935 (and later reprints).

GUNDERT, H. 'Platon und das Daimonion des Sokrates', *Gymnasium*, 1954, 513–31.

GUTHRIE, W. K. C. *The Greeks and their Gods.* London, 1950 (and later reprints).

GUTHRIE, W. K. C. *Plato, Protagoras and Meno*, translated with introduction, summaries, etc. Harmondsworth (Penguin Books), 1956 (and later reprints.)

HACKFORTH, R. *The Composition of Plato's Apology.* Cambridge, 1933.

HACKFORTH, R. 'Socrates', *Philosophy*, 1933, 259–72.

HACKFORTH, R. *Plato's Phaedrus*, translated with introduction and commentary. Cambridge, 1952.

HAMILTON, E. and CAIRNS, H. (ed.). *The Collected Dialogues of Plato including the Letters.* New York, 1961.

HAMILTON, W. *The Symposium by Plato, a new translation.* Harmondsworth (Penguin Books), 1951 (and later reprints).

HARE, R. M. *The Language of Morals.* Oxford, 1952 (and later reprints).

HARE, R. M. *Freedom and Reason.* Oxford, 1963 (and later reprints).

HARRISON, A. R. W. *The Laws of Athens: Family and Property.* Oxford, 1968.

HAVELOCK, E. A. 'The Evidence for the Teaching of Socrates', *TAPA*, 1934, 282–95.

HAVELOCK, E. A. *The Liberal Temper in Greek Politics.* London, 1957.

HEATH, T. L. *A History of Greek Mathematics.* 2 vols., Oxford, 1921.

HIRZEL, R. *Der Dialog.* 2 vols., Leipzig, 1895.

HOGARTH, W. *The Analysis of Beauty*, ed. J. T. A. Burke. Oxford, 1955.

HUG, A. 'Symposion-Literatur', *RE*, VIII. Halbb. (1932), 1273–82.

JAEGER, W. *Paideia: the Ideals of Greek Culture*, transl. G. Highet. 3 vols., Oxford, 1939–45 (vol. I, 2nd ed.).

JAEGER, W. *Aristotle: Fundamentals of the History of his Development*, transl. R. Robinson. 2nd ed., Oxford, 1948 (and later reprints).

JANELL, W. 'Die Echtheit und Abfassungszeit des Theages', *Hermes*, 1901, 427–39.

JOËL, K. *Der echte und der Xenophontische Sokrates.* Berlin, 1893.

JOËL, K. *Geschichte der antiken Philosophie.* I. Band, Tübingen, 1921.

JOWETT, B. *The Dialogues of Plato translated into English with Analyses and Introductions.* 4th ed., 4 vols., Oxford, 1953.

KAHRSTEDT, U. 'Meletos (3)', *RE*, XXIX. Halbb. (1931), 503 f.

KAIBEL, G. 'Aristophanes, der Komiker', *RE*, II (1896), 971–94.

KELSEN, H. 'Platonic Justice', *International Journal of Ethics*, XLVIII (1937–8), 367–400.

KERN, O. (ed.). *Orphicorum Fragmenta.* Berlin, 1922.

Bibliography

KIERKEGAARD, S. *The Concept of Irony, with constant reference to Socrates*. Transl. with introduction and notes by L. M. Capel, *London*, 1966.

KIRK, G. S. and RAVEN, J. E. *The Presocratic Philosophers*. Cambridge, 1957. (Selected texts with introduction and commentary.)

KNEALE, W. and M. *The Development of Logic*. Oxford, 1962.

KOCK, T. *Comicorum Atticorum Fragmenta*. 3 vols., Leipzig, 180–8.

KÖRTE, A. 'Sophron', *RE*, 2. Reihe, v. Halbb. (1927), 1100–4.

KUHN, T. S. *The Copernican Revolution*. Cambridge, Mass., 1957.

LAGERBORG, R. *Platonische Liebe*. Leipzig, 1926.

LEE, H. D. P. *Plato, the Republic: a new translation*. Harmondsworth (Penguin Classics), 1955.

LEISEGANG, H. 'Platon (1) Der Philosoph', *RE*, XL. Halbb. (1941), 2342–537.

LEVY, A. W. 'Socrates in the Nineteenth Century', *JHI*, 1956, 89–108.

LEVY, M. A. *Political Power in the Ancient World*, transl. Jane Costello. London, 1965.

LITTRÉ, É. *Œuvres Complètes d'Hippocrate. Traduction nouvelle, avec le texte grec en regard...accompagné d'une introduction, de commentaires médicaux, etc.* Paris, 1839–61.

LLOYD, G. E. R. *Polarity and Analogy: two types of argumentation in early Greek thought.* Cambridge, 1966.

LLOYD, G. E. R. 'The Role of Medical and Biological Analogies in Aristotle's Ethics', *Phronesis*, 1968, 68–83.

MAGALHÃES-VILHENA, V. DE. (i) *Le problème de Socrate: le Socrate historique et le Socrate de Platon.* (ii) *Socrate et la légende platonicienne.* Paris, 1952.

MAIER, H. *Die Syllogistik des Aristoteles*. Tübingen, I. Teil, 1896, II. Teil, 1900.

MAIER, H. *Sokrates, sein Werk und seine geschichtliche Stellung*. Tübingen, 1913.

MANNEBACH, E. (ed.) *Aristippi et Cyrenaicorum Fragmenta*. Leiden, 1961.

MARCHANT, E. C. *Xenophon, Memorabilia and Oeconomicus, with an English translation.* London and Cambridge, Mass. (Loeb ed.), 1959.

MEINEKE, A. *Comicorum Graecorum Fragmenta*. 5 vols., Berlin, 1839–57.

MERRY, W. W. *Aristophanes: The Clouds, with introduction and notes*. Oxford, 1916.

MEYER, T. *Platons Apologie*. Stuttgart, 1962.

MONDOLFO, R. *Problemi del pensiero antico*. Bologna, 1936.

MONDOLFO. *See also* ZELLER-MONDOLFO.

MOORE, G. E. *Principia Ethica*. Cambridge, 1903.

MOTTE, A. 'Pour l'authenticité du "Premier Alcibiade"', *L'Antiquité Classique*, 1961, 5–32.

MÜLLER, E. *Sokrates in der Volksversammlung*. Zittau, 1894.

MURRAY, G. *Aristophanes: a Study*. Oxford, 1933.

MURRAY, G. *Greek Studies*. Oxford, 1946.

NATORP, P. 'Alexamenos', *RE*, I (1894), 1375.

NATORP, P. 'Eukleides aus Megara', *RE*, VI (1909), 1000–3.

NAUCK, A. (ed.). *Tragicorum Graecorum Fragmenta*. 2nd ed., Leipzig, 1889.

NESTLE, W. *Vom Mythos zum Logos*. 2nd ed., Stuttgart, 1941.

NEUMANN, H. 'On the Madness of Plato's Apollodorus', *TAPA*, 1965, 283–9.

NORTH, H. *Sophrosyne: self-knowledge and self-restraint in Greek literature*. New York, 1966.

O'BRIEN, M. J. *The Socratic Paradoxes and the Greek Mind*. Chapel Hill (Univ. of N. Carolina Press), 1967.

PARKE, H. W. 'Chaerephon's Inquiry about Socrates', *CP*, 1961, 249 f.

Bibliography

PEIPERS, D. *Untersuchungen über das System Platos. Erster Theil: Die Erkenntnistheorie Platos.* Leipzig, 1874.

PFLEIDERER, E. *Sokrates, Plato und ihre Schüler.* Tübingen, 1896.

PHILLIPSON, C. *The Trial of Socrates (with chapters on his life, teaching, and personality).* London, 1928.

POMPA, L. 'Family Resemblance', *Philosophical Quarterly*, 1967, 63–9.

POPPER, SIR K. R. *The Logic of Scientific Discovery* (transl. from German). London, 1959.

POPPER, SIR K. R. *Conjectures and Refutations.* 2nd ed., London, 1965.

POPPER, SIR K. R. *The Open Society and its Enemies*, vol. 1, The Spell of Plato, 5th ed., London, 1966.

REICH, H. *Der Mimus*, vol. 1, parts 1 and 2. Berlin, 1903.

REYNEN, H. 'Philosophie und Knabenliebe', *Hermes*, 1967, 308–16.

RIBBECK, O. 'Über den Begriff des εἴρων', *Rheinisches Museum*, 1876, 381–400.

RICHTER, G. M. A. *Portraits of the Greeks.* London, 1965.

RIST, J. M. 'Plotinus and the Daimonion of Socrates', *Phoenix*, 1963, 13–24.

RITTER, C. *Sokrates.* Tübingen, 1931.

ROBIN, L. 'Sur une hypothèse récente relative à Socrate', *REG*, 1916, 129–65.

ROBIN, L. *Greek Thought and the Origins of the Scientific Spirit*, transl. from *La Pensée Grecque* by M. R. Dobie. London, 1928. (A third ed. of the French was published by P.-M. Schuhl in 1963.)

ROBINSON, R. *Definitions.* Oxford, 1950.

ROBINSON, R. *Plato's Earlier Dialectic.* 2nd ed., Oxford, 1953.

ROGERS, B. B. *The Clouds of Aristophanes. The Greek text revised with a translation into corresponding metres, introduction and commentary.* London, 1916.

ROSS, W. D. *Aristotle's Metaphysics, a revised text with introduction and commentary.* 2 vols., Oxford, 1924.

ROSS, W. D. 'The Problem of Socrates', *Classical Association Proceedings*, 1933, 7–24.

ROSS, W. D. *Aristotle's Prior and Posterior Analytics, a revised text with introduction and commentary.* Oxford, 1949.

SACHS, E. *De Theaeteto Atheniensi Mathematico.* Berlin Diss. 1914.

SCHMID, Wilhelm and Stählin, O. *Geschichte der griechischen Literatur.* 1. Teil, Die Classische Periode, 3. Band, 1. Hälfte. Munich, 1940.

SCHMID, WOLFGANG. 'Das Sokratesbild der Wolken', *Philologus*, 1948, 209–28.

SHOREY, P. *What Plato Said.* Chicago, 1933.

SCHWEITZER, A. *The Quest of the Historical Jesus.* 3rd ed., London, 1954.

SIMETERRE, R. *La théorie socratique de la vertu-science.* Paris, 1938.

SNELL, B. *Die Ausdrücke für den Begriff des Wissens.* Berlin, 1924 (*Philol. Untersuchungen*, 29).

SNELL, B. 'Das früheste Zeugnis über Sokrates', *Philologus*, 1948, 125–34.

STARK, R. 'Sokratisches in den Vögeln des Aristophanes', *Rheinisches Museum*, 1953, 77–89.

STENZEL, J. 'Kyrenaiker', *RE*, XXIII. Halbb. (1924), 137–50.

STENZEL, J. 'Logik', *RE*, XXV. Halbb. (1926), 991–1011.

STENZEL, J. 'Sokrates (Philosoph)', *RE*, 2. Reihe, V. Halbb. (1927), 811–90.

STENZEL, J. *Plato's Method of Dialectic*, translated and edited by D. J. Allan. Oxford, 1940.

STEVENSON, C. L. 'Persuasive Definitions', *Mind*, 1938, 331–50.

Bibliography

STEVENSON, C. L. *Ethics and Language.* New Haven (Yale Univ. Press), 1945.

STRYCKER, E. DE. 'Les témoignages historiques sur Socrate', *Mélanges Grégoire*, II (= *Annuaire de l'Institut de Philologie et d'Histoire orientales et slaves*, 1950), 199–230.

TARRANT, D. 'The Pseudo-Platonic Socrates', *CQ*, 1938, 167–73.

TARRANT, D. 'The Touch of Socrates', *CQ*, 1958, 95–8.

TAYLOR, A. E. *Varia Socratica.* First series, Oxford (Parker), 1911.

TAYLOR, A. E. *Plato, the Man and his Work.* London, 1926 (p. back reprint, 1960).

TAYLOR, A. E. *Socrates.* London, 1932.

THOMPSON, E. S. *The Meno of Plato, edited with introduction, notes and excursuses.* London, 1901 (reprinted 1937).

TREDENNICK, H. Translations of Plato's *Apology, Crito* and *Phaedo.* Harmondsworth (Penguin Books), 1954.

TREU, M. 'Xenophon', *RE*, 2. Reihe, XVIII. Halbb. (1967), 1567–982.

'UEBERWEG–PRAECHTER.' Ueberweg, F. *Grundriss der Geschichte der Philosophie*, ed. K. Praechter. 13th ed., Basel, 1953 (photographic reprint of 12th ed., 1923).

VERSÉNYI, L. *Socratic Humanism.* New Haven, Conn., and London (Yale Univ. Press), 1963.

VLASTOS, G. *Plato's Protagoras: B. Jowett's translation extensively revised by Martin Ostwald, edited with an introduction by Gregory Vlastos.* New York, 1956.

VOGEL, C. J. DE. *Greek Philosophy. A collection of texts, selected and supplied with some notes and explanations.* Vol. I, *Thales to Plato*, Leiden, 1950.

VOGEL, C. J. DE. 'Une nouvelle interprétation du problème socratique', *Mnemosyne*, 1951, 30–9.

VOGEL, C. J. DE. 'The Present State of the Socratic Problem', *Phronesis*, 1955, 26–35.

WEHRLI, F. *Die Schule des Aristoteles: Texte und Kommentar* (Basel), Heft X: Hieronymos von Rhodos, Kritolaos, Rückblick, Register, addenda, 1959; Heft VII: Herakleides Pontikos, 1953; Heft II: Aristoxenos, 1945.

WEIL, R. 'La place du Premier Alcibiade dans l'œuvre de Platon', *L'Information Littéraire*, 1964, 75–84.

WILAMOWITZ-MOELLENDORFF, U. VON. *Aristoteles und Athen.* 2 vols., Berlin, 1893.

WILAMOWITZ-MOELLENDORFF, U. VON. *Platon.* 2 vols., Berlin, 1920.

WILAMOWITZ-MOELLENDORFF, U. VON. 'Lesefrüchte', *Hermes.*, 1927, 276–98

WILAMOWITZ-MOELLENDORFF, U. VON. *Der Glaube der Hellenen.* 2 vols., Berlin, 1931–2.

WINSPEAR, A. D. and SILVERBERG, T. *Who was Socrates?* New York (Cordon Co.), 1939.

ZELLER, E. *Die Philosophie der Griechen*, 2. Teil, 1. Abteilung, *Sokrates und die Sokratiker: Plato und die alte Akademie.* 5. Auflage, Leipzig, 1922 (repr. 1963).

'ZELLER–MONDOLFO.' La filosofia dei Greci nel suo sviluppo storico. Florence, various dates from 1932. (Zeller's work translated and enlarged by R. Mondolfo.)

'ZELLER–NESTLE.' E. Zeller, *Die Philosophie der Griechen*, 1. Teil, 1. Hälfte (7th ed., 1923) and 2. Hälfte (6th ed., 1920), edited by W. Nestle (Leipzig).

ZIEGLER, K. 'Xenarchos', *RE*, 2. Reihe, XVIII. Halbb. (1967), 1422.

INDEXES

INDEX OF PASSAGES QUOTED
OR REFERRED TO

AESCHINES, *orator*
  In Tim. (173), 63
AESCHINES, *Socraticus*
  fr. (10c Dittmar), 75 n. 1; (40, 44), 11 n. 2
[ALEXANDER]
  Ad. Ar. Metaph. (1078a31), 172 n. 1
AMEIPSIAS
  ap. D.L. 2 (28), 40 n. 3
ANDOCIDES
  De myst. (94), 60 n. 4
[ANDOCIDES]
  4 (42), 67 n. 4
ANTIPHON, *orator*
  Tetr. Γα (7), 149 n. 1
ANTIPHON, *Sophist*
  fr. (23–32), 102 n. 2
ANTISTHENES
  fr. (33), 59 n.
ARISTIPPUS
  fr. (1–8 Mannebach), 171 n. 1; (9A, B, D, E),
  173; (22A, B), 177 n. 2; (30–4), 173;
  (32C), 173; (37B), 170 n. 3; (45), 173 n.,
  175; (54A, B), 175; (56), 175; (57A–G),
  175; (67), 173; (72–83), 173; (121),
  174 n.; (125), 174 n.; (126A–C), 174 n.;
  (132), 174 n.; (143), 177; (145), 174:
  (154A), 172 n. 1; (155), 174 n.; (156),
  174, 177; (157), 174; (161), 174; (163),
  174 n.; (181–3), 174; (193), 174 n.;
  (193 ff.), 174; (201), 174 n.; (207–9), 174;
  (208), 174; (209), 174; (210), 175 n. 2;
  (211–18), 176 n. 1; (211A), 176; (211A,
  B), 175 n. 2, 176 n. 1; (212), 175 n. 2,
  176 n. 1; (213A), 176 *bis*; (213A–C), 175
  n. 2; (217), 175 n. 2, 176; (218), 176;
  (227), 177; (231), 172 n. 2
ARISTOCLES
  ap. Eus. P.E. (15. 2), 180 n. 1
ARISTOPHANES
  Birds (1282), 40 n. 3; (1296), 45 n. 1;
  (1553), 40 n. 3; (1554), 69 n. 2; (1564),
  45 n. 1
  Clouds (64), 65 n. 3; (94) 149; (103), 45 n. 1,
  69 n. 2; (104), 45 n. 1; (112 ff.), 51;
  (113 ff.), 43; (137), 124 n. 3; (140–3), 54;
  (143–79), 44; (145 f.), 54; (175), 53 n. 3;
  (198 f.), 45 n. 1; (234), 48 n. 1, 53 n. 1,

(258), 54; (260), 44, 50; (266), 41 n. 1;
  (317 f.), 44; (320 f.), 50 *bis*; (331 ff.),
  50 *bis*; (345 f.), 53 n. 1; (362 f.), 53; (363),
  69 n. 2; (385 ff.), 53 n. 1; (412 ff.), 45 n. 1;
  (412–19), 50; (435), 50; (436), 45, 50;
  (449), 126; (504), 45 n. 1; (520–6), 56;
  (658), 45; (695), 45; (740 ff.), 45; (762),
  46; (837), 40 n. 3; (842), 53; (874 f.), 50;
  (1111), 57; (1148 ff.), 50; (1173), 51 n. 1;
  (1286 ff.), 47, 53 n. 1; (1400), 48 and n. 2;
  (1421 ff.), 48; (1454 ff.), 50; (1482–
  1507), 57; (1485), 54 n. 2
  Frogs (1492), 40 n. 3
ARISTOTLE
  Anal. Post. 2 (ch. 19), 134 n. 1; (71a8),
  106 n. 2; (71a21), 106 n. 2; (81b2),
  106 n. 2; (1006b3), 109 n. 1
  Anal. Pr. (25b33), 134 n. 2
  Ath. pol. (39), 62 n. 1; (60.5), 67 n. 4
  De anima (405b5), 102 n. 2
  De Insomn. (462a13), 67 n. 2
  De part. an. (642a28), 97
  EE (1216b2ff.), 131; (1216b4), 104 n. 1;
  (1230a6), 132 n. 5; (1230a7), 131 n.;
  (1235a35–b2), 38 n. 2; (1235a39) 2, 7;
  (1246 b27), 136 n. 3; (1246b33), 131
  n.
  EN (1096a11ff.), 37 n.; (1096a16), 38;
  (1103b26), 132; (1113a6), 149 n. 2;
  (1113b16), 140 n. 3; (1114a11), 140 n. 3;
  (1116b5), 131 n., 132 n. 5; (1127b2ff.),
  126 n. 1; (1139b18 ff.), 134 n. 1; (1140b
  30 ff.), 134 n. 1; (1141a10), 58 n. 2;
  (1144b18), 132 and n. 3; (1144b29),
  132 n. 3; (1145b25), 133; (1177b27),
  157; (1178a7), 157; (1179b1), 106 n. 1
  GC (323b11), 185 n. 3
  Metaph. (987a20), 97 n.; (987 b1 ff.), 97;
  (987b20), 183 n. 1; (992a32), 39; (996a
  29), 171; (1032a32 – 1032b14), 132 n. 2;
  (1046b29), 180 n. 2; (1078a33), 171 n. 3;
  (1078b17), 97; (1078b24), 112 n.;
  (1078b27), 105; (1091b13), 183
  Phys. (209b13), 39 n.
  Poet. (1447b9), 12
  Pol. (1262a32 ff.), 76 n. 1
  Rhet. (1393b4), 411 n. 3, 429 and n. 1;

194

GENERAL INDEX

Bold figures denote a main or more important entry. The entries for modern scholars are often selective, and as a rule no entry is made where the text has no more than a reference.

General Index

god, gods (see also names of separate gods, providence), moral failings of, 47; replaced by natural forces, 44
Gordon, R. M., 117 f.
Gorgias, 102; refused to define areté, 116
grammar, 120
Grote, G., 147 n. 1, 181 n. 2

Hackforth, R., 103 n. 1, 128, 163 n. 2
Hare, R. M., 153 n. 1
Hedonic calculus, 143, 144 f., 166 f.
Hedonism (see also pleasure); of Aristippus, 174 f.
Heracles, 47; see also Prodicus
Hermogenes, 11 n. 2, 18, 21, 169
Hippias, 126
Hogarth, W., 68
homosexuality, 70 ff.
Hume, D., 90

Ideas, Platonic. See Forms
induction, 105 ff., 111 n. 1, 115 n. 2
irony, 126 f.

Jaeger, W., 6 n. 2
Jesus, 6 n. 2, 7
Joël, K., 135, 139 n. 1, 140 f.

kairos, 111
Kelsen, H., 71 n. 1, 73 n. 1
Kierkegaard, S., 9 n. 1, 126 n. 1
Kuhn, T. S., 32

Lagerborg, R., 72
Lais, 175
Lamprocles, 65
Leon of Salamis, 60
Levy, A. W., 8
lot, appointment by, 91 f.
Lycon, 62

Magalhães-Vilhena, V. de, 3 n. 1, 9 n. 2
Mannebach, E., 171 n. 2, 172
mathematics, 39, 125, 171
Megarian school, 179, 180 f.
Meletus, 61 f., 84
Melissus, 180
Menexenus, 169
Merry, W. W., 56, 57
Metrodorus, 176
Milton, John, 100 n. 4
Moore, G. E., 118
Morality, see relativity, Protagoras
Murray, G. G. R., 49
Myrto, 65 n. 3

natural philosophers, immoral use of, 47 f.
naturalistic fallacy, 118
nature, and necessity, 47

O'Brien, M. J., 137 n. 1

Orphism, 52, 148, 157, 164

Panaetius, 98
Parke, H. W., 86 n. 2
Parmenides, 180, 183
persuasion, 119
Phaedo, 77, 169 with n. 1
Phaedondes, 169
Phaenarete, 58 with n. 1
Philolaus, 169
phrontisterion, 41
Plato (see also Forms), 29–35, 94, 113; visit to Megara, 179; compared to Socrates, 5 f.; Apology, historicity of, 29 n. 1, 158 n. 1; doctrine of eros in, 76; on homosexuality, 76 with n. 1; on wrongdoing as involuntary, 139 f.; Theages, 79 f.; otherworldliness of, 164; and Aristippus, 178 f.
pleasure (see also hedonic calculus), Socrates on, 143, 166; Aristippus on, 174
Polycrates, 11, 26, 62, 63 n. 1, 91 n. 3 (b)
Popper, K. R., 95, 115 n. 2
Prodicus, Choice of Heracles, 46; as natural philosopher, 44
prophecy, see Delphic oracle
Protagoras, 41 n. 1, 46, 51, 176, 177 n. 1
providence, Socrates's belief in, 155 f.
Proxenus, 28
Pythagoreanism, 52, 94, 148, 157, 164

Reich, H., 13 n. 1
relativity, of values, 111, 143 ff.
Renault, M., 70 n. 2, 169 n. 1
Ritter, C., 36 n. 1, 141 f.
Robin, L., 184, 185 n. 1
Rogers, B. B., 56 f.
Ross, W. D., 36, 108, 115 n. 2

scepticism, 111; of Aristippus, 175 f.
Schweitzer, A., 7
self-control, as prerequisite of intellectual progress, 136 f.
s'Gravesande, 111 n. 1
Shaw, G. B., 42
Silverberg, T., 94
Simeterre, R., 137 n. 2, 139 n. 1
Simmias, 52, 169
Simon the cobbler, 24 n. 1
Socrates (see also table of contents), political views, 89–96; belief in a future life, 33 f., 156 ff.; on relativity of values, 111 f., 143 ff.; utilitarianism of, 34, 66 ff., 100 f., 142 ff., 166; teleology of, 66, 122, 146, 152 f.; relation to Sophists, 51 f., 105, 129; 'virtue is knowledge', 130–9; wrongdoing is involuntary, 139 ff.; as intellectual midwife, 17, 58 n. 1, 77 n. 1, 124 f.; poems of 6 n. 1; his divine sign, 19, 79, 80 n. 1, 81, 82 ff.; how far he had a 'school', 53 f.; portraits of, 67 n. 1; compared to a stingray, 82, 127; attitude to the crafts, 88 ff.,

INDEX OF SELECTED GREEK WORDS

Greek words transliterated in the text will be found in the general index